performance **lighting design**

how to light for the stage, concerts, exhibitions and live events

First published 2007
A & C Black Publishers Ltd
38 Soho Square, London W1D 3HB
www.acblack.com

ISBN 978–0–7136–7757–7

A CIP record for this book is available from the British Library.

Note: While every effort has been made to ensure that the content of this book is as technically accurate and as sound as possible, neither the author nor the publisher can accept responsibility for any injury or loss sustained as a result of the use of this material.

This book is produced using paper that is made from wood grown in managed, sustainable forests. It is natural, renewable and recyclable. The logging and manufacturing processes conform to the environment regulations of the country of origin.

Cover and inside design by James Watson

Typeset by Fakenham Photosetting, Fakenham, Norfolk NR21 8NL
Printed and bound in Spain by Graphycems.

STAGECRAFT

performance **lighting design**

how to light for the stage, concerts, exhibitions and live events

NICK MORAN

contents

BULLIE'S HOUSE, PRODUCED BY BORDER CROSSINGS, DIRECTED BY MICHAEL WALLING, DESIGNED BY JAMIE VARTAN, LIGHTING BY THE AUTHOR

Introduction

Lighting design — painting and drawing in space

This book is about designing with light for live performance. Like most design, it is a mix of craft and art. A few years ago the award winning North American lighting designer Ken Billington began a speech by describing himself as 'an artist who can neither paint nor draw'. The award winning British lighting designer Paule Constable talks about not being great at sketching on paper and much more at home sketching with light on a stage. The material of this art form is not the charcoal or the paint of the traditional fine artist, but ephemeral and untouchable light. Performance lighting design has no real lasting product to be hung in a gallery. It does not even really exist independently of the performance it was made to support, but at its best it does aspire to be art — it can change the way we experience life.

Performance lighting design is often described as painting with light. Motivated light helps to turn the everyday into the extraordinary. It can bring to a stage scene something like the difference that distinguishes a snap-shot from a Cartier-Bresson photograph, or a 'chocolate box' reproduction from the original old master painting. It helps to guide our senses and to reveal (or sometimes to hide) additional layers within the stage picture or the *mis en scène*. Light can reveal and alter the form and colour of objects and people. It can guide and frame our vision. It can even give form and colour to the air!

Lighting design is often about edges and boundaries — defining the edge of the performance space with light is common. But the motivated light of performance lighting design helps to make clear the edges and outline of objects and performers on stage. It helps to show the boundaries between one object and another, one space and another, one performer and another — like the pencil line of a sketch it can bring form to an

otherwise flat space. If the lighting designer cannot sketch with pencil on paper, they can sketch with light — highlighting outlines, creating shadow to reveal form, helping to compose a moving living picture from a collection of objects and bodies in space.

This is not something anyone can do alone, sitting in a studio as the professional fine artist might. Like most design, it requires collaboration. Just as the architect must collaborate with builders and engineers, the graphic designer with author, publisher and printer, the performance lighting designer cannot make their work alone. They must collaborate with other members of a creative team — the director, designers of set, costume, sound and video, choreographer, and of course the performer or performers. They must also collaborate with other members of the lighting team who help to realise the design — the production lighting chief, the venue chief electrician, lighting technicians, follow spot operators, programmers, engineers and other experts from the venue and from the manufacturer or hire company supporting the equipment. On larger shows the lighting team may include assistants, associates and other helpers. Then there are the members of other teams whose work also supports the lighting design — stage managers, production manager, technical management, stage crew, fly crew, riggers — the list goes on. On many productions, at least as much of the lighting designer's time and effort is spent managing relations with all these people as with actually lighting the stage. As well as being an artist, the successful performance lighting designer must also be a manager, a communicator, a persuader of the sceptical or unwilling and a listener, responding to and often developing the ideas of others. Sometimes they may have to be referee, attempting to unify the artistic vision of director and set designer perhaps. Sometimes they have to be emergency physician, reviving a piece from near disaster by leading a team already tired and demotivated. Sometimes they will feel that their only contribution to the piece is to interpret the ideas of others, at other times their insights will substantially affect the performance.

Lighting design — craft

What do we mean by the craft elements of performance lighting design? Knowing the equipment, what different lighting fixtures will and won't do for instance, and how to make the best use of each. Keeping track of all the numbers associated with a performance lighting rig, channel numbers, cue numbers, dimmer numbers, patch numbers, colour numbers to name just a few. Focusing the lighting rig to make it work for the production, making sure the right quality of light will fall in only the places we want it too — keeping distractions to a minimum. At the top of the profession, in large scale theatre, opera and dance, or major world tours of bands like the Rolling Stones, there are often teams of assistants doing much of the slog and preparation required before the lighting designer can sit down and 'paint'. However, in almost every other production setting the lighting designer will need to get involved in at least some of these matters. Sometimes they will have a production electrician to help with hanging, plugging, colouring and focusing the rig — sometimes they will have to do some or all of this alone — and still remain an artist!

Scenographic[1] illumination

At the end of the 19th century the Swiss scenographer Adolphe Appia (who worked with the great opera composer Richard Wagner) had some thoughts on what performance lighting design might be capable of:

In itself, lighting is an element that can produce unlimited effects; restored to its freedom ... (from being servant to the tyranny of painting) ... it becomes for us what the pallet is for the painter. Every combination of colours is within its scope. Through productions that can be simple or complex, stationary or shifting, through partial obstruction, through varying gradations of transparency, etc, we can obtain an infinite number of modulations. In this way lighting offers us a means of, so to speak, externalising a large number of the colours and shapes that painting freezes onto flats, and of extending them, brought alive through space. The actor no longer moves in front of painted lights and shadows, but is plunged into an atmosphere intended for him. Performers will easily understand just how far reaching this kind of reform would be.[2]

He was arguing for an end to flat stage settings of painted cloths that decorated the stages at this time ('the tyranny of painting'). He hated the lack of connection between this two dimensional painted world and the three dimensional actors performing in front of it. He wanted a stage where design evoked an equally three dimensional world of performance in which the actors moved, lived and performed. And he knew how important light would be in creating this world.

Appia was writing at a time when the lighting technology needed to realise his vision hardly existed. Through his emphasis on performer, space and light, all at the expense of the traditional representational setting, Appia has directly and indirectly influenced many theatre and performance movements. Most importantly for us, his ideas set stage lighting on to a road where it could aspire to more than simply illumination. He raises the possibility, even the expectation, that light in performance will have a scenographic function as well as an illuminating function. It will be

---

[1] The word 'scenography' comes from the Greek words for stage and for writing or describing, thus literally it means to write or describe something on stage. Where the word is used in English it often refers to set design, though this is much less the case in continental Europe. Whilst I am aware that its use in English is not usually thought to include lighting design, my feeling is that it should. The act of describing 'things' on stage adequately includes designing and making costume, sound and light as well as set, and can be a useful way to discuss some elements of performance too.

[2] Adolphe Appia (1862–1928): actor/space/light, exhibition catalogue, Dennis Bablet, John Calder Books, 1982. p43. Quoted from *La Mise en Scène du Drame Wagnérien*, published around 1895.

required to communicate with the audience, to evoke time and place, to signify doom and dread, delight and wonder, as well as to guide the attention of the audience through the performance.

Working with the others, the performance lighting designer can manipulate how the space of performance is seen by the audience. In a drama, by controlling the length, colour and position of shadows to mimic nature they can 'describe' changes in the time of day, the seasons, or the apparent weather conditions. They can change the perceived colour of objects, costumes, even the performers, for dramaturgical reasons or to add to the visual variety of the show. They can isolate a performer with a follow spot or a 'special', perhaps for a song in a musical or an opera, or for psychological reasons in a play. They can change the apparent height of the stage or turn a single space into several different rooms, all apparently by simply choosing to turn on different fixtures at different times. The competent performance lighting designer, working with the right tools, can truly 'write the stage' as a scenographer.

It is important to remember through this discussion that what we are doing in performance is not a literal representation of reality. Even in the most naturalistic domestic drama, the performance space is not the four walled room it pretends to be, any more than the actors are the people they present to the audience using the words in the script, and it is extremely unlikely that the scene will be successfully lit using only the domestic fixtures that would be present in the 'real' room. Performance is about pretence, whether it is *Hamlet* or the latest pop sensation.

The international theatre maker Peter Brook has commented that whilst film deals in similes, theatre's concern is primarily with metaphor, and this is as true for our scenographic lighting designer as it is for everyone else involved in making live performance. It is not usually possible (or useful) to create an exact reproduction of sunlight or moonlight on an indoor stage. By careful manipulation of the single point of view of the film camera (and the use of very large fixtures not generally available to live performance) film can create images that look like real world scenes lit with sunlight or moonlight. In almost all live performance the show will be seen from many different points of view. Each member of the audience will have a different view, some from the stalls, some from the gallery, some from the centre of the auditorium and some from the edges. For theatre in the round, the audience surrounds the stage, becoming a backdrop for fellow audience members opposite them. Clearly for most live performance the single viewpoint of film is not available, and generally neither is the possibility of a strict imitation of 'natural' light. The performance lighting designer will have to evoke sunlight or moonlight, to present the motivated essence of sunlight or moonlight, rather than try to create an accurate facsimile. This should be taken up as a challenge rather than a limitation. How much more powerful is the boiled down essence of a thing than that same thing diluted? This is, after all, how much of performance works — a play such as Shakespeare's *Hamlet* distils many tempestuous months of a young man's life into a few hours, for example. Scenography for live performance usually works best when it evokes the essence of a thing rather than when it tries to show a literally accurate reproduction of the thing, and this goes for lighting design as scenography too.

About the book

The following eleven chapters aim to provide insight and guidance into the world of lighting design for live performance. Overall the aim is to introduce concepts and offer ways of working in an order that follows the development of a standard production process: from first concept through development of design ideas, planning and realisation of the lighting rig and finally the public showing of the performance. There is also a section on analysing the finished design in order to make the next one better.

The book is not just aimed at those interested in working as lighting designers. There is lots of information to help directors and other designers working with a lighting designer to understand the potential and the limitations of light in live performance. There is also information for anyone working to help a lighting designer realise their lighting design, as crew, as programmer, or as production manager. There are some sections in boxes that go into practical details, outlining safe practice for example, and extensive footnotes explaining technical terms and offering asides that aim to help put parts of the main text into context.

The final chapter takes a very brief look at some things that are already beginning to change some aspects of the way lighting design is done, including growing environmental concerns and developing technology.

No book can provide a complete course in such a practical subject. Please do try things out and don't expect to find all the answers just by reading.

Acknowledgements

This book would not have been possible without a lot of help from friends and colleagues. From my earliest days with the Huddersfield Thespians, in a converted Methodist chapel working with resistance dimmers, through to my time as lighting manager at English National Opera and lecturer at the Central School of Speech and Drama (CSSD) I have been lucky to have worked with some kind and supportive people. At the start of my professional career I was trained on the job mostly by Jenny Cane, Gary Brown, and Andy 'Crusher' Hartley. Later, as a programmer and production chief I benefited from being able to watch some of the world's top lighting designers at work for over 20 years. In my own work as lighting designer, I have been supported by some dedicated and caring staff, in the UK, Europe and North America. There are too many fine people to name individually, but you have all indirectly contributed to this book and I thank you for that.

More direct contributions have come from Gavin McGrath, one of the best and most dedicated chief electricians in the West End — or anywhere else for that matter — who gave invaluable guidance on the chapters concerning getting the rig in place. Also from Phil Engelheart, scenographer, director and teacher, who allowed me to incorporate much of his teaching on text analysis, and who read the whole thing, offering encouragement and suggesting improvements. I would also like to thank Bryan Raven of White Light for his encouragement and proof reading.

This book would not have been possible without the support of friends and colleagues at Central, who covered for me when I was away writing or working, allowed me to bounce ideas off them, and gave encouragement and support throughout, and of course my wife, not least because she gave up the dining table to be my desk for over a year.

Finally, I need to acknowledge the students at Central School of Speech and Drama, especially the lighting students I encountered in my first years as a teacher. They made me think harder than I had ever done before about how and why I work in the way I work and allowed me to develop a logical approach to teaching performance lighting design, which has changed the way I practice lighting design. They showed me new ways in which to make light work on stage, and provided me with many of the pictures as well.

Thank you all.

1

an introduction to light in performance

An introduction to light

To talk about lighting design in performance we first need to establish some common ground. Don't worry if some of this does not make sense to you at first reading — the nature of light and colour has engaged some of the brightest minds of scientists, artists and philosophers over the centuries. Use this section as a quick introduction to some ways of talking about light and colour that are useful to performance practitioners. Come back to it if there are discussions later in the book where the science gets confusing, or if you need to remind yourself or someone else of some basic facts about light.

Many people working with light in performance will already be familiar with the material covered in this section. To those of you with a detailed knowledge of the science of light, I apologise for some of the necessary approximations made here.

What is light?

We can't see light. Everything we see, we see because light, emitted or reflected from objects, enters our eyes and stimulates the specialised receptors there, creating images that are interpreted by our brain. But you can't see light as it travels from source to lit object, or from lit object to eye. What we see is the object, not the light — even though we only see the object because light from it is entering our eyes. When we see images of our solar system, we see planets and moons with black space in between. Much of that black space is 'full' of light from the sun, but it cannot be seen until there is an object for the light to bounce off.

Whenever we can see beams of light, for example in a shaft of sunlight through storm clouds or the beams of light above a rock stage, what we are seeing is light reflected from dust, mist, rain or smoke particles. A beam of light is invisible until it hits something — if you can see it, it is hitting something.

FIGURE 1. BEAMS OF LIGHT MADE VISIBLE IN THE AIR BY WAFTS OF SMOKE AND 'DANCING WATER' SPRAY IN A SCENE FROM AN OPEN AIR SHOW, *BOLLYWOOD STEPS*. LIGHTING BY ALASTAIR NOONAN.

For several centuries scientists argued about what kind of stuff light is. In some scientific experiments it behaved like a wave, in some like a particle. In some philosophies, it travelled with a knowable speed, in others it appeared instantaneously. In the early years of the 20th century, the wonderful duality that is quantum mechanics began to give us a description of light that combined its particle-like and wave-like properties, and Einstein famously predicted that light had a constant velocity in a vacuum.

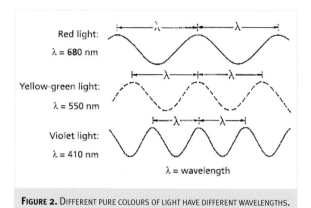

FIGURE 2. DIFFERENT PURE COLOURS OF LIGHT HAVE DIFFERENT WAVELENGTHS.

For our purposes, light is best described as a wave. Like radio waves and x-rays, it is a part of the electromagnetic spectrum. White light is a mix of many different wavelengths of light. For someone with good colour vision, each different narrow band of wavelengths is perceived as a different colour from the rainbow (by analogy, if we could see in the radio wavebands, each radio station would be a different colour). We can use special filters to separate out quite narrow wavelength bands, which we then see as light of a single pure colour. This is like the filters in a radio tuner separating individual radio stations. Visible light has wavelengths between about 700 nanometres at the lower energy red end of the spectrum down to about 400 nanometres at the higher energy violet end of the spectrum. A nanometre is one millionth of a millimetre. To give this some scale, the average width of a human hair is about 250,000 nanometres. The wavelength of the blue light called cyan, which is about 500 nanometres, is 500 times smaller than a human hair.

Scientists talk about the speed of light in a vacuum (about 0.3 billion metres per second) as being a constant know as 'c' — as in Einstein's famous equation $E=mc^2$. When light is not travelling in a vacuum it is slowed down — slightly. In the glass of a prism the average speed is about 0.2 billion metres per second. However, when light passes through almost any

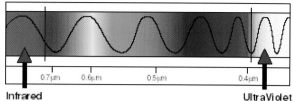

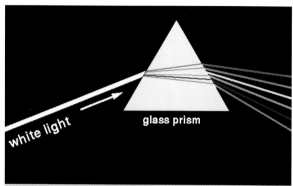

FIGURE 3. ILLUSTRATES A BEAM OF WHITE LIGHT SPLITTING INTO ITS COMPONENT COLOURS BY DIFFRACTION IN A PRISM. EACH DIFFERENT COMPONENT COLOUR IS BENT TO A DIFFERENT EXTENT AS IT PASSES THROUGH THE GLASS, THE SHORTER THE WAVELENGTH, THE MORE BENDING OCCURS.

material, some wavelengths of light are slowed down more than others. Violet and blue light slow down more than amber and red light. So, white light travelling through a prism becomes split up into its component wavelength bands — its colours. This was most famously demonstrated by the 17th century scientist and philosopher Isaac Newton.

It is not just a glass prism that can do this, but any substance where different wavelengths of light pass through at different speeds — this includes the raindrops that give us rainbows, and simple lenses. Unless we take special care, every time light of mixed wavelengths goes through a lens, it will begin to split up into its component colours. This is called chromatic aberration. It can be overcome by coating lenses, and by using special glass, and this is what makers of good quality camera lenses do, but there are limits. For most lantern manufacturers, the extra cost of coating lenses is prohibitive, so most theatre lanterns have a limit to the sharpness of beam they can produce, especially when using white or near white light.

How light travels

Light travels in straight lines. Actually even this is not strictly true. Lenses bend light, and in astrophysics, very dense objects, such as black holes, can be detected from earth because they bend starlight due to their immense gravitational fields. (Light also appears to bend around the earth under certain conditions, but this is a phenomenon due to reflection and refraction in layers of air of different densities which causes effects like mirages.) So, these special cases aside, in the performance space, light travels in straight lines. It will not bend round corners or under a ceiling. But it does bounce!

We perceive light to be bounced, or reflected, from surfaces in two ways; specular reflection from shiny surfaces such as highly polished metal, and diffuse reflection from objects that are not shiny. We can think of light waves carrying information about the objects that emitted them, and the objects that reflect them. The information about an object carried by light includes its shape, colour and relative position. It is the information carried by light, information our eyes and brain interpret, which allows us to discover properties of the objects we see.

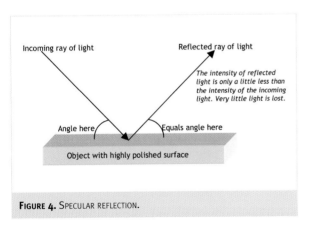

FIGURE 4. SPECULAR REFLECTION.

In specular reflection (illustrated in figure 4) the light bounces off the surface losing little of the information it carried as it hit the surface. We can see a reflection in a mirror, and less perfectly in other shiny surfaces, because the information carried by the light hitting the mirror remains intact as it leaves the mirror and travels towards our eyes. Light bounces off the reflective surface at the same angle that it strikes the reflective surface — just like a ball (with no spin) bouncing off a wall.

In fact light can only behave in this way. Diffuse reflection, where the information carried by the beam of light is disrupted and bits of the beam end up travelling in different directions, is actually specular reflection from a rough surface. The surface may not look rough, but remember we said that the wavelength of light was about 500 times smaller than a human hair. At that level even polished paintwork can look pretty rough!

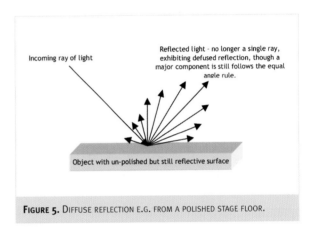

FIGURE 5. DIFFUSE REFLECTION E.G. FROM A POLISHED STAGE FLOOR.

The amount of light reflected by a surface depends mostly on how shiny or dull the object is. The more shiny the object the more light is reflected, hence shiny objects look brighter than dull ones. But shiny objects reflect light primarily in one direction, at the same angle to a line perpendicular to the reflective surface as incoming light. Meanwhile dull objects, whose surfaces exhibit only specular reflection, bounce less light, but in more directions. This means that shiny things will look bright from some angles and less bright from others, while dull things will normally look more or less the same brightness from most angles.

White and coloured light

Not all white light is the same. The white light from the sun is different at different times of day and different times of year. The white light from an ordinary domestic light bulb is different from the white light from a theatre lantern, and different again from the white light of a fluorescent strip light. It can be difficult to establish this with our eyes because unlike a camera, the human eye does not see absolute colour, we see colours relatively. You can, however, see the difference between all these different 'white' lights when you see them side by side. For example, look at the colour of white paper in the beam of a theatre lantern and a domestic lamp. We say the different sources each have a different colour temperature; we will come back to this several times in the following chapters.

If we illuminate a coloured object with white light, the object reflects back to us only the colour of light we see, absorbing all the other colours. If we see a red object in daylight, the object reflects only the red light. All the other wavelengths of light, the orange, yellow, green, blue and indigo, are absorbed by the surface of the object.

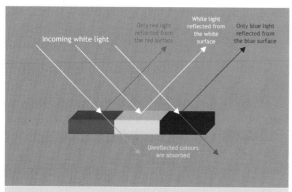

FIGURE 6. WHITE LIGHT REFLECTED FROM A MULTI-COLOURED OBJECT.

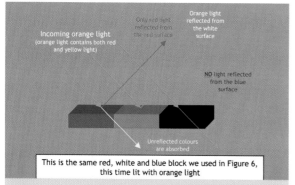

This is the same red, white and blue block we used in Figure 6, this time lit with orange light

FIGURE 7. IN COLOURED LIGHT, WHITE OBJECTS TAKE ON THE COLOUR OF THE LIGHT. WHEN NO LIGHT OF A PARTICULAR COLOUR IS PRESENT, OBJECTS OF THAT COLOUR APPEAR BLACK.

If we illuminate our red object with only blue light of a narrow band of wavelengths, the object will look black, because no red light is available to be reflected off the surface back to our eyes. There are some interesting tricks to be done with coloured light and coloured objects.

Most green pigments reflect both yellow and blue light, so a green object may well appear yellow in a 'red' light. However, if that 'red' light is very pure and has no yellow in it the green object will look black. Even if the 'red' light has some yellow (as it almost certainly will have on stage) if there is nothing to reflect yellow light in the green pigment of the object, it will again look black. Confusing isn't it — but this can explain why some of these experiments may not work for you and why sometimes we get surprising results on stage.

One good place to look at the effect of strongly-coloured light on different materials is back stage during a performance, where non-performers often wear black clothes, and the light is blue. The blue lighting can reveal differences in the black pigments and dyes of different garments, not seen under white light.

Light and human perception

As already discussed, we see something because light either emitted or reflected from it enters our eyes and triggers specialised nerves. But the story does not stop there. The brain gets involved in processing the information from the optic nerves, using information from our past experience to make sense of the information coming in through the eyes. This means that, unlike a camera, what we see at any particular moment is related to what we have just seen and our life experience. One extreme example of this comes from some research where people were asked to wear spectacles that turned the world they could see up-side-down. After a relatively short time wearing the special spectacles, they stopped seeing the world upside down — presumably because their brains 'knew' that the images were 'wrong' compared to the rest of their experience and 're-processed' the images to make them fit with previous knowledge about what the world looks like.

We have already touched on another more familiar example with colour perception. Whilst the different white lights of a domestic fitting and an uncoloured theatre lantern can both look white in isolation, when seen together it is clear that the domestic light in almost orange in comparison to the theatre light, which itself looks much less 'white' when compared to full sun light.

Colour perception can be upset by the use of strongly-coloured light or the presence of large area of contrasting colour. Notice how quickly the colouring effect of even quite heavily tinted sunglasses can wear off as once again the brain part of the eye/brain channel seeks to match current perception with past experience, and for example, render the open sky as basically blue.

The relative nature of visual perception holds for intensity too. A person going from a bright sunny exterior into an interior with no windows, lit only by a single domestic fitting is likely to feel almost blind for a short time in what they perceive to be a dark space. If the same person comes into the windowless room from a candle-lit cellar, their perception of the intensity level in the room will be quite different.

Perception of intensity depends not only on actual intensity but on the observer's immediate prior experience of intensity, and on the intensity of the surrounding visual field — a stage can look much brighter in a darkened auditorium than when the house lights come up. Other factors particular to the individual observer also have an impact on visual perception, including age, tiredness and general state of health.

Summary

If you are now feeling a little dazed, here is a recap of some of the important properties of light:

- Anything we can see is either emitting or reflecting light.

- White light is a mix of coloured light.

- To make 'coloured light' from white light we filter out the colours of light we don't want to leave the coloured light we do want.

- Objects reflect the colour of light we see, and absorb the rest. An example: in light that does not contain red, all red objects will appear black.

- Objects we see as black are reflecting little or no light.

- Light travels in straight lines.

- Light reflected by shiny objects 'bounces' like a ball.

- Light reflected by non-shiny objects is likely to go in all possible directions.

- Human visual perception involves the brain processing the information that comes into the eyes — the eye/brain channel.

- Human visual perception is relative — what we see and the way we see it is affected by experience, both immediate previous experience and life experience.

What makes performance?

Performance is what a performer or performers do. Performance theory looks at interactions between individuals and groups, in day-to-day life as well as in formal planned productions. In this book we will be considering many different genre of *formal performance*, that is formally-organised events, usually performed by trained, professional performers. Formal performance usually happens in a building designed or adapted for performance, usually but not always with a stage or defined performance area. It has become common to provide a technical infrastructure to enable luminaires to be hung, powered and controlled to make performance lighting in these spaces. This technical provision will vary from the very basic few lights and a control board to the sophistication of a modern opera or dance repertory theatre, with many hundreds of lanterns and dimmers, and many skilled engineers, managers and technicians to make them all work.

Some performance spaces are created just for one production, and these can present the most exciting challenges to performance lighting professionals. Site-specific theatre work and touring live music concerts are just two very different types of performance in this category. Live music concerts include orchestral music in purpose-built concert halls, jazz in small clubs and rock 'n' roll' in sports arenas and open-air festivals. The multi-stage Glastonbury Festival and the BBC Henry Wood Proms in London's Albert Hall are both live music concerts, despite their very different styles of lighting and very different expectation of that lighting from both audience and performers. Site-specific work comes in all shapes and sizes too, from community opera in the abandoned shipyards of the River Clyde, to psychological ghost stories in the cellars of Edinburgh or York. Many of these events require ingenuity and imagination just to get lanterns in place, let alone to make lighting for the performance.

Performance lighting techniques are also used in a range of genre with no performers, including exhibitions, interactive displays in museums and *son et lumière* presentations. Designing and planning exhibition lighting involves considerations beyond those normally encountered on the stage, such as ensuring the chosen light sources will not damage the exhibit. However, many performance lighting techniques are used in exhibition lighting.

Large event lighting, including the spectacular ceremonies associated with major sporting events such as the Olympics, use many of the same techniques as theatre and rock 'n' roll lighting, but on a significantly larger scale. Those in charge of the lighting for these events need to consider both the huge live audience at the event and the millions watching at home on TV. The team involved may well be over 100 strong. The amount of equipment and power required can be mind boggling. Managing these resources requires the extensive knowledge of some very talented individuals, and many consider those who do this well to be at the pinnacle of performance lighting practice.

Finally, there are the genres where the distinction between who is performing and who is observing is blurred. I am thinking about spaces where, to a greater or lesser extent, the paying public is invited to take a more active part in what is going on such as at the local disco, large theme parks, hi-tech mega-clubs and shopping centres. Theme parks use many theatrical techniques, from scenic art and costume to the direction of audience attention and the creation of atmosphere, with theatrical lighting and sound. Some clubs have experimented with systems that allow the clubbers to affect the lighting, for example by breaking invisible infra-red beams as they dance, but the majority leave tight control of their lit environment, including video screens and projectors, in the hands of specialist operators. This stuff has too big an effect on the atmosphere of the club to be left to chance operation. Likewise, designers of retail space take great care to ensure they create the right atmosphere in their shops, and lighting plays a big part in this.

Each different genre has its own practical requirements and audience expectations. The audience for a play in a traditional theatre may not have explicit expectations of the performance lighting, but they will normally expect that once the play begins, the stage will be brighter than the auditorium, that they will be able to see the faces of the performers, and that they will not notice or be distracted by the lighting. In contrast, the audience at the main stage of a large music festival will expect to be (sometimes literally) dazzled by in-your-face lighting effects, see the lead performers in hard edged follow-spots, and to be brightly illuminated themselves from time to time as they are either asked to join in a chorus, or be recorded by camera, cheering between songs.

What is performance lighting?

As we have already seen, we need light to see: light bounces off the objects around us and enters our eyes, triggering nerves that send signals to the brain and enable us to see the world.

The English language has many expressions involving light: a teacher throws light on subject; a reporter may help us to understand a situation in a different light or might bring a scandal to light. We talk about people having a light in their eyes or having a smile that lights up their face, or a personality that lights up the room. We talk about the light of experience, and about a person being the light of our life. We talk about the light at the end of the tunnel and about stealing someone's limelight. We use expressions that imply light or its absence, about dawning realisation and false dawn, about being in someone's shadow, shadowy worlds and dark forces. Light is a metaphor for understanding, for clarity and clear perception, and for inspiration, for bringing joy, for excitement. The absence or reduction of light is often a metaphor for fear and danger or for hidden action, often with implications of deceit and dishonesty, or sadness and rejection. With this in mind it is clear that light in performance can carry a great deal of signification, on top of its primary function, that of allowing the audiences to see what is going on.

In English we use, 'I see' to mean, 'I understand', and this is not surprising when we consider how much information healthy human eyes can receive in the right circumstances, that is with adequate light. To see performance in well-directed light is a step towards understanding it. Whether we mean 'see' literally or metaphorically, the literal light will shape our understanding and interpretation of the performance. It will guide our eyes to focus on certain parts of the performance at certain times; it will illuminate some aspects and shadow others and this will encourage emotional and intellectual responses. These may be heightened through the use or absence of colour, of particular directions of light striking objects and performers, and by structure and composition. The audience reads the performance — taking in all the visual, sonic, and other information in the very human attempt to make sense of what is going on, and light illuminates this reading, both literally and metaphorically.

Light in performance

An audience discovers the performance, informed by light. This is the case whether the performance lighting is designed or not. If the performance lighting is designed well, in harmony with the other elements of the performance, then it will enhance the communication between the performers and their collaborators (writers, designers, directors, composers, choreographers, etc), and the audience. If the performance lighting does not work with the other signifiers, it will often have a negative impact on communication and therefore on the performance. If the performance lighting highlights the wrong areas of the performance space or creates excessive and distracting shadows, the attention of the audience may be in the wrong place, or at least not in the place intended by the creators of the production. If the performance lighting fails to get across the time and place of what is happening on stage, perhaps by not making clear the passage of time or a change in location, the audience may be misled, and again the communication with the audience will be diminished. If the performance lighting fails to illuminate the faces of speaking performers, the meaning of the text may be lost.

In the last century, lighting for dramatic theatre was often self-effacing — remaining more or less unremarked on by much of the audience — and prompting the often heard statement, 'Good lighting is when you don't notice it'. The fully engaged audience member may read much of the significance of many elements of the performance sub-consciously, but that does not mean that their presence is unimportant, and what may be appropriate for a naturalistic presentation of a relatively uncomplicated drama may not be appropriate for other kinds of performance.

Audience expectations are changing however. The argument that performance lighting should be unnoticed is losing its once strong grip, even on the dramatic stage. In many genres of performance, we live with an audience that is increasingly able and willing to dissect what they see and hear on the stage and elsewhere, and to find meanings beyond the superficial one presented. Performance lighting can and frequently does play an important role in aiding the clarification of meaning by the audience. In doing this, it also enhances audience engagement with and enjoyment of live performance and the lighting designer becomes an increasingly important member of the creative team.

These three production photographs show light being used for purposes beyond 'mere illumination'.

FIGURE 8. *PROTECTING THE VEIL*, BIRMINGHAM ROYAL BALLET, 1998. LIGHTING BY MARK JONATHAN, CHOREOGRAPHER DAVID BINTLEY, SET AND COSTUME DESIGN RUARI MURCHISON, PHOTOGRAPHER BILL COOPER.

FIGURE 9. PHOTOGRAPH © LOUISE STICKLAND.

FIGURE 10. *DIE WALKÜRE* BY RICHARD WAGNER FOR DEN NY OPERA, DENMARK. LIGHTING DESIGN BY DAVID W. KIDD, DIRECTOR TROELS KOLD, SET AND COSTUME DESIGN ROY BELL. PHOTOGRAPH BY DEN NY OPERA.

Looking natural

As well as the desire to contribute to the signifiers — to be seen and heard — the 21st century lighting designer will frequently want to provide a 'natural light' on the performance stage. What do we mean when we say light looks 'natural' or 'unnatural'? In our everyday world we are used to light from above. Outside in daylight the strongest source of light is the sun, next is the more diffuse light from the sky, and then the light that is reflected or bounced off our surroundings. At night the main source is usually the moon or streetlights, again from above. The dominant sources of natural light outside are above our eye line. We have to look up to see them. We know also that the sun's light is a kind of white, and that light from the moon is a different kind of white.

In most interior spaces, the main light source is also from above us, again with varying amounts of bounce light from walls, floors and ceilings, and other objects in the space. Perhaps there will be subsidiary sources such as task lights and feature spots, but still in most spaces the main light sources will be above the eye line. Again, most of the time this light will be basically white though a different kind of white to the light outside. We live in a world where most of the light comes from above the eye line and is basically white so this is what we think of as natural light. This natural light puts shadows below noses and chins, often highlights the tops of objects and people, and lets us see colours in a particular way. It is so natural that unless we look for these (and other) effects, many people don't even notice them — until they are not there. You may have seen a friend shining a torch onto his face from below his chin. This strong source from below the eye line places the shadows of their faces in different, 'unnatural' places. Changes from the natural draw attention to themselves. This is true for shadows and, as we will see, for colours too.

If the creative team for a particular production want to create a quality of natural light outside for some scenes, the major sources of light need to come from natural angles — above the eye line — and be of a natural colour — not too far from white. If we wish to disrupt the audiences' perception, and draw attention to light or the effect it is producing, we need only to introduce 'unnatural' shadows and colours. Clearly the lighting practitioner needs to have a keen appreciation of what natural light looks like, and a good knowledge of how to reproduce its effects when required.

Learning to 'see'

For anyone interested in creating visual imagery, educating the sense of sight will clearly be important. This is sometimes described as the development from passive 'looking' to active 'seeing' (as in 'I see' to indicate understanding). Since the business of a lighting designer is light, and what light illuminates, seeing is clearly going to be important. All performance practitioners need to be aware of how much visual information is potentially available to their audience, and need to hone their skills in both reading the intentional visual cues, and spotting potentially distracting stimuli in order to eliminate them. Those particularly concerned with the visual elements of performance, for example the set, costume and lighting designers, need to be able to create stimulating images for the audience. In theatre, indeed in most live performance, we steal from wherever we can, and the field of visual imaginary is no exception. Creating stimulating images on the stage requires us to see with understanding and not just to look.

Fine art painting — composition and light

It can be difficult to begin a study of light, a constantly changing environment. Perhaps a better way to begin to develop an appreciation of light — both natural light and unnatural — is by looking at how fine art painters and photographers have captured moments of our constantly moving three dimensional world, within a static two dimensional frame. Fine art paintings and photographs, especially representational works, offer a way to study a single scene frozen in time.

There are many artists who have displayed a deep understanding of light and composition. Good quality poster sized prints can provide excellent examples for studying the handling of light, as can images from the web sites of some galleries. Some of my favourites include examples of Michelangelo's work in the Sistine Chapel, where he uses light in several ways; to help demonstrate physicality and the representation of three dimensions on a flat surface, and frequently as a metaphor. I also find inspiration in much of Rembrandt's work, especially his handling of artificial light sources inside, for example in *The Blinding of Samson*. Most of the few surviving works by Jan Vermeer depict interiors too; wonderfully balanced compositions, to me almost driven by a cool clear light, often from an unseen source to the left of the picture (or in proscenium theatre terms, off stage right).

There are many other inspiring works from many other periods and styles of art. I have a particular affection for the landscapes of two British artists from the early 19th century, J.M.W. Turner and John Constable, both concerned with the play of sunlight and sky, but working in very different styles. In the late 19th century, the Impressionist artists were deeply concerned with the play of light in their work. Many worked in a consciously theatrical way; Edgar Degas drew much of his inspiration and subject matter from the Paris Ballet. Quite apart from the joy of studying these works for their own sake, lighting practitioners need to be able to look at a scene and make a reasonable guess as to the position and nature of each light source affecting it. Even postcard reproductions of paintings can be used to hone this skill.

Whilst these famous, even iconic, works are readily available as reproductions, seeing paintings for real can be more rewarding, and the paintings don't have to be by the great artists to have an impact. It is a good idea for anyone involved in making visual performance to have a reasonable knowledge of fine art, as a reference point for discussions about style and look for a particular production, and this means getting to know the great iconic works, from the past and the present. In addition, for a lighting practitioner, a visit to a gallery or exhibition is more than getting to know a historical style from the works. A more general concern with composition and the handling of light informs active viewing. If you are new to this try these few questions to begin with:

'Where are the light sources within the image?'
'How could that look be reproduced in performance?'
'What am I reading from this image beyond surface meaning?'

Figure 11. One of several paintings by Edgar Degas titled *The Rehearsal*, from between 1873–78. Original in the Fogg Art Museum, Harvard University MA. The artist uses light and shadow to aid the impression of solid form, especially in his rendition of the dancers' limbs. Photograph by Fogg Art Museum, Harvard University Art Museums, USA/Bequest from the Collection of Maurice Wertheim, Class 1906/The Bridgeman Art Library

'How is that information being communicated to me?'
'What role is light playing in my reading?'

If you are a newcomer to this way of seeing pictures, you may be surprised to find that many artists cheat with the sources of light, even in highly representational art. It is not unusual to find inconsistencies used for dramatic or narrative effect, or more often for reasons of composition. A lighting designer may sometimes want to do much the same — for example highlighting different areas of the stage from different directions for compositional or practical reasons. A close study of how old masters get away with it can be useful.

Photography

Photography became the primary mode of representational art in the last century. It appears to be much more instantly available to the practitioner and the viewer than painting or drawing. Because of this it is often disregarded as art, after all anyone with a camera can take a photo. This may be true, but some photographers have the ability to consistently produce powerful images, and it is worthwhile investigating what is different about their photographs compared to the average holiday snap. One of my favourite 20th century photog-

raphers is Henri Cartier-Bresson, who worked almost exclusively in black and white, in the world outside the studio. His photographs demonstrate a technical proficiency with the tools of his craft, the camera, its lenses and shutter, the film, and the techniques of the dark room. But they also demonstrate an ability to connect the viewer with the subject, and to tell a story, and most of that is through choice of subject, and frame — that is composition. On the performance stage, the lighting almost always defines the composition of the stage picture, the centres of interest and the relative importance of background and foreground, the depth of field, the boundaries, the visibility of textures and so on. A study of good photography can help an understanding of how elements combine in powerful ways to communicate more than the sum of their individual parts.

Many lighting designers are keen photographers themselves — both to record their work and for inspiration. There are similarities between photography and lighting design — the same need to balance creative skills with mastering technology, and of course the same basic material — light. Digital photography has considerably reduced the cost of experimenting — it no longer costs so much to take and look at hundreds of shots. You can then spend time developing a technical skill with the camera and an eye for your own photographs as well as those of others.

If you want to develop seeing by taking photographs, try to get hold of a camera with as much control over focus and exposure as you can afford. This kind of machine may be more difficult to master, but once you have done that, any good photographs you produce will be much more your own work rather than the happy accidents of the 'snapper'. Also take care with the colour temperature or white balance setting — auto white balance is not a good option for anyone interested in recording digital images of performance.

Performance and communication

The study of performance gives us tools to speak about and analyse how communication takes place, between stage and audience in both the highly organised context of, for example, a theatrical production and the less formally organised circumstances of everyday life. In most live performance there is a torrent of information, in words and other sounds, and potentially in every other sensory channel, available to those observing the performance. For the most part, the observers will engage in the apparently natural human instinct to make sense of this information. Just how this happens, how audiences make sense of, or *read*, that information is a key element of performance studies. Makers of performance, from avant-garde performance artists to Broadway or West End producers, including designers and performers, will often claim to have an understanding of the ways in which an audience can read a performance. This may be expressed in the academic language of performance studies or as gut instinct gained over years of trial and error. Whatever the source of the understanding, and however it is expressed, it points to the importance of communication between the makers and the audience of a live performance. The makers of performance need to have some idea of what it is they want to communicate to the audience — even if it is apparently something as simple as having a good time!

We have mentioned before the idea of a formally organised performance creating a special place — a place pregnant with possibilities and meaning. For Western theatre this idea goes back to the beginning of formalised performance on the stage in ancient Greece. The concept also appears in other cultures; the idea of performing musicians or priest/performers opening gateways to possibilities not available in everyday life is common to many cultures. An audience for a live performance is very often eager to read meaning into what they hear and see (and perhaps touch, smell or even taste) on stage, and as makers of that performance we need to be aware of that, and be prepared to engage in the generation of coherent meaning in the performance.

Communication and the role of the lighting designer

For those working on the creation of performance, perhaps the only guiding principal should be to remember that everything presented to the audience is capable of being read, interpreted, and given significance by that audience in their normal human desire to make sense of what they are experiencing. This includes all the elements we present intentionally, as well as those elements that slip in by accident or omission.

The work of the performance lighting designer is often of pivotal importance to successful communication between stage and audience. The visual elements of the performance will be seen only if there is light there.

How they are seen (and therefore how they are read by the audience) will be determined largely by how they are lit. Clearly this is a good reason to pay attention to lighting a performance, and for the person or people in charge of doing that, to be fully in tune with the channels of signification used by the production.

Strong signification from stage lighting is rarely possible without careful collaboration with the director, other designers and the performers. Without rigorous effort to integrate the stage lighting signs with the way the performers move,[1] with the scenic design, and with all the other elements of the production, the lighting will no longer have the intended signification, and may be read as 'careless mistakes', producing a negative or unsatisfactory reading of the production. There is more about signification in the appendix on semiotics

Lighting and audibility

On the dramatic stage, lighting the faces of the actors is almost always the first priority for the lighting designer. Research in the fields of artificial intelligence, language teaching, brain function and from elsewhere have all confirmed as scientific fact what many 'old school'

[1] In performance studies, we use the terms proxemics and kinesics to describe in detail the ways in which a performer makes use of space. See E. Aston & G. Savona, *Theatre As Sign System*, Routledge, 1991 for a good introduction to these topics in the context of semiotics.

theatre practitioners have been saying for years. We comprehend language with our eyes as well as with our ears.[2] Thanks to science's ability to map what is going on in our brains, it is now possible to say with some certainty that a good view of the speaker's face aids cognitive processing of speech; in other words, when the audience can see the actor's face, and particularly the area round the mouth, they will be able to process (and therefore understand) what is spoken more quickly than if they cannot see the actor's face. This is not quite the same notion as that 'the audience can't hear if they can't see faces. After all how would radio work if that were true? What some of the research points to is that there are situations where seeing the face significantly improves comprehension. Researchers refer to times when the auditory channel is compromised, which usually means there is an amount of background noise or the language pattern is unfamiliar. For a performance environment, this could mean lighting faces becomes especially important when words are spoken over a sound-scape or background music, or when the words are not the familiar 'everyday' speech we are used to — the blank verse of Shakespeare or the heavily loaded prose of Becket might both be examples of that. Even in contemporary drama using patterns of speech familiar to the audience, delivered in a quiet space, the chances are the words will be more significant than the chatter of 'everyday' speech. A lighting designer needs to have a really good reason if they are not to light the face of a speaking performer. In performance genre where comprehending the spoken word is important, performance lighting influences how well the audience hear as well as how they see.

artists and fine art photographers. We have also touched on elements of performance theory. For anyone who wants or needs to understand a little more about some of the concepts used in performance theory, there is an appendix at the back of the book which provides some thoughts on semiotics for performance.

The rest of this book concentrates on the art and craft of performance lighting, but this is only a part of the knowledge necessary to become a successful designer of light in performance. There are many other useful areas of study for someone aspiring to work in performance lighting, including a study of music of any and all kinds, abstract art, architecture, history and literature. On top of these, any engaged theatre practitioner needs to have a good understanding of the organisational structures and processors of the genres of performance that particularly interest them.

At best, any single book can only provide a part of the knowledge needed by a practitioner, and there is no substitute for experiment and practical research. Please keep this in mind as you continue through this book.

Summary

In this first chapter, we have covered a lot of ground; from an introduction to the physics of light and to fine

FIGURE 12. This photograph shows a student working at a lighting desk in the foreground, while the rehearsal continues on stage.

---

[2] I have found useful work on the links between visual and auditory speech recognition and comprehension in journals ranging from Cognitive Neuroscience to Computer Assisted Language Teaching. For readers who wish to look further into this interesting research field, some key words are 'visual speech' and 'speechreading'.

2

an introduction to the tools of lighting

Overview of a performance lighting system

In live performance, it is usual to want to be able to control the light focused at the stage, to ensure it reveals what the audience should see, and hides what the audience should not see, and to make light work for the performance. The light for performance most often comes, not from 'naked' light bulbs (referred to as lamps by professional lighting practitioners) but from instruments developed mostly for theatre, which are able to focus and colour the light, and to add texture and depth to the stage picture.

Most practitioners will want the light on stage to change over the duration of the performance, even if it is only to become brighter at the beginning and to return to a dark state at the end. To enable this, most lighting systems contain dimmers and at least one controller, or lighting desk. We live in a digital age, and most modern lighting systems reflect this. The link between lighting controller and dimmers, or even between lighting controller and lighting instrument, is most often a digital one. There is a diagram of a lighting control system, showing the path from lighting desk to stage on the next page.

Lighting instruments

The lanterns (or units, or instruments — the three words are more or less interchangeable) used in performance lighting fall broadly into three categories.

1 **Floods.** As the name suggests, these units allow light to flood out over a wide angle, determined by the shape of the reflector and of unit itself. Floods have no lens. In performance, their main use is to light

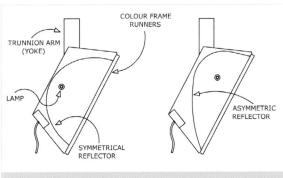

FIGURE 1. SIMPLE FLOODS

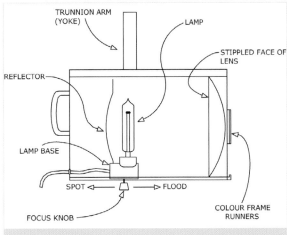

FIGURE 2. PC LANTERN

From the lighting desk
(or lighting console)...

Control signals

SIMPLE 2 PRESET LIGHTING CONTROL DESK

MULTI-PLAYBACK LIGHTING CONTROL DESK, CAPABLE
OF CONTROLLING MOVING LIGHTS AND VIDEO AS
WELL AS CONVENTIONAL LANTERNS

signal cables carry instructions
from the control desk to...

Control signals

ELECTRICAL POWER

VERY LARGE CABLES CARRY
ELECTRICAL POWER TO THE DIMMERS

US TOURING DIMMER RACK
WITH PATCH FACILITIES

A SMALLER TOURING RACK CONTAINING 24 X 10
AMP DIMMERS

...the dimmers, which then feed
controlled electrical power to...

Control signals

LIGHTING MULTICORES

...lanterns (or fixtures) which can then illuminate the performance on stage

FIGURE 3. SCHEMATIC OF A LIGHTING CONTROL SYSTEM.

large items of scenery, such as back cloths and cyclo-ramas.[1] They are also useful as work light and sometimes as audience light, though the lack of beam control can have disadvantages here.

2 Fresnel[2] and PC.[3] Both names refer to the type of lens in these units. They emit a round beam, the size

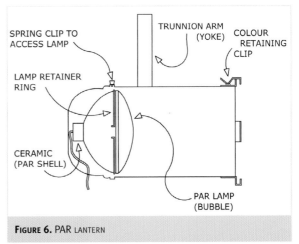

FIGURE 6. PAR LANTERN

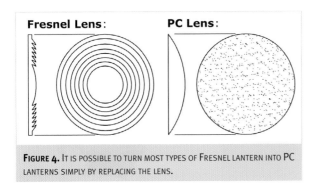

FIGURE 4. IT IS POSSIBLE TO TURN MOST TYPES OF FRESNEL LANTERN INTO PC LANTERNS SIMPLY BY REPLACING THE LENS.

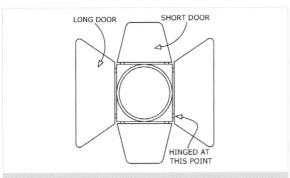

FIGURE 5. A BARN DOOR, USED FOR SHAPING THE BEAM OF PC AND FRESNEL LANTERNS.

of which is adjusted by moving the reflector and bulb assembly closer to (bigger beam) or further away (smaller beam) from the lens. The edge of the beam is 'soft', that is the intensity falls off relatively slowly, so the beams of these lanterns can be joined together relatively easily to make a wash of light, covering a large area. The beams can be shaped by *barn doors* (see below). They are used mostly from a short or medium *throw*, or distance from target, between 2m and 12m.

2a PAR 64s.[4] These are a significant sub-type, providing much the same softness of beam and ease of joining beams together as Fresnel and PC units, but without the same ability to change the beam

---

[1]Strictly, the cyclorama is a plain surface wrapped around a performance space to give the feeling of infinity. It can be fabric, but in some spaces, such as TV or film studios, it is a hard structure with a gentle curve at the bottom and the sides. On many large proscenium stages, the 'cyc' as it is often called, is made from back projection screen material, stretched tight on a frame, as wide and as high as the practicalities of the theatre flying system will allow. The idea is to give the impression of infinite depth to the stage space, to reproduce on stage the feeling of open sky.

[2]Augustine Fresnel (pronounced *fren-elle*) a Frenchman working in the early years of the 19th century, invented this type of lens, originally for use in light houses. The more steps there are in the lens the more even the intensity across the beam.

[3]PC in this context stands for pebble convex, a version of the standard plano-convex lens used in many optical devices such as spectacles and simple telescopes. The pebble refers to small bumps on the otherwise flat surface of the lens which help to diffuse the image of the filament and make the edge of the beam softer. Continental fixtures have a plain plano-convex lens.

[4]PAR stands for parabolic aluminumised reflector. The number after the PAR is the diameter of lamp in eighths of an inch. Thus a PAR 64 has a lamp which is 8 inches in diameter. There are many other sizes of PAR, and many different uses, both within the entertainment industry and outside it. For example, air-craft landing lights (ACLs) and PAR16s — mini-PARs also know as birdies.

angle. PARs have a fixed beam angle. The PAR lamp is a sealed unit containing, along with the filament, the reflector and the lens. These determine the beam angle and its shape which is usually oval. To change beam angle it is necessary to change the lamp rather than simply move a knob. PAR 64s are relatively low cost, robust lanterns. Their reliability and ease of use have made them a favourite tool of many lighting practitioners.

3 **Profiles.** In traditional proscenium theatres, most of the lanterns used front of house[5] will be profiles. They come in many different forms, but almost all have the common features shown in the diagram. They can produce a hard edged beam, by which we

FIGURE 8. ETC SOURCE FOUR PROFILE. THIS SMALL AND EFFICIENT UNIT, WITH A FIXED FOCAL LENGTH, IS VERY COMMON IN NORTH AMERICA AND EUROPE.

mean the intensity of the beam drops rapidly to almost nothing at the edge. The beam can be shaped accurately using shutters. Zoom profiles can be adjusted to give various different sizes of beam. Profiles can be used to project patterns, usually know as gobos (or templates in North America). They can be focused with a soft edge to enable several to be joined into a single wash of light. Profiles are often used as lighting specials (there is more on lighting specials on p. 41).

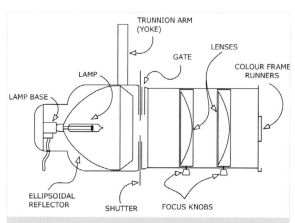

FIGURE 7. SIMPLE ZOOM PROFILE WITH AN ELLIPTICAL REFLECTOR, AN EXAMPLE OF JUST ONE OF THE MANY DIFFERENT DESIGNS OF PROFILE LANTERN AVAILABLE.

Pre-use checks

Anybody who plugs in any piece of electrical equipment has a moral and legal obligation to check, as far as they can, that it is safe to use. This is especially true of performance lighting instruments which will usually need to be focused by someone while the lantern is switched on, increasing the risk of electric shock to the person focusing, who will often be some metres above the ground. Also lighting instruments are often hung

[5]Front of house, or FoH, refers to the space where the audience are, as opposed to back stage, the stage house, or rear of house. FoH lighting positions in older theatres will normally have been created many years after the theatre was first built, and often are not the ideal solution, merely the least impractical one.

above people, audience or performer, who could be badly hurt if even part of the instrument fell from its rigged position.

With this in mind, it is essential that anyone using lighting instruments exercises proper care. This includes pre-use checks for electrical and mechanical soundness. If you don't know how to do this, either find someone who can show you, or don't use the equipment!

Check for a compliance mark, especially on unfamiliar equipment. In the European Union this is the CE mark, in North America the UL mark. Also check that the equipment will work at your voltage, and won't blow the fuse on the circuit you are using.

It is also good practice to have some indication of when the equipment last had a detailed inspection and test by a competent person, and when it should be tested again (usually as PAT sticker in the UK. PAT stands for portable appliance test). It is not advisable to use equipment that is beyond its test due date, and it is illegal to use equpiment that has been declared unsafe by a competent person.

Here is a list of some basic pre-use checks.

■ The unit is clean and in a good state of repair. Not only can a build up of dirt cause a fire, dusty lanterns are usually dim lanterns. Check that the case of the unit is undamaged, and that all the screws and nuts and bolts are in place. If you are unfamiliar with the particular type of unit, ask someone who knows, or get a drawing, for example, from the manufacturer's web site.

■ The plug of the unit and the socket it is to be plugged into are compatible, and are both undamaged.

■ The cable feeding power to the unit is undamaged and there are no nicks, frays or cuts in any of the insulation. The point where the cable goes into the unit is often most vulnerable to damage, and needs to be inspected carefully.

■ The suspension clamp(s) are up to the job. Ideally all suspension equipment should be clearly marked with its safe working load limit, and all equipment should be marked with its weight. In practice you may sometimes have to use your own skill and judgement where these marks are absent or unclear. It is good practice to use a secondary suspension device, such as a steel wire rope safety bond, on all lanterns suspended at height. If the clamp is unrated, ensure the safety bond is rated to hold the full weight of the unit.

■ All accessories are secured to the unit in an appropriate manner, with clips or bonds, and that these do not impede the functioning of the accessory, e.g. you can still turn the barn doors of a Fresnel lantern.

■ **And finally: check it works!** For example, for a profile lantern, the lenses and all the shutters move as they should. If it is possible to 'flash out' i.e. to plug in the lantern and switch it on to see light coming out of it, then do. Replacing a lamp or fixing a unit on the ground is faster and safer than trying to do the same later from the top of a ladder.

Remember this is the minimum. Checks should become second nature but never lose their importance, since one mistake can result in serious injury or even death.

Other sources for performance lighting

The majority of the lighting instruments described above use incandescent lamp technology. The light is produced by electrical heating of a tungsten filament in a quartz glass envelope filled with halogen gas, hence tungsten halogen, or sometimes quartz halogen. When the full design voltage is applied across the filament, the tungsten glows white hot and emits light. For anyone with a reliable electrical supply, this is a very easy way to make light. It is also relatively easy to control the intensity of that light. By reducing the applied voltage across the lamp, we can reduce the amount of current flowing through the filament and thus the heat, and light, produced by the lamp. The light gets dimmer and changes in colour as the voltage drops, and the filament gets cooler. There is proportionally more red and less blue in the white of a relatively cool filament than in the white of a very hot filament. Psychologically, we perceive the light with more red in it, coming from the cooler filament, to be warmer than the light coming from the very hot filament, with a higher proportion of blue in its white. This seeming paradox is the situation most current lighting practitioners have grown up with. As we dim our incandescent lanterns, the light coming from them appears warmer. As we increase the intensity by increasing the applied voltage, the filament gets hotter and the light appears cooler.

What an outsider might consider a huge inconvenience has been turned in most cases, to a positive advantage, for example, enabling the same lanterns to act as both a dim warm and a bright cool wash simply by changing their intensity. Theatre practitioners have become used to seeing the dimming light on stage 'warm up', and for stages to feel cooler as intensity builds. It may not always be this way, however.

The modern tungsten halogen filament lamp, although much more efficient than its predecessor, is not an efficient way to produce light. Much of the energy consumed by a tungsten halogen lamp is wasted as heat. If that were not bad enough, this waste heat often has to be removed from the performance space, consuming more energy in ventilation and air conditioning plant. Environmental and commercial pressures have already made it very hard to use tungsten lighting in new build commercial premises. Performance lighting is probably safe for some time yet, but as practitioners looking to the future, we should be aware that the days of rigs with predominantly incandescent lamps will not last for ever. So what else is out there?

On the left, the lamp is dim and the light from it is warm. On the right the lamp is brighter and the light is cooler.

More scientifically, the higher applied voltage on the right produces light with a higher intensity and a higher colour temperature.

FIGURE 9. CLOSE-UP OF AN INCANDESCENT LAMP: THE APPLIED VOLTAGE IS ABOUT 10% OF THE FULL DESIGN VOLTAGE.

FIGURE 10. THE SAME INCANDESCENT LAMP: HERE THE APPLIED VOLTAGE IS CLOSE TO 100% OF THE FULL DESIGN VOLTAGE.

A brief guide to colour temperature

As we have already discussed, white light is made up of a mixture of colours. There are different 'whites' each containing a different proportion of the colours in the rainbow. Physics tells us that the proportion of each colour, or wavelength, of light emitted by a perfect black body radiator is dependant on the temperature of that radiator. This creates a scale of white light emitted from bodies of different temperatures, expressed as the colour temperature, and measured in degrees Kelvin. For our purposes, the light from a tungsten halogen lamp is similar to that from a black body radiator. Both produce a continuous spectrum, with none of the colour from the rainbow missing. A tungsten halogen lamp at full brightness usually approximates to a black body temperature of 3200 degrees Kelvin, written as 3200K. At around 80% intensity the filament gets a little cooler and the colour temperature falls to around 2700K.

Light from a candle sits as just under 2000K on this scale, while the noon day sun ranges between about 5000K and 7000K, depending on the time of year, weather conditions and latitude. There are more values of colour temperature for different sources in the table on the right.

Many other types of light source do not produce a continuous spectrum, and therefore the light they emit can only approximate the continuous spectrum of a black body radiator. Colour temperature is not a full description of the quality of the light — some of the frequencies (colours) present in light from a black body radiator of the same colour temperature may be missing. One consequence of this is that colours may appear different under the light of a tungsten source and, say a fluorescent source, or the discharge lamp of a follow spot. The colour rendition index (CRI) of a lamp gives an indication of how 'complete' its spectrum is.

Blue sky, sunny day 12000° K to 18000° K
Overcast sky ~ 7000° K
White LEDs 6500° K to 9500° K
Xenon or HMI daylight lamp ~ 6000° K
'Photographic' daylight 5500° K
Warm white fluorescent 4000° K
Tungsten/halogen incandescent 3200° K
Sunrise/sunset ~ 3000° K
100W household lamp 2900° K
Gaslight ~ 2100° K

Discharge lamps

This is a large category, including some types of source that have only very specialist uses. It includes many industrial sources, used for street lighting and in large work spaces. Although performance lighting practitioners do use some of these lamps with narrow spectra, for the moment I will focus on lamps designed specifically to give us light we can usefully call white. Discharge lamps are more efficient than incandescent lamps — more of the power going in comes out as light. It is not possible to dim discharge lamps in the same way that incandescent lamps can be dimmed. Instead, the lamp stays on and some form of mechanical shutter opens or closes either inside the fixture or in front of it. Discharge lamps produce heat, often considerable amounts of heat, which requires fans to remove it from the fixture. This can make fixtures with discharge lamps unsuitable for some venues, and fan noise remains a problem in many others.

Where the problems of dimming and fan noise can be overcome, or at least side stepped, discharge lamps are widely used in performance lighting. Most follow spots, projectors and moving lights use them. Opera and the film world have embraced high wattage discharge lamps to light large areas with a single source, thus producing single shadows. The issues raised by the use of discharge lamps in performance lighting are twofold.

1 The 'white' of most discharge lamps is significantly bluer than the 'white' of tungsten lamps, even when the tungsten lamp is at full. This means that light from instruments with discharge lamps looks different to that from instruments with incandescent lamps.

2 When you do dim discharge sources (e.g. by putting remotely controlled louvre shutters in front of the lantern) the beam does not respond the same way as a conventional incandescent lantern. Unless you have high quality shutter systems, the results of a slow fade can be disappointing. In situations where the face of the lantern is visible to the audience this can create greater distraction by drawing attention away from the stage and towards these bright beginnings of light.

For these reasons the beams from discharge sources stand out from those in the rest of the rig.

In high wattage discharge lamps the light comes from a sustained spark, or arc, contained by a quartz glass bulb filled with a tightly controlled mix of gasses. Rather than the continuous spectrum of colours produced by an incandescent source, the spark produces discrete spectral lines, which means that there may be some colours present in light from a tungsten source that are not present in a discharge source. The function of the gasses is to help spread the spectral lines and fill these gaps, but the technique is not perfect, and the spectrum from a discharge source is noticeably different to that from an incandescent source. Most noticeable is the dominance of higher energy frequencies of light, in the blue, violet and even ultraviolet range. UV light needs to be filtered out of the beam of theatre lanterns using discharge lamps to ensure that it does not damage the eyes or skin of performers.[6]

The relative dominance of blue light in the spectrum of most discharge lamps means that their light most closely compares to light with a colour temperature somewhat higher than that of standard tungsten halogen sources. This, along with the relative lack of red in their spectrum, helps to give the light from discharge lamps a different quality or feel to that of tungsten halogen lamps.

The differences in spectral composition can make some colours look dull under discharge light. As the technology behind spreading the spectrum of discharge light gets better, this becomes less of a problem, but it is worth checking important colours used in scenic elements and costume under the light sources the production will be using, in order not to be unpleasantly surprised.

The difference in quality of light between tungsten halogen lamps and discharge lamps cannot be ignored by the lighting practitioner or the rest of the creative team, whether the lamps are in the large fixtures favoured by opera and film, or in moving lights, or specialist projectors. Handled with care, these differences can enhance the lighting states, and the performance. Handled clumsily the qualities can clash, and the different ways in which the different sources dim can draw attention away from the desired focus of that moment of performance.

Fluorescent lighting

Fluorescent tubes, once confined to the factory and office, are increasingly common on the stage. Strictly speaking fluorescent light is another kind of discharge light, but there is much less heat involved. Fluorescent lamps are energy efficient, produce a smooth soft light, and the technology now exists to successfully dim fluorescent tubes, from full down to zero, without the distracting flicker such systems used to be prone to. The

---

[6]Technicians and others working on units with discharge lamps need to guard against exposure of their eyes and skin to damaging ultraviolet. Severe sunburn and a condition called 'arc eye' will result from careless exposure, for example during maintenance work on discharge fixtures.

Some typical values of colour rendition index

Light source	Daylight	Tungsten Halogen Incandescent	Fluorescent (including compact and T2 tubes)	Metal halide (e.g. HMI or Xenon)	High pressure sodium	Low pressure sodium (orange street lights)
Typical CRI	100 (by definition)	95 to 100	75 to 85	65 to 85	25	0 to 18

colour temperature of the light remains constant throughout the range of intensity, unlike incandescent lamps. As with other discharge sources, colour temperature here is an approximation, because to a greater or lesser extent, light from fluorescent lamps does not have the continuous spectrum of an incandescent source. Colour rendition index (CRI), a measure of how well colours are rendered under different light sources, varies across the range of tubes, and, as with the discharge sources, technological advances are improving performance.

Tubes can be wrapped in coloured lighting media, mounted in banks of three or four, and successfully used to light small to medium sized cycloramas. Fluorescent tubes are also fitted in some soft light fixtures used in lighting for cameras. Here the constant colour temperature is a real advantage. Fluorescent tube fixtures can also be used for set lighting, and soft,

FIGURE 12. THIS LED FIXTURE FROM MARTIN PROFESSIONAL IS BASED ON AN RGB CELL, AND CAN BE BUILT INTO LONG ROWS FOR CYC LIGHTING OR BLOCKS FOR DISPLAY.

even and discrete footlights from the front edge of the stage.

The light from these fixtures is diffused, with a wide spread — no beam as such — so it can be hard to contain, resulting in 'spill' illuminating things we would rather stayed in the dark. This diffuse light is good at filling shadows, which can be a positive or a negative, depending on the particular situation. It has a distinctive quality, which, like the light from discharge sources, when handled appropriately, can be very effective.

Light emitting diodes

Light emitting diodes (LEDs) have been the big news at most of the lighting trade fairs of the last few years. Every year they become brighter and more affordable, and yet as I write, they have made little impact on theatre lighting practice. At Showlight 2005 in Munich, leading UK based opera and theatre lighting designer Paule Constable said 'They don't smell right', and most of the people in the room knew what she meant.

FIGURE 11. LIKE MOST FLUORESCENT UNITS, THIS FLUORESCENT SOFT-LIGHT FROM DE-SISTI CAN BE DIMMED TO AROUND 20% OF FULL ON STANDARD DIMMERS OR USED WITH A PROPRIETARY DIMMING SYSTEM.

Coloured LEDs are a very efficient source of light,[7] but limited in size. This means LED fixtures often use clusters of LEDs. Many manufacturers have now successfully produced LED cyc floods, with a mix of three or four colours of LED. These units enable a lighting designer to produce a huge range of colours and other effects on a cyclorama, with considerably less power than would have been required by incandescent units. The white produced by these units however does indeed 'smell odd', and multiple sources in each unit produces multiple different coloured shadows, both factors that hold back their use for lighting people at present.

Moving lights

Moving lights used to be toys, used primarily for effects, not for lighting performers. Then they became the tool of choice for live concert lighting and light entertainment TV — both genre heavily dependant on follow spots to light 'the money', that is the principal performer or performers. The moving lights were used — often very effectively — to create an energised space in which the principal performed, lit by a follow spot. While some moving lights are still used in this way, many large-scale theatre and concert performances use moving lights as their main lighting tool, for lighting the set, for creating exciting effects, *and* for lighting the performers. Competition amongst manufacturers and advances in technology have both contributed to greater availability and to an expanding range of moving lights. In the West End and on Broadway, large musicals use as many moving lights now as they used profile lanterns 20 years ago. They are increasingly being integrated into the repertory rigs of opera houses and state theatres, and even occasionally make an appearance in London fringe venues and off-Broadway shows. In the live music industry, almost every venue with its own rig has moving lights, and touring bands playing one nights in clubs frequently travel with their own 'movers'. They even make their appearance in concerts above a classical orchestra or choir, provided they are the kind without fans, since noise is still a problem for many environments.

Even though prices have fallen in relative terms, they are still not cheap, and a budget conscious production may have to make considerable sacrifices to pay rental and maintenance costs. We have already touched

FIGURE 13. THREE MOVING LIGHTS FROM MARTIN PROFESSIONAL. THE MAC 700 PROFILE AND THE MAC 700 WASH, BOTH MOVING HEADS, SIT EITHER SIDE OF A ROBOSCAN, A MOVING MIRROR FIXTURE ALSO KNOWN AS A SCANNER.

[7]White LEDs however are presently no more efficient than household incandescent lamps, though many research hours are being invested in improving their efficiency.

briefly on the light source used in most moving lights — discharge lamps, and how the differences in the quality of the light and the way it dims can cause problems. Many moving lights are poor at reproducing the pale tints favoured especially by lighting designers working in theatre. Moving lights require more complex control systems than dimmers, and often require a dedicated programmer and technical support. With all these potential problems, why are they so popular? What do they offer that makes them worth the money, the difficulties with matching beam quality and dimming, and the poor colour performance?

Benefits of moving lights

The original London production of *Miss Saigon* was amongst the first commercial theatre shows to use moving lights for more than just effect. Lighting designer David Hersey found himself with hardly any space to hang lanterns, most of the grid having been taken up with scenery and bridges. He used the Vari*Lite™ II hard-edged moving lights and Vari*Lite™ IV colour wash lights as re-focusable specials and as individual elements of several washes, replacing between them the function of many generic units, which in any case he had nowhere to hang. As the production developed in the theatre — in common with many large scale musicals of the time, there was an extended devising and rehearsal period on the stage — other advantages of the moving lights became apparent. It was possible for the lighting department to respond almost immediately to blocking and other changes on the stage. Whereas before it would have been necessary for a person to climb up to a lantern and change its colour, position, beam shape or gobo, now it is only necessary to pass a comment to the moving light programmer, who with a few key strokes can accomplish all this from behind the lighting desk in the auditorium. Ideas can be tried out with minimal fuss. Those that

worked can be integrated into the show; those that do not can be abandoned, with minimum wasted effort.

More recently, lighting designer Rick Fisher and his programmer Vic Smerdon were able to extend this practice on the London production of *Billy Elliot*. Using powerful moving lights with remotely adjustable shutters, they were able to create boxed off isolated areas on the otherwise open stage with ease, and change them quickly in response to new ideas from the creative team.

What moving lights do and don't do

There are several ways to divide moving lights. First is the split between those that move a mirror in front of a fixed body and those that move the whole lantern, or head, usually by means of a motorised yoke attached to a box housing electronics and the power supply. In the early years of moving lights, moving mirror lights were faster and more reliable, but moving head fixtures have now caught up and their increased flexibility has made them by far the more popular of these two types in most applications.

Next is the divide between 'projectors' also called 'hard edged light' and 'wash lights'. The first have similar optics to a traditional profile lantern, and can be used to project gobos. The second have similar optics to a PC or Fresnel, and are used primarily to provide coloured washes of light.

Colour systems provide a further way to divide moving lights. The split is between discrete colour changing and continuous colour changing. Discrete colour changing uses either an internal wheel loaded with dichroic[8] glass filters which can be remotely inserted into the beam, or by an external colour scroller, as shown on the Revolution™ moving profile lantern. Continuous colour changing also uses dichroic glass colour filters in three colours; cyan, yellow and magenta (CYM). A variety of patented methods in introducing dif-

[8]Dichroic glass colour filters use thin film technology to produce intense colours, and are frequently used in moving lights. They can be made to allow only very narrow bands of frequencies through, resulting in very pure colours of light. Their production requires stringent quality control, and when this is absent, it can be impossible to match colours in adjacent moving lights.

ferent amounts of each filter into the beam can produce a large range of colours. These CYM moving lights can also be made to change the colour of their beam in a 'fade' as opposed to the 'bump'[9] colour change of a colour wheel.

Lamp type provides a further split. While most moving lights use discharge lamps, some use incandescent lamps. These are much easier to integrate into a generic lighting rig of instruments with tungsten halogen lamps. The quality of light is similar, and they behave in the same way as they fade intensity.

Beam shaping provides another differentiator. The number of gobos available and how many of them rotate could be important in deciding on a particular unit for an effects-heavy show. The presence and accuracy of beam shaping shutters and 'frost' effects will be important for other shows. Some units offer a zoom function — especially useful for lanterns at the side of a stage whose targets may be close on their own side or far away on the opposite side of the stage. Most units offer some kind of remote adjustment to the beam edge and quality, however the compact design of some units seems to lead to limitations in this area at times. Most lighting designers will want to assure themselves that beams will merge seamlessly if required, even if the intended use for the units presently only as individual specials.

It is very important for the lighting designer to know just how accurately the effects they ask for can be repeated, especially if the show is destined for multiple performances. The lighting designer needs to know that when a performer 'hits their mark', the lighting will also. A lighting effect that perhaps highlights only the hand of a performer is possible, but only if the instruments involved can be relied on to put the light in exactly the same place every night, and of course the performer puts their hand in that same place. This is true of moving lights just as it is for conventional lights, but it

is only recently that this level of repeatability of both position information and beam size could reasonably be expected from moving lights. Improved accuracy, along with smoother movement and better colour systems are beginning to open up new ways of working with moving lights, especially in drama and music theatre.

Several different systems exist to track the position of the performer on stage, data from the tracking system can then be fed into the lighting desk and used to control the position (and other parameters) of moving lights. These systems need to be set up with care, and even then they do not really replace good follow spot operators, but they can be very effective in some situations.

Moving lights offer many benefits to the creators of performance lighting. The range of instruments gets bigger each year. The quality of many moving light products has improved to a point where they can be seamlessly integrated into a conventional rig of static instruments with tungsten halogen lamps. The lighting rigs of many large commercial musicals are dominated by moving fixtures, and in the live music concert world moving lights have dominated rigs for some time.

Fan noise and cost remain major factors preventing wider use of moving lights in many performance environments. In 2004, following complaints from audiences and performers, all moving lights with fans were removed from the auditorium of Britain's National Theatre. Few promoters of classical music concerts will allow instruments with fans near the audience or the musicians. Many medium-scale performance spaces have invested in dimmers and conventional lanterns, and are reluctant to spend again on moving lights they often still see as 'just toys'. Manufacturers are trying to remedy both these concerns, and it is most likely that the coming years will see the introduction of moving lights into many more performance spaces.

---

[9] Fade and bump are both used to describe the time taken for a lighting cue to happen. A fade happens over a given time, which may be very short or extremely long. Some fades continue over a whole act of an opera. A bump happens as quickly as the technology will allow — ideally in zero time!

Choosing moving lights — some considerations

Question	Potential response
Is there money in the budget?	No point going much further if the answer is no — let's assume it's yes.
Do we have the knowledge available to make best use of movers?	This will usually mean someone who is experienced at putting a system together, programming moving lights, and someone who can fix them and solve system problems.
Let's assume we have a good enough reason to use movers (which might be a wish to experiment with something that is new to you) and you can negotiate sufficient resources to allow you to use them. What next? How do we choose which ones to have?	
Colour	
Does the design call for pale tints from the movers?	If so this may well eliminate some types that are not good at producing tints. It may also mean that a scroll will be needed rather than dichroic colour of (most) CYM systems.
Do you want specific colours? (A secondary question may well be do we know enough about the design to know what colours we want? For some large shows the equipment choice has to be made too early to know all the answers.)	Mostly yes. So you will need to check that your movers will produce the colours the design calls for. Even the best CYM systems have colour 'blind spots' — colours they just won't produce. If the movers have to blend with other units, they will need to produce light at least similar in colour. Make sure you see a realistic demonstration if it matters.
Do you want to be able to fade between colours (and chose colour from a wide pallet as opposed to from a list of say 10 to 20 colours on a scroll)?	Beautiful and powerful effects can be gained through changing colour 'live', but a well-planned colour scroll can do this too. It can be difficult to match colours across the rig with some CYM systems (see below).
Is it important that precisely the same colour is produced by every unit? (For some, if a few moving units are to be used as individual specials, this is not a problem. If you need the movers to produce an even colour wash then it's a different story.)	If so, this will rule out many of the older (and cheaper) units because they are not reliably consistent. It may also lead to questions about how new the lamps will be — since many lamps change their colour as well as their brightness with age. (This is a problem that most lamp manufacturers are keen to solve, so it should become less of a problem in time.)

Movement	
Moving heads or mirrors? What range of movement is required? Are targets to be followed?	Moving heads generally have more range of movement than moving mirrors. However, for automatic follow-spot systems and some other applications, moving mirrors have a big advantage — they can move smoothly from any position to any other in a straight line. Moving heads get into difficulties trying to follow targets directly underneath them.
Does the design call for fast moves (either 'live' or to rapidly reset ready for the next action)?	Moving mirrors move the fastest. Many modern moving heads move very quickly too, but . . .
Does the design call for very precise moves or very smooth slow moves?	Not all the quick fixtures are good at very slow moves, and some are not as good as others at hitting exactly the same spot on stage every night. Ask for a demo in a realistic space, i.e. somewhere with a throw similar to that on your stage.
Noise	
Establish how important quiet operation is to others involved in the production — even rock 'n' roll performers have been known to complain about the noise of the moving lights!	There are usually at least two separate problems: noise produced when the units move (or change colour/gobo, etc) and background fan noise. As ever, the best advice is to be prepared, you may have to fight to keep your noisy lights but you may also lose.
Do the fixtures run in a quiet mode? If so what other restrictions does this put on the fixture?	Part of being prepared is knowing stuff like this. If you can quote the noise reduction in dB, it shows you are at least taking an interest in the problem.
Beam	
Gobos: how many? Glass or metal? If glass, black and white or full colour (or any of the other options in between)? How much will they cost, and how long will they take to be delivered?	Different moving lights have different ways of mounting gobos, need gobos of different sizes, and sometimes different materials. Don't assume gobos from one sort of fixture will fit in another, or that if they do the resulting image will be the same.
Beam size: moving lights will usually need to be useful over a large part of the performance area so the throw will change. Can your movers cope?	Beam size can be adjusted by 'zoom' and by 'iris'. Zooming concentrates the intensity into a smaller beam, while irising just cuts down the size. If you have significant differences in required throw distances for a single fixture, zooming is much better.

Does the design call for shutters?	How precise will they need to be, and how repeatable, and how easy is it to adjust them on the chosen control system? How will the programmer see to make the adjustments? Some shows have used a camera to give the programmer a bird's-eye view of what they are doing on stage.

This brief table by no means covers everything you need to think about when choosing moving lights for a show. It is always wise to ask for a demonstration of any equipment you are not completely familiar with. Take advice — it is likely you can contact others who have experience of the kit you propose to use. Find out what the kit can and cannot do, what it does well, and what poorly, how much noise it really makes, how long the lamps last, how well they survive touring, etc. Decide what is important — there is no fixture ideal for every role. You will need to decide what is most important for the realisation of the lighting design, and the production as a whole. It is not a simple choice to decide to base a lighting design on moving lights. Time will be used differently — often less time focusing but more time creating lighting cues — with the right preparation (and that includes making sure the rest of the creative team understand the implications of working with moving lights) problems can be minimised.

Programming moving lights

Most performance lighting is plotted with *cue states* during rehearsals. This is when the lighting designer, hopefully working in collaboration with other members of the creative team, uses the lighting rig to create performance lighting in the performance space. It is usual for a lighting cue state to have a defined time in the piece where it happens, called the *cue point*. This cue point may be called by a stage manager following a script or score (as in the UK and US theatre tradition) or taken by the lighting operator, who has a good knowledge of the show (as in live music concert lighting). Making sure the lighting does what the lighting designer requires at each cue point and throughout the show is usually accomplished by storing each cue state in a computer-controlled lighting desk, and then playing them back on command during the performance. The storing of each cue state, that is all the control information required to reproduce that lighting state from the lighting rig, including the intensity of each lantern, any colour, pattern or position changes and the time each change should take, is referred to as programming. Whenever the lighting rig has colour changers, moving lights, or certain other devices, it is usually necessary to *preset* these, to make sure they are ready to do whatever the cue state requires **before** the intensity is faded up. This is also part of programming, as is

maintaining a back-up of all the stored information, and ensuring the production can continue as designed, with replacement units, in new venues, or with a different cast.

Imagine a lighting control system with just 12 dimmers, each with at least one lantern. No other technology — no colour changers, no gobo rotators, no remotely controlled movement. Imagine that the lighting desk is very limited, and will only let us set intensity levels of full, half and zero. Even with this small limited lighting system, to try out every possible cue state, at the rate of one state per second, would take more than six days' constant plotting!

Imagine how many possible states there are in a more realistic lighting system, even without moving lights — and we have not even begun to talk about transitions and the variables of both cue time and cue placement, both of which can have a significant affect on the effectiveness of performance lighting. Once we introduce moving lights into the rig, the possibilities, and technical complications are multiplied many times. It is usual in these circumstances for the lighting designer to delegate some of the control of these myriad possibilities to others, the first of these being the *lighting programmer*. At best, the lighting programmer provides the lighting designer with a link between their artistic vision of the light for each moment of the performance and its technical realisation. To do this the lighting designer and programmer must establish a good working relationship. This can allow the lighting designer working in the performance space to free themself of the constraints of thinking channel numbers, colour numbers and exactly how an effect can be executed, to focus maximum attention on collaboration with the rest of the creative team, for example the director, other designers, choreographer etc, and the appropriateness of the light at each moment of performance. This does not absolve the lighting designer of the need to have a good knowledge of the lighting rig and what it is doing, but it does mean that they need not be tied to a single position in the auditorium during lighting rehearsals, or to merely receiving and interpreting instructions from the director.

Preset focus — palettes — focus groups

If one single thing has made using moving lights in performance lighting practical it is the ability to recall positions, colours and beam patterns, not as a set of numbers, but by using definable names that make sense in the context of the production. For the computer lighting desks that we use to control the moving light, the instruction to point a moving light towards the centre of the stage, with a small beam in pale pink, is a set of perhaps 24 8-bit binary numbers. To work quickly the lighting designer needs to be able to say 'Unit X, centre stage, small beam, pale pink' and to have that happen. Palettes make this possible, however it requires some preparation.

The lighting programmer has to record each of these palettes, and many more, into the lighting desk. The lighting designer and the programmer need to agree how they will refer to each parameter of the moving lights, usually divided in four groups:

■ Intensity — which may also include strobe functions.

■ Focus — that is the position of the lantern, how much pan, how much tilt.

■ Colour — continuous CYM mixing and discrete colour wheels.

■ Beam — including size, pattern or gobo and shutters.

Focus can be referred to by named targets ('drummer', 'Lady M hand washing special'), by stage area ('down stage centre', 'up stage right') or by a previously agreed grid system. Colour might be referred to by conventional lighting get numbers ('L181') or gel names ('Congo') or by close match to colour scroller frame numbers ('frame 12'). These and other choices are all valid, as long as all involved agree on which one they will use. Once agreed they can be recorded logically in the lighting desk and the relevant text attached.

During the plotting of lighting cue states the chief advantage of palettes is that they enable the lighting designer and programmer to work quickly and efficiently, using a natural common language to create lighting cue states.

Another advantage of palettes is that they can be used to rapidly update a show if blocking changes, or there is a need to change colours or beam patterns in more than one cue state, or if the show moves venue (as in a live music concert tour). Each cue state that uses a palette or palettes refers to the stored value of that palette. This means if you *update* a single palette, say 'drummer' because the position of the drums on stage is altered, all the cues containing lanterns positioned on the drummer and using the 'drummer' palette, will be automatically updated too. By changing one palette, all the cues using that palette are automatically updated. (This can lead to pitfalls, best avoided by careful naming and use of palettes.)

There is more on the implications of working with palettes in later chapters.

Note. Some lighting desk manufacturers have copyrighted words associated with lighting programming; palette and preset focus are just two, hence the title of this short section. This practice has made it harder to communicate common concepts within the lighting industry, and in my view should be reconsidered.

An introduction to washes and specials

Now we know what some of the lanterns are called, it is time to try to define a few more terms commonly used in performance lighting, starting with two that have crept into the text already — wash and special. Unfortunately, like so many terms we have come across already, and others we have yet to meet, these two important concepts in performance lighting do not have universally-defined meanings, and you may find many disagreements about what either means in detail. In general terms, a wash illuminates a broad area while a special illuminates a smaller one. Another way to define these two words is that a special has a sharp edge to its beam and a wash has an ill-defined edge. Most often, a wash is made up of several instruments or lanterns working together, quite often called wash lights, while a special is most often the effect of a single instrument. Many lighting designs are made up of washes and specials.

Imagine a lighting design for a nativity play. The lighting designer may employ washes of differing colour and differing angles to the stage to help to signify the changes in place and time through the story. For example, cool open washes for the open air times and places. Warm more contained washes would help signify 'interior' for the stable scenes, whilst a more open feel would be required for the shepherds' hill. The lighting designer may include specials for the appearance of angels, the infant saviour or for other dramatic reasons, as agreed with the director and other design collaborators.

Notice that each scene will normally require more than one wash. It is normal think about a wash being light from just one direction, or at least to appear to be from just one direction.

The lanterns that make up a wash may be referred to as a *system* (although again this word may have slightly different meanings for different practitioners). Since it is likely that the lighting designer will often want to use all the component lanterns of a particular system together, control of their intensity may be linked in a *group,* which is also the name most lighting desks have for several channels under a single controller.

By appropriate planning, the lighting designer can often use elements of the wash as specials from time to time, highlighting smaller areas of the stage by carefully controlling the relative intensity of each lantern in the wash group. Whilst the group control enables the whole wash to be adjusted quickly, individual control allows the lighting designer to be more subtle, and often to make each unit perform more than one role. To do this though, each unit (or instrument or lantern) needs to have its own control channel and its own dimmer.

It has been common practice to have several washes, or systems, from the same direction, each with a different colour or tint. Many lighting rigs designed for proscenium theatre contain three washes from each side of the auditorium, focused to provide illumination to the performers' faces on stage. These washes might be tinted straw or pink, that is 'warm', very pale blue, that is 'cool', and either left open or tinted pale lavender, that is 'neutral'. Using combinations of these washes provides variation through the piece, which could perhaps signify the difference between scenes set inside and outside, in winter and summer, two different parts of the world, or two different psychological moments. A similar method is used on many concert stages, where banks of PAR cans are arranged in systems of different colours, each system providing a different coloured wash on stage.

FIGURE 14. ACT I SCENE 2 OF *THE MASKED BALL* AT THE ENGLISH NATIONAL OPERA IN 2003.
THE CHORUS IS LIT IN A RED WASH WITH ULRICA (PRINCIPAL) IN A SPECIAL.

As moving lights get more sophisticated and prices drop further, we may see an end to the need for rigging multiple systems of instruments to produce multiple washes from each useful direction. What will not change, however, is the need to use groups of luminaire together to produce a wash on stage, and to be able to use individual control of separate units within the system producing the wash to enhance the performance lighting. There will be more about planning and focusing systems of lanterns into a wash in later chapters.

Learning how to use the tools

Chapter 1 looked at some useful properties of light, at communication in performance, and at learning to see and understand rather than just to look. This chapter has looked at some of the tools used to realise performance lighting design; different lanterns with their different beam pattern and different uses, different lamp technologies and some of their pros and cons. It has also introduced us to the first member of the lighting designer's team — the programmer.

Lighting design is about light; controlling its quality, quantity, and its signifying potential. To do this effectively, a practitioner needs to be able to see the difference between different light and to have a knowledge of how that light is produced, controlled and modified. Just as a sculptor must learn to see their sculpture before it is made, and at the same time must learn about materials and tools, about armatures and castings, so it is essential for a performance lighting designer to learn how to see the lighting state before it is created on stage and also to be confident with the tools that will create that light. Practice improves almost all practitioners, and the aspiring lighting designer needs to find places to practice both seeing and making light.

3

describing performance lighting

FIGURE 1. *THE MASKED BALL* BY GIUSEPPE VERDI BY ENGLISH NATIONAL OPERA, 2003. LIGHTING BY THE AUTHOR, SET BY ALFONS FLORES, COSTUME, MERCE PALOMA, DIRECTED BY CALIXTO BIEITO. PHOTOGRAPH BY ENO LIGHTING STAFF.

Describing and controlling light

A designer of performance lighting should be able to talk about light in the context of the production with the other members of both the creative team and the team that will realise the lighting design. It can be hard to describe light and therefore hard to discuss it, but it is not impossible. Having the words to discuss light is clearly important for anyone wishing to be involved in lighting for performance. I would argue that this includes directors, choreographers, and designers of set and costume as well as lighting people. Often it is up to the lighting people to provide the basics of that language, just as the choreographer will provide the basic language for a discussion about dance and the musical director for a discussion about music. Clearly any discussion of a specialist aspect of performance among a team including non-specialists will use more general language than a discussion between specialists. Dancers use specialist terms when talking about dance to each other that most non-dancers do not fully understand. The same is true for musicians talking about music and for lighting people talking about performance lighting.

Specialist practitioners learn specialist terms as they train (either formally or informally) and these can be intimidating to the outsider. Lighting designers working in live performance often need to develop two ways of talking about their specialist subject — the specialist language to be used amongst fellow lighting practitioners and a more general language to be used with other members of the creative team. We have already come across some specialist terms and some ways to talk about light in more general language. This chapter introduces some more examples of both types of language, once again highlighting how important communication skills are to a lighting designer.

The fundamental physical properties of light cannot be altered, they underpin all discussion. However, as we look at light for performance in more detail, it will become clear that there are matters relating to the

45

constraints of most performance situations and the workings of human visual perception that must also be taken into account.

Intensity, location, colour, beam and time

The properties of performance light at any single moment fall relatively easily into four interrelated categories.

Intensity — a measure of how much light is present.

Location of the beam in 3D space — where the light comes from and what it hits and illuminates on the way to its target, how it strikes the target, and what happens afterwards, especially in terms of shadows cast and other things illuminated. In the Vari*Lite™ tradition, this is referred to as focus, but the property should not to be confused with the sharpness or softness of image.

Colour — well we know what that is, don't we? Coloured light is usually the result of filtering some colours out of white light. Different lamps produce different 'whites', and the white light of nature is actually different colours at different times of day and year, and in different places on the earth.

Beam — including edge, pattern across the beam, and light quality of the beam. The main difference between the output of different fixture types can often be described in terms of beam. For example, a conventional profile fixture has a 'flat' beam with 'sharp' edges i.e. there is relatively even intensity across the beam and at the edge the intensity drops off very quickly. In contrast, the beam of a conventional Fresnel fixture is 'peaky' with a soft edge i.e. the intensity drops more or less continuously from the central 'hot-spot' to the indefinite edge of the beam. A conventional PC fixture has a beam somewhere in between these two, flatter than that from most modern Fresnel fixtures but with a less well defined edge than the beam from a profile fixture.

These are the same categories mentioned in the section on moving light, and this is not a coincidence, but it should be understood that this is only one way to think about the properties of light. It is current in part because that is how many moving light desks, and those who use them, work, and so it will give us a common language with which to describe the light from conventional lanterns and from moving lights.

Time — the ever-present fifth element of performance lighting; on stage, as in nature, light changes over time. Very few live productions keep the same lighting state throughout the performance, and even if they did, for reasons to do with the way human eye/brain channel works, the audience perception of the light may well change over time anyway. Time affects each of the other properties — human perception seems to be largely based on an ability to recognise changes, and changes happen over time. It also has its own discrete role to play in the creation of performance lighting on stage and we will come back to time frequently in rest of the book.

Intensity

Intensity is a measure of how much of light is present. We know that for the audience to see anything there must be some light present. For performance lighting what we are usually interested in is how much light is bouncing off things and available to enter the eye of the audience member (or go down the lens tube of a camera). In the metric system, we measure intensity in Lux, the number of Lux giving the intensity of light at a particular point.[1] Lumens, the unit most usually quoted for luminaires and projectors, is the total light output at the source. Since the beam from most sources spreads out as it gets further away from its origin, the intensity falls off too, and so an intensity measurement for a single source will decrease the further away you are from the source.

Many cameras allow the user to measure relative intensity using the light meter within the camera, but an

---

[1]The equivalent unit in the imperial system is the Foot Candle. One Foot Candle is about 10 Lux.

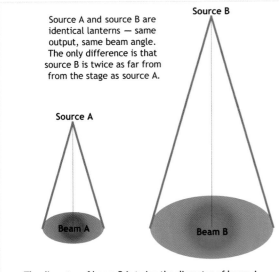

Source A and source B are identical lanterns — same output, same beam angle. The only difference is that source B is twice as far from from the stage as source A.

The diameter of beam B is twice the diameter of beam A. The area of beam B is 4 times the area of beam A (area is proportional to the square of the diameter of a circle — 2 squared is 4).

Intensity is a measure of the amount of light present. Compared to beam A, the light in beam B is 'spread' over 4 times the area, so the intensity in beam A is 4 times the intensity in beam B.

FIGURE 2. INTENSITY DECREASES AS THE SQUARE OF THE DISTANCE FROM THE SOURCE OF LIGHT. DOUBLE THE DISTANCE FROM THE SOURCE AND THE INTENSITY HALVES.

incident light meter will provide an absolute reading in Lux or Foot Candles which can be essential when working with video or film cameras. It is not common practice to measure intensity on stage for live performance, unless cameras are involved, when contrast must be more strictly controlled. Generally people can tolerate much greater differences in intensity with the visual field than cameras. A light meter can, however, be a useful tool for training your eye to spot relatively small changes in intensity, establishing an idea of what is acceptable contrast between, for example, foreground and background and in gaining an understanding of how much light is 'dim' or 'bright' in a particular situation.[2] Do not be afraid to use one if you think it will help you.

Humans can cope with an incredible range of light intensity, from 100,000 Lux of a snow field on a clear bright day to 0.00005 Lux of starlight. Unlike cameras, humans perceive relative intensity not absolute intensity. We reference intensity to what has gone before, and it takes some time for our eyes to become accustomed to radically different levels of intensity. If you went quickly from the 100,000 Lux snow field into a normally-lit room, at say 300 Lux, you would perceive the room to be very dark. If, on the other hand, you came into the room from a moonless starlit night, you would perceive it to be painfully bright. It is said that after 90 minutes under starlight the visual perception adjusts sufficiently to make it possible to read!

Although we can operate in this huge range of light intensity, we can't see detail in objects of very different intensities at the same time. Our visual perception will attempt to set its sensitivity to the average intensity level of what we are looking at. This is not the same as the average intensity level of the whole visual field; we can clearly see a bright image in an otherwise dark visual field, even if that image makes up only a small proportion of the total visual field, as is often the case when we watch a stage show from the back of a large theatre, or a rock show from the back of a sports stadium. Within the area of audience focus, we need to control the relative intensity, that is the contrast.

Intensity: glare, distraction and directing audience attention

Although we can cope with a wide range of intensity within the visual field, if there are particularly high contrast areas, especially if the very bright area appears small in the visual field, it creates discomfort. The effect is known as glare and most people will have experienced it at some time or another — looking into low sunlight or very bright car headlights on a dark road. In extreme cases glare can cause physical pain but more often it is just unpleasant and reduces visual acuity —

[2]It can also be useful for balancing the intensities of follow-spots, when grey neutral density filters can be placed in the beams of the brighter units until all intensities are the same, which is usually what we want, at least to start with.

not usually helpful to the lighting practitioner. Glare can result from any number of sources in the performance environment, from lanterns shining into the eyes of the audience, either intentionally or unintentionally, from highly reflective surfaces on the set or costume catching the light, or from extraneous light sources, such as the gap between the colour frame and the lantern on some units (particularly PAR cans) or from poorly implemented emergency lighting. The attentive lighting practitioner, whether designer or not, will endeavour to eliminate all unintentional sources of glare.

Our visual systems have evolved with a good ability to see detail in the centre of the visual field, and a refined ability to detect movement at the periphery of our vision,[3] a reason for dimming the house lights, and lighting the stage. Everything else being equal, we use the part of our vision most able to see detail to examine the brightest part of the visual field. The focus of visual attention is normally directed to where it is brightest so long as the contrast is not so great that it creates glare. This makes the ability to selectively control intensity hugely important in performance lighting design. We can use selective control of intensity to direct attention within the performance area, to point the attention of the audience towards the particular area of the stage we want them to focus on. The technique of directing the spectator's attention by using selective intensity is extensively used in the field of fine art, notably by some of the old masters of painting. Look at Renaissance paintings of interiors for the way in which the masters handle the depiction of light and shadow, and use it to draw attention to the main subject, and then to broaden the attention of the spectator into the surrounding shadows.

Big changes in intensity can leave the audience almost blind for several moments, or sometimes longer, while their eyes readjust to the new level of illumination.[4] Our attention may be directed by even relatively small increases in relative intensity, though at the same time as we have said, we are easily distracted by even relatively low points of illumination at the edge of the visual field, especially so when the point is not constant — either physical movement or flickering intensity for example.

It follows that performance lighting needs to be concerned with control of relative intensity across the performance area, and the elimination of distractions in the visual field of the audience, both within individual scenes and from scene to scene through the performance.

Intensity as a signifier

In nature, we take many signals from the intensity of the light surrounding us. For example, we are used to night being darker than day outside and the reverse inside. For anybody who has spent some time in the open air, there will be many more signals, the darkening that heralds a storm, the brightness of mid-day against the lower intensity of early morning light, the bright intensity of direct sunlight in an open space or more diffused daylight reflected from many tall buildings in a city's financial district, or through trees in a forest. Inside buildings, light intensity gives other signals. In many bars, relatively low intensity light is replaced by bright light at the end of the evening, signalling closing time. Lower intensity light can be seen as romantic in some settings or as threatening in others. High intensity can be used to help signify clean and efficient in some public spaces, or cold and uncompromising in others.

---

[3]This is said to have been evolutionarily useful to our distant ancestors, both when hunting and when being attacked. Whatever the evolutionary origins, it is very unhelpful when members of the audience are distracted by the peripheral sight of an usher's torch in the middle of an important speech from the stage.

[4]Compared to most camera technologies humans are able to tolerate a relatively high level of contrast within our visual field. Take a look at shadows against a bright sky on the screen of most digital cameras, and your eye will see more detail in the shadow than the camera will.

Think about the way intensity is used in fast food outlets and romantic restaurants.

What often gives the major clue to a change of time, place or location on stage is intensity. When resources are in short supply (and often even when they are not) intensity may have to carry most of the signification of time and place, and of mood. In each of these examples (and in the many more I'm sure you can think of) there are other properties of the light that change along with the intensity — the colour of light at night is different to that in the daytime, the shadows are strong in direct sunlight and weak or absent in defuse reflected light — the properties of light are interconnected, in the natural world and in performance, yet intensity remains perhaps the strongest single signifier available to the performance lighting designer.

By controlling relative intensity throughout the performance, the lighting designer can use the simple idea of the indexical sign (see the appendix on semiotics for more on indexical signs), pointing the audience towards what is important on the stage. They can use variations in intensity across the stage to signify something about how one area relates to other areas. Intensity can be varied through time, and so can be used to signify changes in the relationships between different spaces or changes in the space as a whole; changes in stage time or location. It also follows that selective use of intensity can define the size of the performance space at any particular moment.

To achieve many of these effects we need to be able to separately control the intensity of light in different areas of the performance space. One of the most important decisions to be made in the evolution of a lighting design concerns the number and shape of these separate areas, and how many areas will be illuminated at each point of the performance.

Focus — the location of light in space

If intensity is about the quantity of light, focus[5] in this context, is about which part or parts of the stage the light hits, and the direction from which the light comes.

There are two distinct parts to this property. The more apparent is usually defined as the angle of incidence and has an effect on our perception of objects illuminated on or near the performance space. The angle of incidence of a beam of light on a target object or performer describes the relationship between the direction from which light comes and the direction from which the audience is observing.

The second part I will call the throw. This is to do with where the light originates and the path it takes to the stage — with the path between the source of the light and its destination.

Angle of incidence

Lit objects create shadows, and in nature it is often these shadows that give us the best visual clues as to

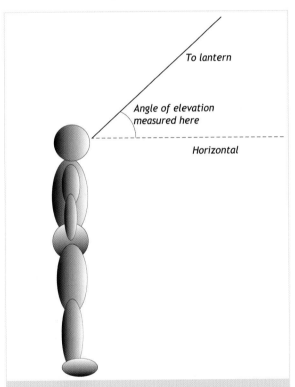

FIGURE 3A. ONE OF TWO ANGLES USED TO DEFINE THE ANGLE OF INCIDENCE OF A BEAM OF LIGHT TO THE PERFORMER FACING STRAIGHT OUT: THE ANGLE OF ELEVATION.

---

[5] The word focus is used in several different ways in performance lighting. As well as the present context, it can be used to describe the size, shape and edge quality of the beam from a luminaire, and the point of stage intended to be the centre of audience attention.

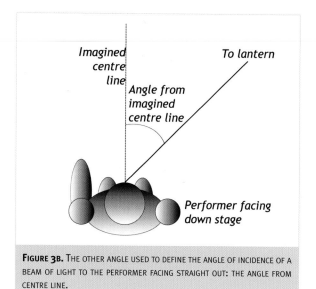

FIGURE 3B. THE OTHER ANGLE USED TO DEFINE THE ANGLE OF INCIDENCE OF A BEAM OF LIGHT TO THE PERFORMER FACING STRAIGHT OUT: THE ANGLE FROM CENTRE LINE.

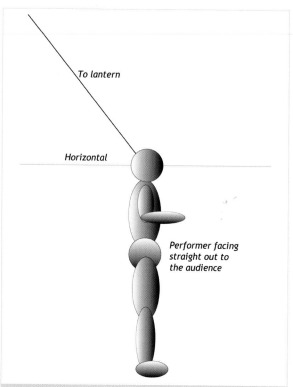

FIGURE 4A. BACK LIGHT COMES FROM BEHIND THE HEAD OF A PERFORMER FACING DOWN STAGE.

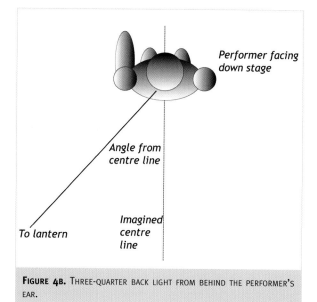

FIGURE 4B. THREE-QUARTER BACK LIGHT FROM BEHIND THE PERFORMER'S EAR.

time of day, location, and to the three dimensionality of the people and objects we see. Where those shadows fall, their size and shape depend on the object, where the light is coming from, and the position of the spectator. These last two define the angle of incidence. Although frequently constrained by the architecture of the performance space, the angle of incidence of the beam to the performance area will ordinarily be the most important consideration when the lighting designer comes to decide where each lantern should hang.

Conventionally, when performance lighting practitioners talk about angles, they refer to the angle of incidence to a performer facing straight out towards the centre of the audience. There are two angles involved: the angle of elevation, taken from the plane of the stage, which is assumed for these purposes to be flat, and the angle the performer would need to turn from looking out to centre, in order to face the lighting position.[6] High or steep angles are close to directly overhead and low or shallow angles are close to or even below the eye line of an upright performer. Up light as

---

[6] I should say that few practitioners get out equipment for measuring angles in these discussions, and any angles mentioned are rough approximations.

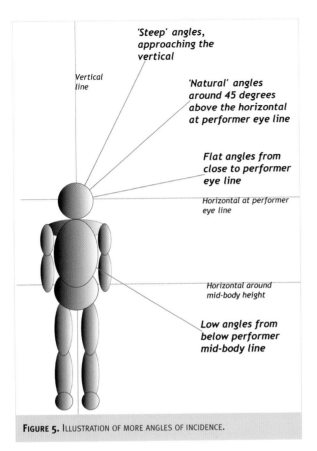

'Steep' angles, approaching the vertical

Vertical line

'Natural' angles around 45 degrees above the horizontal at performer eye line

Flat angles from close to performer eye line

Horizontal at performer eye line

Horizontal around mid-body height

Low angles from below performer mid-body line

FIGURE 5. ILLUSTRATION OF MORE ANGLES OF INCIDENCE.

its name suggests is from well below the performer's eye line, for example footlights. Back light comes from behind the performer (180 degrees or ½ a turn for the performer), side or cross light from the side (90 degrees or a ¼ turn in either direction) and top light from directly above. All these terms can be modified or combined to describe different lighting positions relative to the subject or to the performance area. For example, a ¾ steep back light for a performer would be in a direction roughly behind their ear, above them, and further away vertically than horizontally (see diagram).

A low cross light could be to the performer's left or right side, it would probably be below waist level, and may be pointing slightly up. This position has a special name in dance lighting where is called a shin buster because of the potential hazard the lantern becomes to the legs of those working on the stage.

It is clear that the part of the beam that does not strike the performer continues past that illuminated performer and lights up the stage floor or the set or whatever else is in the beam of the lantern. Light from any angle of incidence other than directly above the performer, illuminates a larger area of stage floor than the

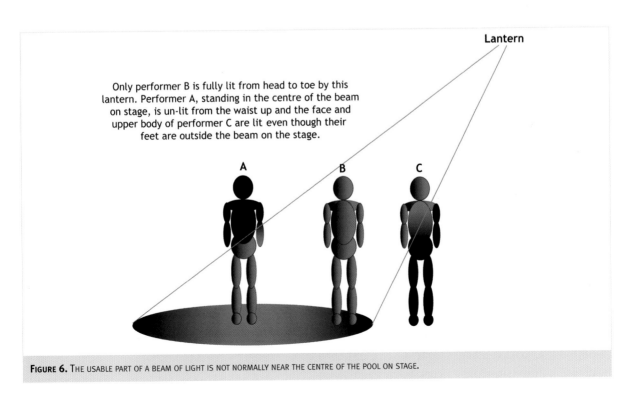

Lantern

Only performer B is fully lit from head to toe by this lantern. Performer A, standing in the centre of the beam on stage, is un-lit from the waist up and the face and upper body of performer C are lit even though their feet are outside the beam on the stage.

A   B   C

FIGURE 6. THE USABLE PART OF A BEAM OF LIGHT IS NOT NORMALLY NEAR THE CENTRE OF THE POOL ON STAGE.

area useable by a performer (see figure 8). The steeper the angle, the smaller the illuminated area or stage floor or set, the less spill outside the usefully illuminated area. Steep angles provide more tightly defined areas, which in turn gives the lighting designer a better opportunity to use selective intensity to guide the attention of the audience. However, steep angles often don't illuminate the performers' eyes — the performers' brow creates shadows that stop the light getting to the eyes. A compromise must be made between the steep angle that gives well-defined areas for selective illumination and superior modelling, and the shallower angles that get light into eyes and under noses, helping the audience to see the facial expression of the performers more clearly, but tending to flatten the stage picture, illuminate parts of the stage floor and set that we would prefer to leave unlit, or create potentially distracting shadows.

All these positions assume we are in a more or less traditional proscenium theatre space, or at least that the audience has more or less the same end on view of the performance area. If the performance space is not laid out like this, the description of lighting angles gets a little more complicated. For example, if the audience surrounds the stage, for a performance in the round, front light on the performers for some of the audience, is back light for others, and side light for the rest!

Front light

FIGURE 7. TWO QUITE DIFFERENT EFFECTS ACHIEVED WITH DIFFERENT APPROACHES TO FRONT LIGHT.

On the left, lighting student Jenny is lit by ¾ front light, warm from stage right, cool from stage left.

The combination helps to model her face. (The effect of the coloured light on her face is somewhat exaggerated by a camera. In live performance, our eyes are more willing to accept small deviations from white.)

On the right, Jenny is lit with a steep front light and a soft back light. This combination increases the impression of depth and of the figure having three dimensions in space, but the steep front light tends to hide her eyes.

Straight on front lighting

Some of the first lighting positions installed for electric stage luminaires were on the front of the circles and galleries of the 19th century play-houses. This is a good position from which to give a more or less natural look on the faces, but it does little to model the body. As originally installed in most theatres, light from these circle front positions complemented the foot light, which had until then worked almost alone to light the performers. Light from above the heads of the performers helps audiences to see the performers' eyes and mouths clearly, so long as the angle is not too steep. If front light is from too shallow an angle, it can lead to large distracting shadows on the set. Shallow front light used in isolation tends to flatten the stage picture. Used in moderation with the fine attention to detail of, say multi-award winning UK lighting designer Mark Henderson, low angled front light 'lifts' facial features just enough to allow the audience to see eyes and mouth in an otherwise steeply focused, very area specific, rig.

Three-quarter front light or gallery booms

Many 19th century theatres in the UK and elsewhere have had adaptations built into the ends of the top gallery seating area (or the gallery boxes in traditional play houses) to take theatre lanterns. Almost all proscenium theatres with electric light for the stage have been designed to accommodate these lighting positions. The ideal position is considered to be about 45 degrees up from horizontal and about 45 degrees to either side of the centre line of the stage and the audi-

FIGURE 8. THIS STUDENT IS FOCUSING ¾ FRONT LIGHT NEAR THE PROSCE-NIUM. YOU CAN SEE THE LIGHT SPILL AND HER SHADOW ON THE PROSCENIUM WALL TO THE RIGHT OF THE PICTURE.

the header is not in the way, the angle becomes less steep the further up stage the light is focused, and so the 'spill pool' gets bigger and the performers' shadows get longer. If there is a back wall or an up stage area that should be dark, this solution will not work. Finding positions for ¾ front light lanterns over stage can be difficult, especially so in theatres with a lot of flown scenery. The German tradition has addressed this problem well, and most large proscenium theatres there have a structure of perches and a bridge behind the proscenium to provide a comprehensive selection of rigging positions.

Breaking away from the ¾ front system to light up stage areas can make matching the feel of the lighting up stage and down stage difficult, giving the impression that we have two different worlds on stage — one world down stage with a ¾ front light look, and another up stage with a different look. It is better to try to find a solution that allows for some rigging positions for ¾ front light over the stage if the intention of the production is to attempt to show a unified space over the whole depth of the stage.

One further problem with ¾ front light on relatively small performance spaces is the increased size across

torium.[7] For much of the 20th century, this is where front light for performers' faces came from, and for very good reasons. Light from this direction provides good illumination of the performers' faces and a degree of modelling, so it is good for achieving visual acuity. For lighting a performance staged behind the frame of a proscenium, it is as near to perfect as can normally be achieved. However, once the area of performance is pushed through the frame of the proscenium, we begin to have a problem. How do we light the performers at the down stage edge without breaking the illusion of the proscenium frame by illuminating that as well?

Another problem with ¾ front light is how to continue it further up stage. On a proscenium stage, the header, which comprises the top part of the proscenium frame, gets in the way of using ¾ front light positions from many gallery box booms further up stage. Even when

FIGURE 9. THE SHADOW ON THE STAGE FLOOR GIVES ONE OF THE BIGGEST CLUES TO THE DIRECTION OF THE SOURCE OF LIGHT — BOTH WHERE IT LIES AND HOW LONG IT IS. STEEP ANGLES, LIKE THAT ON THE RIGHT, RESULT IN A SHADOW SHORTER THAN THE TARGET, WHILE ANGLES BELOW 45 DEGREES RESULT IN A SHADOW LONGER THAN THE HEIGHT OF THE TARGET.

[7] 45 degrees is half a right angle, i.e. the same angle you get when you draw a line between the opposite corners of a square.

stage of the 'spill pool' compared to straight in front light (see fig. 9). This can make it harder to define separate areas of the stage across its width, just as straight in front light can make it hard to separate up stage and down stage areas.

So for conventional front lighting positions, there is rarely an ideal solution that successfully solves all the problems set by an evolving performance lighting design. Perhaps this explains the frequent use of follow spots for larger-scale performance. The well-placed, well-operated follow spot can be used to subtly lift key faces out of steep area lighting. This is a common technique in opera and for live music concerts, where the primary role of the lighting is often to make a statement and to light the sometimes grandiose set. In ballet, the primary role of the lighting is usually to emphasise the physicality of the dancers (the faces of chorus are less important) and here follow spots are frequently used to highlight the principal dancers.

Light from below the performer's eye-line
With the arrival of focusable electric light for the stage, most theatres threw out footlights for the 'unnatural' shadows they created and the barrier they made between performer and audience. However, many lighting designers have now re-introduced light from the down stage edge of stage, though usually in the form of small single units rather than the obtrusive floats[8] of old. Light from this position has proved very useful. It can create unnatural shadows, which may be an intentional effect. It can also get light into the performers' eyes in otherwise difficult situations, such as when wide-brimmed hats are worn on stage, or when the available positions for front light all result in steep angles.

Light from the sides
Side or cross lighting emphasises angularity and is good for modelling the body. It helps the audience's per-

ception of depth. Cross light can be used to create strong shadows on the body, emphasising physicality, especially useful when lighting dance. To further emphasise the body, complementary colours can be used in the cross light from each side of stage. Low level cross lighting is very often arranged to cast no shadow of the performer on the stage (the shin busters mentioned above). For most classical ballet, the stage is arranged with wing flats, set to hide both the source of the cross light (rigged on vertical pipes or towers called booms) and to contain the shadows of the performers. On an open performance area the shadows from cross light can become a distraction, especially with low side light when the shadows are over life size, but the effect can also be used selectively to the advantage of the performance.

FIGURE 10. THE LIGHTING FOR MUCH CLASSICAL BALLET AND OTHER DANCE FORMS RELIES HEAVILY ON THE MODELLING EFFECT OF LIGHT FROM BOOMS AT THE SIDE OF THE STAGE TO ENHANCE THE PHYSICALITY OF THE DANCER'S BODIES. THE OCCASIONAL SHADOW ACROSS A DANCER'S FACE IS A SMALL PRICE TO PAY TO ENABLE THE WHOLE AUDIENCE TO SEE CLEARLY HER BEAUTIFUL ARMS.

Perhaps more than any other genre of live performance, ballet, and to a lesser extent dance in general, has a set of rules concerning position and focus of lanterns. There is a requirement to produce light that shows the

---

[8]In the 18th and 19th centuries, floats was the name given to foot lights consisting of wicks floating in a trough of oil. Later electric versions replaced the wicks with a row of incandescent lamps, similar to the ones in common domestic use today. Both types had a reflector-cum-glare guard perhaps 200mm high mounted behind the bulb or flame, which effectively cut off any view of performers' feet for much of the audience.

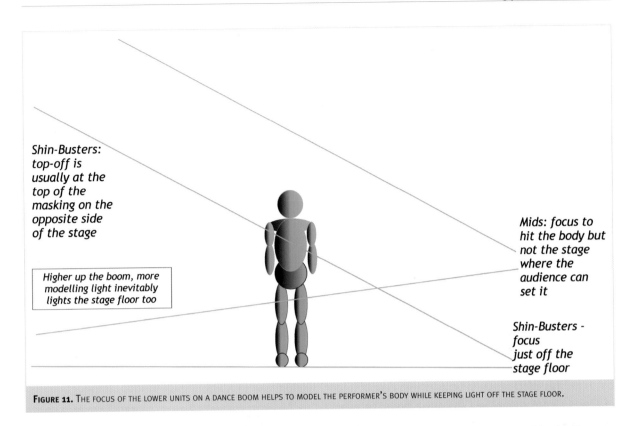

Shin-Busters: top-off is usually at the top of the masking on the opposite side of the stage

Higher up the boom, more modelling light inevitably lights the stage floor too

Mids: focus to hit the body but not the stage where the audience can set it

Shin-Busters - focus just off the stage floor

FIGURE 11. THE FOCUS OF THE LOWER UNITS ON A DANCE BOOM HELPS TO MODEL THE PERFORMER'S BODY WHILE KEEPING LIGHT OFF THE STAGE FLOOR.

physicality of the dancers to best advantage over the whole stage, and to do this an arrangement of side or cross lights has developed and has become almost universal. Anyone wishing to practice lighting for this genre needs to understand how and why this system works. The diagram gives an idea of the focus, but as in other areas of performance lighting, there is no substitute for hands on practice.

When wing flats are not available to mask booms and extraneous shadows, and sometimes even when they are, many designers use high cross light to provide modelling, and sometimes to introduce coloured light. In music theatre, it is common to see pairs of lanterns rigged at the end of the lighting bar and pointing more or less across stage. These are referred to as pipe ends.[9] This position can be especially useful when there are a lot of bodies on stage, for example the large chorus of an opera or a musical, where light from lanterns rigged

lower down on booms would be blocked by the first one or two performers on each side of stage.

Paule Constable and David Hersey, among others, make extensive use of cross light outside the dance genre. In confident hands, it becomes a tool to allow the lighting designer to develop painterly scenes, where the main intensity comes from the side producing an effect close to the chiaroscuro of Dutch and Italian Renaissance painting. The shadows are delicately filled with just enough light to provide an appropriate level of visual acuity, enabling the audience to see facial features. This kind of work cannot be accomplished without a significant level of co-operation between performer, director and lighting designer.

Top light or down light
Top light makes the figure seem more massive, creates very short shadows, and can often seem to shorten the

---

[9] 'Pipe' being the North American equivalent of bar or fly bar in the UK, and the name reflects the origin of this practice.

body. When the lanterns are too close to the performers, it can make the top of a performer's head the brightest part of the stage, which is not usually helpful. When there is enough height between performers and luminaires, it is a good position from which to add colour to the stage, and especially to shadows on the stage floor.

Shadows are created when a part of the beam of a dominant light source is blocked by a person or object. This often means that the light from less intense sources is more evident in shadows, and when that light is coloured, the shadows take on that colour.

Top light is frequently used to colour the stage floor itself. Very often in musical theatre, a coloured top light wash is faded up slightly ahead of the rest of the lighting for the scene, presenting a more saturated colour to the audience for a few moments before the rest of the light dilutes the effect.

Top light can also be used to add intensity to a scene without substantially changing the balance of face light, but again this effect needs to be used with care. If some of the audience cannot see the stage floor the effect could be substantially different for them. It is possible that sources of glare will be introduced for audience members who can see the floor, especially if the floor is highly polished and therefore very reflective. Such dif-

ferences in audience experience for different sections of audience is not limited to the use of top light, or even to lighting effects. Conscientious members of the creative team will usually try to see the performance from as many different audience positions as possible to discover such differences.

Tight pools of top light are often used as specials. In smaller performance spaces, it is sometimes only necessary to have the performer look up slightly to provide sufficient illumination for visual acuity. Sometimes it is possible to cheat and rig the special unit slightly down stage of the performer's position, or use the performer's costume to bounce light into their eyes. Sometimes we can use the light reflected from the floor to fill the shadows just enough. More often, if it is appropriate to see the face, a low intensity, secondary source will be needed, and this could perhaps come from a foot light position. Using a top light minimises the spill required to create an area of useful illumination, and so is ideal for some kinds of 'special'.

Top light is of limited use in concert lighting in sports arenas or open air festivals. Most of the audience cannot see the floor, and the structural effect of beams is less pronounced with top light than with back light. For classical concerts, however, top light can be used to

FIGURE 12. LIGHTING STUDENT LIBBY IS SEEN HERE IN THE SAME TOP LIGHT SPECIAL IN BOTH THE ABOVE SHOTS. IN THE FIRST SHOT, HER FEATURES ARE HIDDEN IN SHADOW. IN THE SECOND SHOT, ON THE RIGHT, LIGHT IS BOUNCED OFF WHITE PAPER TO REVEAL HER EYES AND OTHER FACIAL FEATURES.

illuminate the music and the instruments with the minimum of glare and extraneous shadow, good for both the players and the audience.

Back light

Light from the side of a performer or from immediately above a performer has some impact on the audience's ability to see the facial features of the performer. Light from behind the body of a performer facing the audience clearly does nothing to illuminate that performer's face, so why is it considered so important by almost all performance lighting designers? What back light does for performance lighting design is to further emphasise the three dimensional physicality of both the performers and the performance space. Back light, by illuminating the edges of performers and objects, especially curved objects with hairy edges (such as the head of a performer) helps the spectator to perceive depth in the individual objects and separation between objects and background.

Human stereoscopic vision only works over a relatively short distance. In large spaces, we need help to work out the relative distance to the various objects in our field of view. Because of this, back light is an important tool for the performance lighting designer, especially in large performance spaces, such as the sports arenas and festival sites where rock and pop acts perform. Live concert lighting rigs are often dominated by backlight sources. Standard video and film cameras, having only one 'eye', have no stereoscopic vision, and often back light provides the only visual cue separating performer from background.

Just back light on a performer can help to produce very dramatic effects, perhaps because the presence of the body is emphasised without giving the audience sight of the face — there can be no direct reading of the face so suggestion can be used to full effect. Concert lighting, especially for rock music, makes huge use of these effects, concentrating attention on shapes on stage rather than details.

Whenever there is dust or smoke in the air above stage, back light reveals itself, an effect more concerned with throw than angle of incidence, but important nevertheless.

Using angle of incidence

Angles of incidence can be used to help enhance mood and atmosphere. For example, shadows produced by light from directions not normally found in nature draw attention to themselves and can signify the supernatural or dreams. The long shadows cast by lanterns at or below performer eye-line can be very atmospheric, as can strong back lighting. A strong single source, such as the large discharge Fresnels favoured by many opera lighting designers, can create massive scenographic statements almost on their own, and getting these units in just the right place can be the key to success in this type of design work.

More often, changes in angle, causing changes in where shadows fall and in shadow length, are used to signify changes in time of day or season. The light of dawn and sunset comes from close to the horizon and produces long shadows, while the light of midday produces short shadows. The problem here is that very often urban dwellers don't notice these things, so the sign may not be widely read by the audience.

Each different direction of illumination can provide a different sign, or set of signs, to the audience, concerning the physicality of the actor/character, and may be used to signify aspects of the character's psychological make-up or relationship to other characters. It might be possible, for example, to show a particular kind of power relationship by lighting a dominant character from the side or diagonal, emphasising angularity, whilst the submissive character is lit primarily with top light, tending to shorten the figure. Such uses of particular lighting angles for different characters, however, can be hugely restricting. If both characters were on stage at the same time, they could not use each other's areas of stage without a fairly obvious lighting cue for each movement, and they would not be able to come close to each other without being lit by the light designed for the other. This kind of effect could be used at the entrance of each of the two characters, but again it is more likely to be read as artificial or a mistake if not perfectly integrated into the production.

The throw

A performance lighting rig usually needs to work with the aesthetic of both the production and the space. Visible beams can draw attention to the source of illumination and away from the performance on the stage. Whilst a massive lighting system can become a dominant element of the design, especially when it comes to concert lighting, some productions ask the audience to willingly suspend their disbelief in the 'staged' nature of the piece and the sight of lighting instruments and the beams they produce could be at odds with this aesthetic.

Usually the audience accept that they are watching a staged performance and that means they will see some lighting and other technical equipment around the performance area. They will not want the presence of this technical equipment to be distracting though, or for there to be sources of glare from unmasked lanterns. One of the key design decisions in most theatre work on a proscenium stage is whether the lanterns will be visible above stage, or will they be masked, for example by flown borders? Either decision presents the lighting designer with possibilities and problems about the placement of lanterns, that is, the choice of throw.

There are other factors to be considered in decisions relating to throw. A strong beam, apparently from an unseen source far away in the heavens, has been a strong signifier of the presence of a deity in Western art since pre-Renaissance times — clouds part, revealing the hand of God. But was that what the lighting designer wanted the audience to read into their use of a big back light? Perhaps less dramatically, we might want to

FIGURE 13. A 'CURTAIN' OF LIGHT HAS AN ARCHITECTURAL EFFECT, CREATING SOMETHING ALMOST SOLID IN THE SMOKY AIR BUT ALSO CREATING A BRIGHT POOL ON THE STAGE. THE LIGHTING DESIGNER WILL NEED TO BALANCE THE TWO EFFECTS. PHOTOGRAPH BY ANA VILAR-BERGUE.

evoke a confined interior on an open stage. If the audience can see beams from distant lanterns in dust or haze above the stage, even sources high above the performers, will they understand the scene as confined interior?

Visible beams of light can have an architectural presence on stage. Stage designer Josef Svoboda working in Prague in the last century, created curtains of light. The beams were made more visible by filling the air with tiny droplets of moisture, creating vast three dimensional shapes in space, which could appear and disappear with the push of a fader. Architectural effects such as this have been used with great effect to signify abstract notions such as the isolation of a single performer or the grandeur of the gods. Visible beams of light can be used to signify physical structures, and they are the stock in trade of concert lighting designers, used to modify the audience's perceptions of the size and nature of the performance space.

Such use of light draws attention to its self, foregrounding the language of stage lighting, potentially distracting the audience from the main action on stage. Conversely, strong architectural lighting can evoke place or atmosphere, aiding the production. As with any potentially dominant theatrical sign, the use of strong architectural lighting has to be thought out and fully integrated into the language of signs within the production.

Where the lantern hangs in relation to the stage is usually defined by what it has to illuminate, how the target will be illuminated, and the physical constraints of the space. Large numbers of very visible lanterns in the auditorium or over the stage say something to the audience about where they are and what sort of experience they may be in for. It seems clear that the decision to hide or show the lighting will have an impact on the audience's expectations of the production. In the semiotics of the French philosopher Roland Barthes, it will alter the decoding grid used by an audience.[10] It should therefore be a matter for the whole of the production team, not just the lighting designer. Having said that, often the only way to illuminate a particular element of a production is to use lanterns that show their presence to the audience, and the lighting designer must be prepared to argue that the ends justify the means — providing that they do!

Colour

In performance lighting, we can colour light with thin sheets of coloured film in a gel frame placed in the runners at the front of most theatre luminaires. These thin sheets are still referred to as gels, harking back to the original coloured gelatine, though these days plastics of various kinds are used. The major manufactures of lighting filters, Rosco, Lee Filters, GAM and others, produce swatch books of their colours for reference, some of which include graphics for each colour in the range, indicating the proportion of light filtered at each wavelength. It is relatively easy to get hold of these sample swatch books at trade fairs or from the sales counter of any decent lighting hire company.

When we use sources of light that are essentially white we create coloured light by filtering out the frequencies we don't want. The dyes, held in either plastic gels or in longer lasting but more expensive glass sheets, allow selective transmission of the various wavelengths of light. A red gel or a red glass absorbs all the wavelengths of light that are not red, letting any red light present through. The filter does not 'make' red light so if there is no red present in the original light, then no red light will emerge.

---

[10]Barthes introduced the idea of a decoding grid to semiotic discussions in 1970 with his book *S/Z*. His original ideas have been considerably elaborated upon since then both by himself and others. In essence, the decoding grid is the assumptions and other information we as audience use to make sense of what we see, hear, feel, etc. In this case, someone who regularly attends a range of performance types would assume a different style of presentation from an open stage with the lighting rig in clear sight and from a naturalistic interior setting with full masking.

FIGURE 14. EXAMPLES OF LIGHTING COLOUR SWATCH BOOKS.

plastic filters. However, glass is more fragile and the initial costs are much greater, as is the cost of the lighting designer changing their mind about the colour they want.[11]

Dichroic filters, used in many moving lights, work in a different way and as a consequence can produce a different quality of light. Dichroic filters are usually made with heat-proof glass coated with a very thin layer of material. They allow some light frequencies to pass through (just as in a plastic filter) but rather than absorb the rest, the other frequencies of light are reflected. A red dichroic filter may look green on the surface and does not look red unless you look through it. The band of frequencies passed by a dichroic filter can be precisely controlled in the manufacturing process. This can result in much more a-chromatic light — light of just a very few frequencies — an effect which is impossible to achieve with dyed plastic or glass filters, hence the potential for a different quality of light with dichroic filtering.

Human response to colour

Our perception of colour is subjective. What we have just seen, and what we see alongside a particular thing, has an effect on the colour we perceive that thing to be. When talking about light and colour on stage it is also worth remembering that we cannot distinguish between a neutrally-coloured object illuminated with coloured light and a coloured object illuminated with neutral light.

Much of our response to colour is also subjective and/or culturally specific. We may respond well to colours we associate with pleasant early experiences. These responses will be unique to the individual and therefore unavailable to performance practitioners wanting to communicate to a whole audience. However,

The more light a filter absorbs the less gets to the stage. To some extent, all lighting filters reduce the intensity of the lanterns that they are used in, and using deep colour in lighting filters can dramatically reduce the amount of light reaching the stage. Strongly-coloured plastic filters tend to absorb a lot of infra-red (heat) from the light source, which makes the filter more prone to fading, and in some cases melting, over time. To some extent, this problem can be overcome by using specially dyed glass filters, which last much longer than

[11]The subtractive way in which colour filters work can lead to some perhaps unexpected results, for example when using two sheets of the same colour in a single gel frame. If the chosen filter removes 20% of all blue light present, the first sheet leaves 80% of all the blue light in the beam. The second sheet removes a further 20% of what is left — not of what you started with — so adding a second sheet of filter usually has a smaller effect than you might suppose on increasing the depth of the colour on stage whilst often removing more useful light thus reducing intensity. It is usually better to choose a single colour rather than double up filters.

scientific work has been done to show that some responses to colour are more general in the population. Here are some examples.

- Heart rate speeds up in response to the colour red, and slows in response to the colour blue.
- Advertisers have found that yellow is often associated with fun, red with passion, blues and greens with calm and security.
- Purple is often associated with dignity, for example, the regal purple of ancient Rome and the medieval era in Europe.
- In the West, black, brown and grey are associated with sadness and black is the colour of mourning. In some Eastern cultures white is the mourning colour.
- Most people associate the adjective 'warm' with colours near the red end of the spectrum, including orange and some yellows, and 'cool' with the blue end of the spectrum but . . .

Warm and cool

These two terms are frequently used to describe light in performance, the atmosphere and mood as well as the colour. It is as well to be sure everyone understands the same things by these words before basing a discussion around them. Here is what I mean by warm and cool.

Warm — as in the comforting light of a domestic fire, the glow of a sunset in fine weather, the atmosphere between contented lovers or amongst a happy family or group of friends. In performance lighting terms I mean soft shadows, orange, red and yellow tints, perhaps relying on incandescent sources at lower intensity to increase the proportion of red light in the white. All skin tones glow and look healthy.

Cool — as in the light of a clear bright winter day, the light of clinical or scientific spaces, the atmosphere between recently separated lovers or amongst a family split by arguments. In performance lighting terms, harsh and revealing, lots of pale blue tints and no hints of reds or orange, perhaps making use of fluorescent and white discharge sources, or incandescent lamps at full. Shadows where they are present are hard edged. Pale skin tones look starved of blood. All skin tones begin to look lifeless, but this light can animate the facial features with its harder shadows.

If we are to use these notions as signifiers in a lighting design, everybody concerned has to be using the words in more or less the same ways. It is worth thinking about what your version is, and what others you are working with mean by these terms.

Red and blue and focus

Our eyes have a single lens. From Chapter 1, we saw that different wavelengths of light bend by different amounts in a lens or a prism — that is behind the formation of a rainbow, the splitting of white light into component colours by a glass prism and chromatic aberration in cheap camera lenses. For our eyes, the physics means we cannot focus both red and blue light from the same distance at the same time. In technical terms, there is a difference in the focal length of red and blue light for a simple lens system. This shows up in some moving light applications. For example, a gobo focused sharp in blue may look soft in red, requiring a lens adjustment between the two colours if sharpness is required for both.

This effect is what can make the stage of a rock concert, bathed in pure deep blue light from moving lights with dichroic filters, seem slightly fuzzy and out of focus when we are looking at the solo artist in a followspot. It is quite fun to play with the effect and with a bit of planning can be used in other places than the rock stage. To get the full effect, the saturated background light has to be close to one end or the other of the visible spectrum (blue seems to work best) and other frequencies of light (i.e. other colours of light) have to be removed — dichroic filters do this better absorptive filters. Then you need a strong central image to focus audience attention, lit to provide good visual acuity.

Colour theories and complementary colours

The colour of light can be described in a number of ways. We have seen that the different colours of the spectrum have different frequencies. However, coloured light is usually composed of a mix of frequencies. It is possible to define a colour of light by the relative intensity of each frequency present, as some filter manufacturers do in their swatch books.

Another way of describing a colour is the CIE colour model. Developed in France by the Commission International de L'Eclairage (CIE), in the first half of the last century, this model relates more directly to the way our eyes work. It uses three terms to describe colour: hue, saturation and value. The system was designed to describe the colour of pigments rather than the colour of light, with value representing the relative lightness or darkness of a pigment. In light terms, value can be replaced by intensity. Hue is closest to what we ordinarily call colour: red, blue, green, yellow, magenta, cyan, orange, purple, turquoise, etc. In this system, six colours are called the primary and secondary colours; for light, red – green – blue are the primary colours; cyan – magenta – yellow are the secondary colours. Saturation is a measure of how much hue is present. Deep red is highly saturated, deep pink is less saturated while pale pink has a very low saturation.

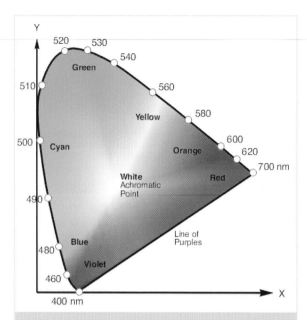

FIGURE 15B. THE CIE COLOUR MODEL MAPPED TO TWO DIMENSIONS. SATURATION IS HIGHEST AT THE EDGE OF THE COLOUR SPACE AND LOWEST (ACTUALLY ZERO) AT THE A-CHROMATIC POINT. HUE ROTATES AROUND THE EDGE OF THE COLOUR SPACE. THE LINK BETWEEN RED AND VIOLET HAS NO BASIS IN PHYSICS AND IS PURELY FOR THE CONVENIENCE OF REPRESENTATION. THIS CAN LEAD TO SOME DESCRIPTIVE PROBLEMS.

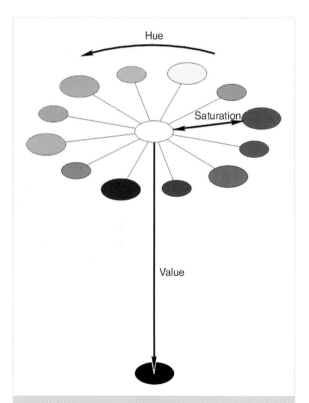

FIGURE 15A. CIE COLOUR MODEL IN THREE DIMENSIONS TO DESCRIBE PIGMENT. IN LIGHTING, WE CAN SUBSTITUTE VALUE FOR INTENSITY.

So how does this relate to the practice of performance lighting? Many moving lights are able to mix colour, using a variety of systems. In theory these units can produce any colour of light from the two-dimensional CIE diagram. In practice there are a number of limiting factors, including the colour temperature and colour rendition index (CRI) of the light source, and the precision with which the filters are manufactured. Many moving light consoles are now offering practitioners the opportunity to pick and adjust the colours they use with controls for hue and saturation. The hue control selects the base colour and saturation control the depth of that colour.

Warm from one side, cool from the other
It is common practice in theatre lighting to fill the shadows created by the main light sources with less dominant sources in a complementary colour, but what are complementary colours in light? For most performance lighting practitioners, complementary colours of light are those that, when added together, make something close to white light. The complementary for any

colour of light should be on a straight line through the achromatic point of the CIE colour diagram. However, our visual perception does not function quite like that, and the best results are obtained by experiment.

For the practice of lighting performers from either side in different colours, we are usually looking for complementary tints which don't look too unnatural on their own. These pairs will be found near the achromatic point. This technique enables fuller illumination of the subjects, without losing too much of the definition created shadows (see figure 7).

Back light is often more strongly coloured than front light and this can lift the performers away from the settings, providing a degree of colour contrast. Because back light does not generally fall on the faces of performers, there is less chance of disturbing the audience with 'unnatural' colours. As we have said, back light illuminates the fringes of people and objects, so if it has a strong colour, objects can appear fringed in that colour. We are used to seeing the blue of the sky as a background to our world, and perhaps this is why audiences appear to accept blue back light so easily. Whatever the reason, blue back light is almost ubiquitous in Western performance lighting.

Using complementary tints from each side of stage and more strongly coloured back light is primarily a functional sign. It is a technique that helps the audience to see better without really being conscious of how much visual acuity would be lost without its use. This is not to say that the use of tints from the sides, or stronger colour from the back light, cannot be used to indicate other things; the cooler light of winter against the warmer light of summer, the yellow tint of candle light against the white of sun light, the 'naturalness' of blue back light against the 'magicalness' of say purple back light. All of these can be employed as signifiers of

time and place and mood, along with aiding visual acuity.

Each of the colour signifiers above is presented as part of a pair, and this comes back to the way we perceive each colour in comparison to the other colours around at the moment of perception and in the immediate past. We have to have some other colour to compare each newly perceived colour with. There appears to be no colour equivalent to perfect pitch, where some individuals can hear a musical note and immediately place it accurately on a scale. This fact has some fundamental implications for the performance lighting practitioner. Here are just three things to consider.

- Looking at lighting states out of sequence can give a false impression of what the audience will perceive. (This is true for intensity too.)

- Some tints, such as pale lavenders, can be made to seem warm or cool depending on what other colours are dominant at the time.

- Large areas of strong colour, for example from the set, or even more so from a brightly lit cyclorama, will have a significant influence on the audience's perception of other colours.

Colour clearly plays an important role, but for now here is a brief description of two potentially disruptive colour effects.

Colour fatigue

This effect leads to the apparent 'dilution' of strong colour over time — as little as a minute — even when no actual change in the colour occurs. Several conceptual artists have used this effect. For example Dan Flavin[12] and Olafur Eliasson[13] have both used arrays of discharge lamps whose colour cannot change, and yet an

---

[12]Flavin has used fluorescent and other cold cathode lamps (for example neon lights) to create art works that although unchanging appear to the observer to change over time.

[13] The weather project installed at the Tate Modern in London in 2003/4 had a large sun, powered by low pressure sodium lamps of the kind used in street lighting. They emit a very narrow band of yellow light, unvarying in its colour. Despite this most observers perceived the colour of Eliasson's sun to change over time, due in part to the effect of colour fatigue.

observer perceives that the colour (and intensity) does change.

Colour adaptation

This is the effect where our perception 're-sets the white balance' of the eye to help to make sense of the world. This happens when we wear coloured sunglasses. Very quickly, we perceive faces and other objects we know well to look a natural colour. If you take a photograph through (non-prescription) coloured sunglasses, you will see how distorted the colours really are, but your brain refuse to be 'fooled' by tinted glasses.

Colour as a signifier

For many traditions of performance lighting, colour provides only subliminal cues, aiding audience perception of space when used in conjunction with other variables. Important for the variation and depth that it helps to add to the stage picture, the use of strong colour can be problematic due to the subjectivity of audience response, and the perceived anti-naturalism it evokes. Generally we do not see strongly coloured light in nature, so when we do see it, we become aware of both the light (which most people hardly ever notice except when it is not 'natural') and its colour. As with other ways in which light in performance makes its presence directly felt, strongly-coloured light needs to be handled with care.

Beam and movement

Glory be to God for dappled things
***Pied Beauty**. Gerard Manley Hopkins*

Long before the birth of modern moving lights, Adolph Appia[14] was trying to persuade the great opera composer Richard Wagner that dappled light could be a more powerful sign of a forest than any number of painted cloths. Since then this notion has been enthusi-

astically taken up by lighting designers working in many genre of performance. Gobos[15] are usually cut from metal or etched on to glass, and placed in the gate of the lantern. The image etched or painted on the gobo is then projected in the beam of the lantern.

FIGURE 16. THREE BREAK-UP GOBOS, USUALLY USED TO ADD TEXTURE TO SET OR STAGE FLOOR. THE LOWER TWO GOBOS HAVE BEEN USED IN LANTERNS. THEY SHOW THE MARKS OF THE HEAT GENERATED IN THE GATE, THE SLOT IN WHICH THE GOBOS ARE POSITIONED. GOBOS FREQUENTLY GLOW RED HOT WHEN IN USE!

To use the formal language signs, semiotics, which is further explained in the appendix, the gobo has become a prominent signifier in much of British and American performance lighting. Hard focused and thus clear and distinct, or soft and impressionistic, these patterns projected in light have been used in many different ways, to 'paint' New York fire escapes onto a plain brick wall, to depict flashing neon signs, to signify the sun shining through a tall window (all iconic signs) or to provide the gently moving dappled light signifying a forest (perhaps a more complex sign, iconic of light in a forest, index of 'hidden' trees and often symbol of something else — fruitless searching or pastoral tranquillity perhaps).

---

[14]Adolph Appia (1862–1928) worked with Wagner at the composer's theatre in Bayreuth. He argued that the scenographer should create a three dimensional world for the performers to inhabit rather than a set of two dimentional painted cloths for the performer to stand in front of. Along with Gordon Craig (1872–1966), Appia is frequently cited as the one of the fathers of modern scenography.

[15]Gobos are referred to as templates in North America.

The lighting industry provides several ways to animate the image projected from the gobo, so we can create the gently rippling light through trees dreamed of by Appia, or imitate light reflected from a canal, without any water on stage.

FIGURE 17. THIS PROFILE IS FITTED WITH AN ANIMATION DISC, WHICH, AS THE NAME SUGGESTS, IS USED TO ADD AN IMPRESSION OF MOVEMENT IN THE BEAM. USUALLY USED IN CONJUNCTION WITH A GOBO, ANIMATION DISCS CAN HELP TO IMITATE THE LIGHT REFLECTED FROM WATER, OR LIGHT FROM A FIRE, OR APPIA'S LIGHT FILTERED THROUGH A FOREST CANOPY.

The present generation of moving lights have multiple gobos, often able to rotate, and often on two or more wheels, so that patterns can appear to dissolve, or morph, from one image to another. Some moving lights incorporate an animation wheel, which can be selected remotely. The promised next generation of moving lights will have a video gate. This technology offers the possibility of lanterns projecting virtually any image, still or moving, onto the stage, or wherever the beam can reach. This concept, sometimes called digital lighting, is covered later in the book.

Shutters

Shutters, the beam shaping blades of profile luminaires, have recently been added to several hard edged moving lights. The ability to remotely and dynamically shape a box of light on stage is an exciting prospect for many performance lighting practitioners. Accurate remotely-controlled shuttering allows the possibility of creating and manipulating spaces on a stage with much more fluidity than is possible with conventional flown or trucked scenery. It offers a new dynamic on the performance stage, potentially more powerful than anything moving lights have brought us so far. The round edge of a beam on stage remains just that — the edge of a beam. A sharply-defined square or rectangular beam, however, can signify the edges of a real or imagined space — and when those edges can move, more possibilities present themselves. This is a rapidly-evolving area of performance lighting practice. There is sure to be some resistance to this very noticeable use of light, and it is a technique that could easily be overused. The potential in many genre of performance is exciting however, whether remotely-controlled shutters are used to compensate for last-minute changes to blocking or to dynamically manipulate the audience's perception of space.

Quality

Beam quality is used with at least two different meanings in performance lighting. The first we have already touched on and refers more to the colour composition of the beam, how much of each frequency of light is present. We talk about the quality of light from an incandescent lamp being different to that from a discharge lamp, and by that we usually mean that the balance of light frequencies in each beam is different. Architectural lighting practitioners use the colour rendition index (CRI) of a source to give a measure of how 'complete' the spectrum of the source is and how similar its light is to idealised sunlight. CRI is often quoted in lamp data sheets and on the packaging of some lamps. In light from a source with a CRI at or very near 100, colours look as they would do in sunlight. In anything else there will be some differences for some colours; the lower the number, the more noticeable the differences.

The second meaning refers to the pattern of intensity across the beam of a luminaire, how the intensity falls off towards the edge of the beam, and the crispness of the shadows produced by that luminaire. This gives us words to describe the difference between the light from, for example, a Fresnel luminaire and a profile luminaire,

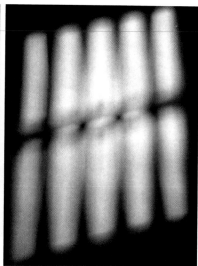

FIGURE 18. THREE VIEWS OF THE BEAM OF A PROFILE LANTERN WITH A GOBO, SHOWING TWO DIFFERENT VERSIONS OF A SOFT BEAM EITHER SIDE OF A SHARP BEAM.

between a unit with a lens and a soft light, and between a profile luminaires focused in several different ways. In this context, we use the words 'focus it' to mean how the lens or lenses of the profile lantern are adjusted, as opposed to how the light hits the stage and objects on it (angle of incidence) or the path the light takes to the stage (throw).[16]

Soft and hard edges are important in performance lighting. Soft-edged beams are easier to blend into one another, hard-edged beams stand out, drawing attention to themselves. Hard-edged beams seem brighter than soft-edged ones because we are more sensitive to the sharp changes in intensity that occur at the edge of a hard-edged beam. Most performance lighting will make use of both, for example, the soft edges for lanterns used in a wash and the hard edges for those used as specials. In a proscenium theatre, soft-edged beams front of house can lead to too much spill or flare, unintended light illuminating the auditorium and causing distractions.

Describing performance light – a summary

Once again we have covered a lot of ground in this chapter, about the mechanics of lanterns and lantern placement, a little of the history of performance lighting, some useful stuff on human visual perception — what we might call the psycho-physics of human perception — and the beginnings of how choices of lantern and position impact the images we produce on stage. Here are some points to carry with you into the following chapters.

■ It is useful to consider performance light in terms of four interrelated properties, intensity, focus, colour and beam, but remember that time as a variable impacts on everything we do.

■ The mechanics of human visual perception are just as important as the physics of light and light production.

■ Humans are able to concentrate on detail in a relatively small area of our visual field — we can watch the show from the back of a large theatre or stadium,

[16]Unfortunately this multiple use of the word focus is widespread in performance lighting practice, amongst native English speakers and beyond. Context will usually define which meaning is intended, but there will be occasions when it becomes necessary to distinguish between 'focus the unit' meaning change its pan and tilt, and adjust the relative position of lenses and other optical elements.

even though the action only occupies a small proportion of what we can see.

- It helps if the rest of the visual field is dark so dim those houselights, especially in large auditoriums.

- We are distracted by small areas of light, and especially movement, at the edge of the visual field — keep an eye out for flickers from faulty emergency lighting and extraneous light spilling from the lighting fixtures.

- Human eyes can make more use of both lower and higher intensities than many cameras, but there are limits. We are not great at dealing with both very low and very high intensity at the same time (but we are better than most cameras are at this).

- Humans don't perceive absolute intensity. A candle flame that is bright in a windowless cellar is barely visible outside in daylight. Perceived intensity depends on what went before. A black-out is usually only relative. If the audience has become accustomed to a bright state on stage, they will perceive a stage with enough light for a scene change as blacked out.

- We don't have an absolute reference for colour either; for example, lavender light can appear warm in comparison to blue tints and cool in comparison to amber tints.

- Adding colours together in light tends towards white. Overlapping the beams of three lanterns each with a different primary colour filter will result in white light (providing the intensity of each beam is matched).

- One way of describing complementary colours in light is to say they add up to something close to white. This is useful when it comes to combining light from two sides of a performance space to achieve a natural colour where the two sources combine and the shadows that help with modelling where they don't.

- Dimming the intensity of an incandescent lamp changes the colour of the light it emits. Lower intensities have proportionally more red light — they look warmer. At or near full power, not only is there more intensity, there is proportionally more blue in the light — and the light looks cooler.

- The closer a luminaire is to the stage, the brighter its beam on stage. Generally if you halve the distance between stage and luminaire you get four times the intensity.

- Different angles of incidence allow different proportions of light to be reflected towards the audience, thus affecting perceived intensity. Front light usually presents the audience with most usable intensity, and back light with least.

- Light from some angles can counteract the effect of light from other angles. For example, light from directly above a performer can make them seem squat, and can hide their eyes. When sufficient light from below is added, eyes are revealed, and the performer can be made to seem gaunt.

- Our eyes have a different sensitivity to different colours, so a particular intensity of yellow light will seem brighter than the same intensity of blue light.

- Almost any change we make to the beam of a luminaire will affect its intensity, that is the amount of usable light that hits the stage and the people and objects on it including introducing a gobo or changing the edge quality (focusing the lenses).

- Filtering white light with glass or plastic lighting filters or dichroic filters reduces the intensity of light reaching the stage.

As we saw in the last chapter, what we are used to seeing we perceive as natural and generally don't consciously notice. Things we perceive as unnatural can draw attention to themselves. Performance lighting can make use of this, and can be tripped up by it too. When the lighting for a performance creates shadows that are too different from those the audience perceive as natural, when the colours used are too far from those seen in nature, the audience will begin to read the lighting. If that is the intention, then all is well. If it is not, then the lighting practitioners on the production may be in trouble. As always, anyone concerned with performance lighting must take care to ensure that what is read by the audience is in harmony with what is intended by the whole creative team working on the production.

4

from text to concept

Introduction — what is a text?

Most works of performance begin their life with a text. A group of people, the production team, assemble with some ideas about something they want to put in front of an audience. In theatre, the text is most often a piece of writing, either words alone or words and music. The text may be new writing or it may be a representation of an existing work. The intention may be to base the performance closely on the text or it may be to use the original writing as a jumping-off point for a devised performance, or something in between. For many live concerts, the spur for performance may be recorded music — a band's demo recording or new album. This may be augmented by the band's vision for their music, or by a commercial marketing strategy. For a dance performance too the initial inspiration is often a musical score, but it may also be a response to poetry or prose, to a painting or another work of art or a particular event. We can think of making performance as a way of getting something extra out of these texts; something that the audience would not get from experiencing the original text alone.[1]

Creating the world of the performance

The design for the performance space creates a world for the performers to inhabit. That world may be an outlandish fantasy of the immense stages designed for the stadium rock shows of the Rolling Stones,[2] or may be an evocation of part-real and part-imagined spaces such as those seen on many opera stages, or the stunning set of the National Theatre's production of *An Inspector Calls*,[3] or the relatively bare and open space 'pregnant with possibilities' of many dance works. Of course, the world of the performance may be many other things. The one thing it is not is the everyday world. Perhaps the best way to illustrate this is to look at performance in non-theatre spaces, where the space of performance is the *found space* of environmental theatre or site-specific work. This kind of performance takes place in cellars, in disused buildings, in open country and other surprising places. Simply by becoming a performance space, we, as audience, are asked to see it differently. Several companies which make environmental theatre have used empty depart-

---

[1]Once it exists, the performance itself becomes a text too.

[2]Sets by Mark Fisher, lighting by Patrick Woodroffe.

[3]Set by Ian MacNeil, lighting by Rick Fisher, directed by Stephen Daldry.

ment stores, for example. The randomly half-dismantled display stands and abandoned artefacts in a closed-down department store were just incidental yesterday. In the moment of performance they become potential signifiers, triggering memories or colouring the audience response to other aspects of the performance, capable of telling their stories about past uses and past users of the building. The incidental becomes potentially significant: a set of pegs with the names of past employees may conjure up, in the imagination of the audience, ghost images of those people at work. An abandoned cutting table with a brass measuring edge marked off in feet and inches, reminds older audience members of a past before metric measurement. A blueprint of the developer's plans for the old store's future, left on the floor by someone, can take the audience's imagination somewhere new. By taking on the role of audience, we are made to look harder, to see a kind of beauty in the pattern left by years of dust rising from a radiator, or tragedy in a once fine ceiling rotted by years of neglect. We invest in the performance and in the evocation of its world. If this is true in an abandoned shop, where the 'set' is largely unpremeditated by the production team,[4] how much more true should it be on a performance stage?

When it works well, performance turns us from casual observers into active audience, exercising our human instinct to make sense of the world, and this places a responsibility on everyone concerned with everything that is seen and heard on a stage. Set design may be the beginning of that signification process; every object choice, every colour choice, every choice about the shape of the space is potentially able to either re-enforce or undermine the creation of that world of performance. For the lighting designer too, each shaft and each wash of light is capable of influencing the audience's reading of the world created for that performance, by what light reveals and fails to reveal, by the way it reveals, and for itself.

In almost all work for live performance, the performers inhabit this world of the performance. Along with practical considerations, usually including the provision of entrances and exists, and ensuring they can be seen by their audience, performance design is there to support the performers communication with the audience.

Jerzy Grotowski, the influential Polish director,[5] placed the relationship between actor and audience at the centre of his Poor Theatre. His practice pared away set, props, structured lighting and artificial sound and even the separate performance area, to concentrate on the audience's intimate experience of the actor. This relationship between performer and audience is at the centre of almost all successful performance, and though the Poor Theatre aesthetic is not appropriate to every style of production, a designer working on the creation of a performance should question any aspect of the design that gets in the way of this communication.

What can light do?

A child is working on a drawing, talking about what they are doing and why as they are drawing lines and choosing colours. A second child looks over their shoulder, watching what they are doing, listening to what they are saying and occasionally asking questions and making suggestions. At a certain moment, the first child hands the drawing to the second one. At this point the second child can do one of two things — they can either scribble all over the drawing, obscuring the original intent and making a mess or they can add marks that complement the original, working with the colours and lines already on the paper. In case you have not already guessed, lighting designers often find them-

[4]The environment of environmental theatre is never entirely accidental. Choices have been made; first about the space its self, and then about which parts of the space the audience will see, and in what order, and how they will be illuminated. Very often, especially in abandoned buildings, a lot of work is done both to make the space safe and to present it in a particular way. Lighting projects like these are amongst the most challenging and rewarding of roles available to a lighting designer.

[5]Born 1933, died 1999.

selves in the position of that second child. Light in performance is most often required to support the performance, to help tell the story, to add an extra dimension, to guide the focus and mood of the audience, occasionally to play directly on the emotions of the audience, but always in support of a wider objective. Making a good lighting design for a production requires the lighting designer to work in sympathy with others, working with 'lines and colours' that have already been established. Hopefully the lighting designer will have a chance to influence choices made about those first lines and colours too, but that is not usually the primary focus of the role.

When light does lead design decisions, exciting things happen. Perhaps the most famous exponent of lighting-led scenography was the Czech sceneographer Joseph Svoboda. Working in the middle years of the last century, he pioneered several influential techniques, including the creation of apparently solid objects using fine mist and 'curtains' of intense back light, and the use of projected images (still and moving) on stage. A more recent exponent is Patrick Woodroffe. Perhaps best known for his work with Mark Fisher on stadium rock spectaculars for the Rolling Stones and others, his lighting-led design for the opera *Romeo and Juliet* for the Vienna State Opera in 2001 is well documented in John Offord's book.[6] Even when lighting design takes this leading role, however, it is still the servant of the text and the performers.

Designer as problem solver

Successful design of any kind is about finding solutions to problems. The problem may be how to make a saloon car exciting to drive and run on less fuel, or how to present the ghost of Hamlet's father on stage without getting unintentional laughs. It is likely that neither problem will be solved by a single person working in isolation. Just as many designers and engineers will work together to solve the car problem, so the director and performers, the designers of set and of costume, of light and of sound, and the wider team who realise the designs, will all contribute to successfully staging the ghost scenes in Hamlet.

Finding the key — why will the audience stay to the end?

In almost any live performance, those making it need to answer the question, 'What will keep the audience there till the end?' Narrative work, including most drama, opera, musicals and much dance, has at its centre a question. In Shakespeare's *Hamlet*, it could be how will the Prince deal with the death of his father? In *Swan Lake*, will the Prince get together with the Swan Princess? In *Don Giovanni*, will the wronged father of the Don's Act One conquest have his revenge? In each of these pieces, there is a single scene where the answer is provided and the fate of the characters is more or less sealed — will Hamlet 'take up arms against a sea of troubles'? Yes, and there will be many deaths as a result. Will the Prince marry? No, but the wicked perish, the rest of the swans are released and the lovers ascend to paradise. Does the murdered Commendatore return? Yes and ultimately drags the Don to down to Hell.

In each of these classic stories, the key question is posed early in the piece, influences much of the action building to the key scene, and the answer determines how the piece ends. Clearly the scene where the key question is resolved will be an important scene. The moments when the question is asked, which may be many, will also be important. Many of the other moments may be ornamentation, or distraction, necessary for the structure but of less central importance. So how will we find out what is the key dramatic question and which scenes are which?[7] The answer in

---

[6]*Lighting For Romeo And Juliet: Patrick Woodroffe at the Vienna State Opera*, John Offord, Entertainment Technology Press, 2002.

[7]My question is not the only one in the piece, and there have been successful productions where other questions have been central. It is a good idea, however, for all the production team to agree on what the key question is, since this will determine the main focus of the performance.

The title *(and possibly a sub-title) of the piece often gives a good indication of what the piece is about.*

The author's name *. Is the name well known, and do you know any other works by the same playwright? What sort of plays does this person write, comedy, tragedy, farce? Does the playwright have a reputation for a particular political outlook or a particular mode or genre of production? What is their nationality, and do they aim to speak for a particular section of that nation or a wider social or political grouping? If you don't know, find out.*

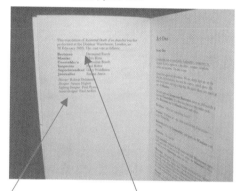

Translation. *If the play is translated, you might need to dig a bit deeper. What is the literal translation of the title? Often the English version changes the meaning; what was the original meaning? Was the play translated by a language scholar who would ordinarily want to get the words as close to the original as possible; a playwright who you might expect to be more concerned with making a play that works, perhaps at the expense of some losses elsewhere, or a poet, who might be concerned to make the words work again as poetry in their new language? If you have one type of translation (literary, stagy or poetic) can you get hold of a different type?*

The list of characters appearing (the dramatics personae *and often a short description of each. The list may be in order of appearance on stage, or in order of importance (to the playwright or editor).*

Date of first publication, subsequent revisions and editions, translations, editied editions etc. *You find out how old the piece is, which then gives a context with which to interpret the piece. This may help with particular words like 'gay' which have radically changed in meaning since the 1920s, or with more general aspects such as the expected role of women in past times. Many plays and other published works are set 'in the present day'. If they are not brand new works, one of the first tasks of the production team will be to decide is which 'present day' they are going to set their production in, the time when the play was written, right now, or some other time.*

Many play scripts are published as the 'prompt copy' of the professional production, and include the production credits for that production. This gives a further indication of how the piece was seen at that time. Did it receive its first performance in a large commercial theatre or at a subsidised repertory company? With a little research, the size and configuration of the original stage can also be found. Was the play written for a well-equipped proscenium space, or a studio space? These and other considerations from the first performance may be written into the published text, but may not be essential to the successful re-presentation of the piece in your performance space with your particular production infrastructure. In this case find out about the Donmar in 2003. What sort of space was it? What was its artistic policy?

How long is the piece? Although it is easy to get this wrong, for many 'straight' play scripts, a guess of between 90 seconds and two minutes per page of dialogue will give you an idea of how long the piece is likely to run. Some scripts give timing information, usually from the first professional production.

FIGURE 1A. FIGURES 1A AND 1B SHOW WHERE TO FIND BASIC INFORMATION ON THE COVERS AND IN THE OPENING PAGES OF MOST PLAY SCRIPTS.

Promotional material (often on the back cover). *Leave nothing out when searching for a way to get into a script. If the publisher has reprinted a review, or offered a quick synopsis, read it but bear in mind that its primary purpose is to sell copies of the script.*

Other versions of the text can be useful for research too. A copy of an earlier translation may yield additional insights. Beside the 2003 copy is a script from an earlier production, a different translation. The earlier copy has a preface by the playwright, giving some background to the incidents mentioned in the play.

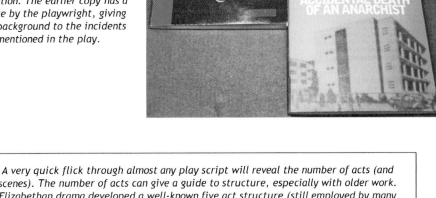

A very quick flick through almost any play script will reveal the number of acts (and scenes). The number of acts can give a guide to structure, especially with older work. Elizabethan drama developed a well-known five act structure (still employed by many Hollywood film writers) whilst playwrights in the 19th and early 20th centuries often wrote in three acts. In recent times there have been a number of plays written to be seen without a break which has an impact on how the piece will be staged — no interval means no extended scene change taking 15 or 20 minutes. Other playwrights use the unexpected arrival of an interval to heighten suspense.

FIGURE 1B.

most cases is to read the text — the script/original story/libretto. Not just read the text as a casual reader though, we need to do some analysis. The process of text analysis can be intimidating to practitioners who see themselves as having a practical focus, but it need not be, and it is necessary work for anyone wanting to play an active part in discussions relating to the making of the performance. A good knowledge of what happens when and where during the piece, as well as some notion of why what happens does happen, not only helps with design decisions, but is necessary in order to engage in intelligent discussions about the piece.

Initial text analysis[8]

With a published text such as a play script or music score and libretto,[9] a lot of information can be gained from the opening pages of many printed editions. A similar amount of information can be gleaned from sleeve notes of a recording, say of an opera, musical, or band.

Once you have gleaned what you can from the covers and introductory pages, the next task is to read the script or listen to the recording (or possibly both), at least twice; first with your heart, then with your head — taking notes. Plays do not take long to read, even a three hour epic is only three hours of speaking, and most people can read at least as fast as normal speech. If it is a play with a lot of characters, especially if they have unfamiliar names, it is a good idea to copy the page near the front of most play texts that gives the character list and a brief description of each character.

I find it useful to read a script through quite quickly the first time, making few if any notes, reading or listening for a first impression — with my heart rather than my head. I will record this first impression in rough note

form, perhaps including brief character sketches, locations, and plot elements. If you own the script, you can write directly onto it, for example simple under-scores or stars in the margin where there are sections that excite you or for laugh lines.

As I read or listen to the text again in more detail I will occasionally refer to my initial notes, both to see how my impression of the piece changes, and to help highlight important areas of the text likely to be missed or misread on first reading or hearing, remembering that most audience members only see a performance once.

For a play text or other written work, I read the text again, I make more detailed notes on each scene, often using a table such as the one opposite. A story told through a play text usually contains far fewer words than one told in a novel or short story. In a play script we don't usually get full descriptions of places and people, and we hardly ever get information about what the characters are thinking. This means we often have to work harder on a play script to find out what might be going on underneath. When the play is eventually staged the actors will help the audience read extra layers of meaning through voice, movement and gesture, supported by the production design. When we read a play script through we don't get any of that help but as designers of the world that this production creates for the play we need to find a way into the structure and meaning of the text. This first table enables us to look at the how the story is told.

This format would work for a play already divided into scenes, with multiple locations and nine different characters. The table will have a different layout for each text. As we work through the text, a table like this one begins to provide a map of the piece and to give an idea of the key moments in the story; scenes where the

---

[8]My thanks to director, set designer and teacher Phil Engelheart, for this approach to analysis.

[9]The score is the notes of the music written down, and the libretto is the words for a music theatre piece, normally just the lyrics or the songs, though it may include short spoken sections. For musicals with extended spoken passages, there is usually a document called the book as well, and this is very like a play script. It is clear that music is integral to all forms of music theatre, including opera, operetta and musicals. If practitioners are not able to read the music score, other ways of learning the music will have to be found. There is more on reading a score in the next chapter.

TABLE 1. A WAY OF DISPLAYING THE STORY OF A TEXT

Act/Scene/Page	Location	Time of year/Time of day	Purpose	Atmosphere	Character 1	Character 2	Character 3	Character 4	Character 5	Character 6	Character 7	Character 8	Character 9
1/1 p.1	A courtroom?	Early morning (pre-dawn?)	Exposition and sentencing of a suspect or defendant	Fateful	On	On	/		E		e/l	/	/
1/2 p.7	The port — outside	Not much later	More exposition & set up	Bright but wary			On		On L		On	On L	E/L
1/3 p.25	The market square	A bit later	First mistaken identity	Bright	/	/	On	On L		E	/		E

Brief key: On = on stage from the beginning of the scene
On L = as above but exits (Leaves) during the scene
E = enters during the scene
E/L = leaves during the scene
Lower case = of minor importance (e.g. speaks fewer than two lines)
/ = that character is mentioned but does not appear

plot simply unfolds, and scenes where the course of events is changed. It helps to identify that key dramatic moment, the key scenes in the piece when things change, and what they change from and to.

Once we have an idea of the dramatic structure of the piece, we can start to do more detailed analysis. Many drama scripts can be read on a number of different levels, and at this stage it is important for our process to access as many of these levels as we can. For example, to discover more about the relationships between characters we might begin by reading any description given by the writer in the play text. If the character has an historical or mythical basis we can research that too. Back in the play text we can note everything they say about themselves and what others say about them and any specific behaviour detailed in the stage directions.[10]

[10]Stage directions are the words in the script that the performers don't speak. In much Elizabethan drama they are short instructions, such as *exuent* (plural of exit) or *he kills her*. In some more modern plays the stage directions are extensive and quite prescriptive (e.g. the plays of Eugene O'Neill or George Bernard Shaw) but they are not always written by the playwright. Many acting editions of play scripts are taken from the prompt book of the first professional production. In these the stage directions may be as much the work of the original director as the playwright. Debates about how much weight should or should not be given to stage directions rage in academic circles and amongst professional theatre makers, so they should be treated with caution. Talking with the director and researching the practice of the playwright and those involved in the first productions may well make it easier to decide how you treat particular stage directions.

Doing this for each of the main characters in the piece can give you an insight into the structures that underpin the relationships, both those presented as *real* to the audience and those that might only exist in the minds of one or two characters. It can answer questions such as who is in charge in a particular scene or act or who might be secretly in love with whom?

Another way into the text might be to examine the choice of any specified locations given by the playwright. Again real or mythical places can be researched outside the script (though many editions of modern works include useful information about period and place chosen by the playwright). Back in the script itself, noting what is said by the characters about the places and times mentioned will often provide inspiration to the visual designers of a production.

Choosing which tools of analysis to use on a particular text will depend on many factors, including what type of text it is, how much time is available, and the preferred working style of designers, director and others involved. I like to have started to get inside the text before any detailed discussion with the director takes place, but many practitioners work successfully in other ways. Whatever the approach taken, good work usually depends on collaboration between all those responsible for the look of the performance. This will clearly include the director, set designer, costume designer and lighting designer, but may also include a choreographer, projection designer, sound designer, musical director, performers and others. At this early stage in the process of making a production, your ability to bring ideas to the group is severely limited if you do not have a thorough knowledge of the script.

Working with a director and other designers

Generally performances are made by groups of people. In most performance genre there is an established hierarchy to the group. In current Western theatre practice,

at or close to the top of that hierarchy is the director, who usually has the ultimate responsibility for, and thus power of veto over, everything that happens in front of the audience. Outside of theatre, this role is often less well defined, but it usually still exists — opera producer, dance choreographer, pop manager for example. It is usually the director who will determine how the key dramatic moment will be built up to and presented, and how the consequences will be played out.

Once in rehearsals, the director's primary role is usually to work with the performers to develop their performance. There are directors who involve themselves in the details of the design,[11] but usually after broad concepts have been agreed, the work of making coherent designs for set, costume, light and sound etc. becomes the responsibility of these designers. So how are these broad concepts arrived at? Most often through meetings of the creative production team. At first this may be only the director and the set designers, or set and costume designers, but whenever possible, the lighting designer should be involved too; the 'second child' looking on and listening and asking questions as the 'drawing' is begun, and the first choices are made.

Hopefully after reading the script or listening to the work a few times (initial text analysis) the lighting designer has a thorough knowledge of what happens when and where during the piece. This will not only help with design decisions, but is usually the 'entry price' to discussions about the piece. Without a good knowledge of what happens, when, where and why in a piece, it is not really possible to take an active role in talking about *how* it will be presented. Going back to the children's drawing, it will be as if the second child does not know why the drawing is being made.

So having found out the when, where and why, it is time to begin active discussions with the director. For most lighting designers, at the heart of these discussions will be the question, spoken or unspoken, 'What could lighting do for this production?' or it could be rephrased, 'What does the production gain by having

---

[11]For examples of contemporary directors who take on design responsibilities for their work, see Robert Wilson or Robert Lepage.

directed light rather than flat white light of most rehearsal spaces?' The director or the set designer may already have an answer in which case the next question is; do you as lighting designer understand that answer, and are you happy to work with it? You may have an answer, or a partial answer; can you sell it to the rest of the team? There may be no answer at initial meetings, or a confusion of answers, some of which may be contradictory, but the lighting designer must keep the question in mind as the production (and the lighting design) evolves.

Selling your ideas

Not every collaboration is perfect and even some pretty good ones have troubled times. When the director and a designer disagree, on a point of interpretation or realisation, we can talk, diplomatically perhaps, about creative tension and how great work comes out of a clash of strong personalities. By and large, resolving these different opinions requires rigorous examination of why each party might be right, illuminating and informing more thoughtful final choices. Many lighting designers often find themselves becoming a mediator between a strong-willed set designer and director, working to somehow help realise the slightly contradictory dreams of both into a coherent production concept. This generally works best when the lighting designer is informed by their own rigorous research. (Here is another indication of the range of skills often needed to work as a professional lighting designer, which include an ability to mediate and negotiate, as well as to research.)

Often when a designer is selling an idea to a director and the other members of the production team, their best support comes from research. A concept supported by intelligent and rigorous research — of the text and beyond — has much more appeal than some piece of whimsy proposed because it might look nice. After all, the director is going to have to work with the design concepts that establish the world of the performance to help the performers create their performances. The director must believe in that vision of the performance world at least as much as the designers do, so the designers have to provide as much underpinning material to support and justify the design decisions as they can. The producer is going to have to find the

Meeting the director

For many designers (both lighting designers and others) meeting a director, especially for the first time, can be an intimidating experience. It is worth having in mind the old saying, you only get one chance to make a first impression. Think about how you want to be perceived by the director and the rest of the production team. Will you be solid and technically competent, will you be full of artistic vision and flair? Will you be seen as being able to facilitate other people's ideas and visions, as an originator of new ideas, and as a contributor to an exciting end result? Will you be seen as someone with whom the others can work or as a potentially dangerous independent who will only do things your way?

Wear an outfit that says the right thing about you and that you are comfortable with. Make sure you know the exact place where you will be meeting and find out as much as you can about all the other people who will be at the meeting. If you have seen work by any of these people, be prepared to say a something about your impression of that work. Have your own CV in your head so you can talk about your work and make sure you have everybody's contact details — and that they have yours. Always turn up on time.

Finally, bring a notebook and a few pens, not just to take notes, but also to draw with — many ideas can be expressed better in a quick drawing than with 15 minutes of chat and arm waving. Try not to leave before you are sure you understand all the concepts the director and other designers want to include, and that they understand yours and that you all know when and where the next meeting will be.

money to pay for the creation of this world, so they may need convincing too.

Through all the almost inevitable arguments (friendly or otherwise) that accompany the evolution of a production, we need to remember who is ultimately in charge. In most cases this is either the director, who carries artistic responsibility for the production, or the producer, who carries the financial responsibility. In theatre it is rarely any of the designers! In most situations, when the lighting designer and the director significantly disagree, the lighting designer has only two real choices — do what the director asks or quit. If the lighting designer and the director maintain a good working relationship, the likelihood is that a practiced lighting designer will be able to persuade the director to their point of view, especially if that point of view is backed by research — so keep researching and keep talking.

Of course, there is no reason other than tradition why the designers cannot lead the interpretation of the text onto the stage. There are working designers at all levels whose contribution to live performance goes far beyond providing a setting, costume, lighting or sound. Although these designers are by no means the majority, they may well be a vanguard for a new practice that will refresh live performance for a much more visually orientated generation. The basis of this practice is, more often than not, rigorous research, not only into the text and all that is implied by the text, but into the audience (its experience and expectations, the venue) its facilities, history and perhaps unconventional use of its spaces, into technology, both old and new, and of course the art and practice of the performer — still at the heart of almost all performance. These designers are taking on some or all of the role of director, following in the footsteps of Appia and Gordon Craig. To be part of this movement, a practitioner must research widely, looking outside the confines of their own specialist area, be that set, costume, sound or light.

Further research

Whether or not the designer is taking on some of the traditional role of director, most productions will benefit from the some research beyond the original text. Some indication of useful areas of extended research have already been given but almost any reading around the author of the text, the period in which it was written, and the period in which it was originally set will be useful as background. Some playwrights have created a definite style of presentation for their work, for example Bertholt Brecht's Epic Theatre style, particularly as practiced at the theatre he helped to found, the Berliner Ensemble, or the opera composer Richard Wagner's Gesamtkunstwerk[12] style, as practiced at his Festival Theatre in Bayreuth. Even if the style is inappropriate for the current production, some knowledge of the author's original presentational intentions is often useful in deciding on an appropriate style for a contemporary production, and in deciding what to keep and what to throw away from the text as written. For example, discovering that a particular stage direction or scenic description is likely to have come from a particular production rather than the author, will often help the production team decide how closely to follow it.

Period choices

One of the early key decisions for a production team is in which period to set the piece. Many scripts state a particular date and refer to specific historical events, and this usually takes the decision out of the hands of the production team. But what happens in the case of a play written say in the 1960s, and set 'in the present day'? The production team may choose to use the original dates, to bring the whole thing forward to the present present day or choose some other date. Each choice will have consequences for the visual design (and probably for the editing the script too).

....

[12]Gesamtkunstwerk literally means total-art-work, and encapsulates Wagner's concept of many elements coming together to make a greater whole — music, poetry and visual elements. The word came to stand for the house style of the Bayreuth Festival Theatre during Richard Wagner's time there, and for many years after his death too.

....

For older works, including those often referred to as classic texts, choice of period can offer the audience a different perspective of what might be a well-known story. Take as an example the case of a production of Shakespeare's *Macbeth*. It could be set in 11th century Scotland, the historical time and place of the story Shakespeare used. It could also be set in the time when it was written and first performed, when the king was James I of England and VI of Scotland. However, the play has successfully been set in any number of other times and places; in contemporary times in an unspecified Western democracy or quite specifically the Uganda of African dictator Idi Amin. It has been set in the confusion after the Great War and in the American West of the early 19th century, and no doubt will be set in space if it has not been already.

When the creative team are deciding on a period, it is important to understand the context of the author's original choice and its impact on the piece. It is likely that Shakespeare chose medieval Scotland for a number or reasons, including the fact that the period was sufficiently distant from his own troubled times for the authorities to find it difficult to accuse him of making trouble for the reigning monarch. But *Macbeth* cannot be set literally anywhere — there has to be a power structure to be subverted.

Often with a play such as *Macbeth*, no specific time frame is given for the production, allowing director and designers to play with ideas from historical and contemporary experience. This choice has its own problems too. A definite period means choices can be informed by historical research and there is usually a 'right' and a 'wrong' answer. Without a definite time to reference, what is right or wrong for the piece can be much harder to determine.

When the production choice is for no specific time and place, every item on stage — every prop, every costume and every scenic element — is open to be read for its greater significance. For example, why is the king armed with that particular gun, well-known as the weapon of choice for a particular real person or group? Why do his personal guards wear those particular uniforms, a stylised version of a particular present day or historical army? What is being alluded to here? Is the audience being asked to draw parallels between the action on stage and the individuals or groups referenced in the choice of weapon and uniform? These extra meanings, perhaps offering an audience insight into their own present or recent past, can easily be enhanced or undermined by light. What would be the point of the particular choice of weapon if it is always in deep shadow and the audience never sees it? Clearly the lighting designer needs to be an active collaborator throughout the design process if the audience is going to benefit from the depth of meanings offered.

Sometimes the lighting designer will have a more direct need to do historical research. One of my first mentors, a set designer, told me that if you put something on stage that should not be in that world, it will upset some members of the audience and spoil their experience of the performance. He was talking about my proposed use of a fluorescent fitting in a domestic kitchen set for a play set well before fluorescent fittings were invented.[13] Historical research for lighting designers might begin with which light sources can and cannot legitimately be used on a set representing a particular period. It might go on to finding out what the light from period fittings looked like — the light from gas mantles, for example, has a pale greenish tint. Collaboration with set and costume designers might include an investigation of what were the fashionable and available colours for clothing, for wall coverings and for furnishings at that time and in that place. As we have already said, it can usefully extend

....

[13] GE began selling fluorescent lamps in North America in 1938. It did not take long for their use to spread, partly because of the relatively high cost of electricity in many markets. But you can't authentically put one in the kitchen of a play set in 1925 (not forgetting that they looked quite different in 1938 to the ones you can buy at the electrical wholesaler today!).

....

into more general information about the period — many working designers would agree that any research is useful and the more you know the better informed your work is.

Locations too will often require research. The light inside a particular building or outside at a particular time of day and season, can be quite specific. To evoke that place and time, the production may well wish to reproduce that quality of light on stage, so the lighting designer will need to research what it should look like. Often it is not the exact light of a particular place we need but the essence of that light, perhaps as captured in an iconic image — a photograph or a painting. The essence of the specific light of a place and time can be very hard to explain in words, and many of the words that a lighting designer might use to do so would not be understood in the same way by other theatre professionals. We have already mentioned the potential confusion surrounding the use of warm and cool to describe light. Almost every lighting designer I have talked to has at least one story where a director misunderstood their verbal description of light, so use pictures. Two people looking at a flat still image may still not have the same expectations of a realised version of the light in that image, but high-quality images will allow discussions about light, with all parties much more confident that they are talking about the same thing.

Several designers I have talked to try to introduce something they have not worked with before into each new performance design. This could be part of their research into technology (in its broadest meaning) and could include resurrecting some old piece of stage machinery or magic just as easily as it could mean using the latest digital projector. The point is not to come into the production with technology for its own sake, but to ensure that whatever means are chosen to realise production ideas they serve the creation of the world of the performance. It is worth remembering that stage technology rarely 'does exactly what it says on the can' so some of your research will be into finding out exactly what your new kit does and how — preferably before the increasingly time pressured rehearsals in the venue.

How much work does the audience do?

Performances at Shakespeare's Globe theatre, both the original 16th century building and the modern recreation on London's South Bank, generally use the minimum of representational cues to evoke hundreds of different locations and times; from the castles and courts of Macbeth and the English kings, to the Roman forum of the Caesars, from the gardens of Padua and Verona to the Blasted Heath of Lear and dozens of battlefields. All of these many locations are presented at different times of day; from pre-dawn through morning, afternoon and evening, to mid-summer's night. For the successful productions on the Globe stage the audience reads the time and place through the action of the performers and the language of the play; and this is possible on other stages too, and with writers other than Shakespeare. It may be considered easier to successfully present narrative work with very little representational set or lighting when the stories are already well known, and when the language is powerfully provided by the world's greatest dramatist. Certainly costume helps the audience to enter and comprehend the world of the performance offering information about period and relative status of the characters. The present-day Globe company put a great deal of effort into getting costume right. But the audience for live performance, for theatre especially, are very often willing and able to fill in the gaps around the performers. The British stage designer Jocelyn Herbert working at the Royal Court in London from the 1960s onwards, with others including lighting designer Andy Philips, with director John Dexter, pioneered a style of stage design where the right table and chair sitting on an otherwise bare open stage, could represent a whole room if not an entire house, with walls, doors and windows. The audience did the work of creating whatever was necessary for the world of the performance around the images Herbert and Philips put on stage, made 'real' by performers and director.

When we watch recorded performance, on film and television, design generally provides an accurate and detailed representation of the world of the performers

— live performance does not always need this. The willingness and ability of an audience to imagine part of the world of performance, above and beyond the 'missing' fourth wall of proscenium theatre, can provide designers with a freedom of expression not usually available to designers working in recorded media. Design for live performance can often do much more than represent time and place, providing an emotional context and visual interest, as well as giving the audience something to think about. Even when the chosen aesthetic is to recreate as closely and completely as possible a very particular world, there are choices open to the design team which allow their work to convey more than simply time and place to the audience.

Expectations and genre

Design for performance, as we have said before, exists to support the performers. This means that there will always be some practical constraints on performance design. Almost all performances need at least one entrance/exit on the stage, if for no other reason than to just get the performers on and off. Productions which feature dance will need room for the dancers to move, and lighting positions to provide good modelling of their forms when they move. Designs for performances that feature amplified sound will need to incorporate the technical requirements of speaker and microphone placement, and if there is a band on stage, all the equipment that goes with the production, control and separation of sound too.

There are constraints on design imposed by the expectations of particular genres. The majority of the audience for musicals, some opera and ballet, and most rock and pop concerts, are often said to expect the stars to be lit by follow spots, and it can be difficult for a lighting designer to argue against their use. Other types of drama demand that no performer is ever seen by the audience in anything but full light no matter what the dramatic time or place may indicate. Either of these conventions can be accepted and worked with or challenged, but the lighting and other designers are not likely to be able to challenge convention if the only argument is 'I don't like that way of doing things'. If the design concept is moving away from the conventions of the genre, realisation of it will often produce something new and exciting, but it still has to be sold to the creative and production teams, and quite likely the performers too, in order for it to ever get on stage.

Audience expectations can be a difficult matter to discuss. Many commercial producers seem to believe that their audience will invest little in filling the gaps of a non-representational design. Short of designing and carrying out your own research into audience expectations (perhaps by presenting a non-representational design and recording audience response) this can be a difficult argument to counter. After all, successful producers make their money by understanding what the public wants, and ensuring they get it. However, almost every child makes fantasy worlds out of the most minimal of props — a castle under the kitchen table is one my mother teases me about — and at times we can be brought back to that joyful state by live performance. Again if designers are going to push at these expectations (assuming that they want to) they will need well researched rigorous arguments.

Next steps

So by now we are a little less than half way through a design for performance process. A 'we' has been established, a creative team which has begun to imagine this piece in a performance space. We have read the text several times; know what happens where and when, and why it happens. We know each of the characters in the piece and what function they serve — hero, villain, love interest, lead guitarist, drummer etc. We have a good idea about the structure of the piece, where the climax is/are, which bits are there for comedy, for exposition, for character development, and maybe for ornament. We have some design concepts, based on rigorous research both of the text and of other things that have proved linked, useful, or just interesting. As lighting designer, you will have started to collect some visual material to illustrate discussions about these design concepts — certain qualities of light perhaps required for particular parts of the piece — perhaps some photographs or a reproduction of an iconic art work. But we are still a long way from a realised production, and as lighting designer you are still some way from a lighting plan, let alone a set of lighting states that go with cues in the piece. The performers may not even have been hired yet (though if this is the case the costume designer may be getting nervous). Here are a few things to bear in mind as we enter the next stage of the design process, first about the concept.

■ The concepts we take into the next stage of the design process should be free to grow and evolve during their development, and respond to what the director and the performers are discovering during rehearsals.

■ Very soon, however, the concept will need to become firm enough to provide a framework in which all can move towards a coherent realisation. In many genre of performance a scale model of the performance space and the set will have been made by the set designer, it will often prove useful to the lighting designer. In any case scale drawings of the space (the ground-plan and section) will need to be made, showing the proposed position of the set and per-formance area, the audience, and as much of the technical facilities as necessary.

About the nature of (almost all) live performance.

■ It will be seen by many audience members at the same time observing from different angles, and often from a distance — you can't get away with a design that is dependant of a single point of view.

■ The stage is not the real world — even in verbatim theatre[14] — performance demands a heightened reality even if it produces it itself.

And about choices and time.

■ Choices diminish as the first night approaches, which means, for example, that six months from the fit-up the lighting designer may have had special equip-ment made just for the show. Six weeks from the fit-up, they will probably have a choice of equipment that exists already maybe in other towns or cities, maybe in other countries. Six hours before the fit-up they will have to work with what is on the truck, in the space already, or perhaps in the hire shop down the road and six hours before the first night, they work with the cue structure they have and the equipment that is rigged and focused, and they make small (but frequently important) changes only.

■ With this in mind, at each stage, try to agree amongst the production team what is fixed and what may still change, be prepared for surprises, and try to build flexibility into your design.

---

[14]Verbatim theatre uses the recorded words of real people and presents them on stage. Examples include re-enactments of infamous trials or enquiries, and dramatic investigations into disasters. This is perhaps the style of theatre where there is often the greatest wish to represent an unmediated reality on stage. However, we should remember that even in the verbatim presentation of an enquiry, some necessary editing of the total content available has taken place to produce a text that makes sense to an audience in a single evening, and there are justifications for taking the same approach to the visual design.

5

evolving the concept

Developing a cue structure

Design ideas begin to be made real

For most mainstream theatre productions, we would now be at the stage just before rehearsals begin. The set design has been more or less completed, and a scale model of the set has been made. Ground plans have been drawn and construction of major scenic elements will probably have begun. The cast has been hired, and the costume designs are already being realised in the workshops but we are still some weeks away from anything happening on the performance stage, and production ideas will evolve and change as the director rehearses with the cast. While the major scenic elements are now fixed, and some costumes have been made (and can therefore not change without extra budget being found) lighting, sound and sometimes projected design elements can still evolve as the production does. This possibility will often give lighting designers (and sound and projection designers) both considerable creative freedom to respond to the evolving production ideas, and huge headaches trying to balance creative freedom with practicality. At some point soon, the lighting designer will have to submit a request for equipment and personnel but hopefully not quite yet.

Some practical considerations

Once the lighting designer has devoured the text and met with the rest of the creative team to establish common approaches and goals, they should have some idea of the answer to the question, 'What does lighting do for this production?' There are practical matters to attend to. These relate to:

- The size and configuration of the production space(s), usually documented on a venue ground plan and section, or better still (for some of us) a 3D CAD model ready to be viewed on computer.[1]

- The production infrastructure of the venue(s), sometimes know as the in-house facilities. This includes such things as number and position of installed dimmers, available power supply, lighting and other equipment available for the production, and often most importantly, the personnel available.

- The overall budget and the expectations of the people or organisation providing the money. Do they see this as a highly-polished extravagant spectacle, a rough and ready rapid response, or something in-between?

- Time. A lighting designer will need a very different approach for a show that must be in, up and out in a

---

[1]Any number of computer programmes allow us to create a model of our performance space in virtual 3D space — from the formality of AutoCAD to the user-friendliness of Sketch-Up. Programs such as Cast Software's WYSIWYG or Vector Works Spotlight allow us to light the virtual model with a virtual rig. There is more about the pros and cons of this approach later in the book.

day, to one that has a month of rehearsals in the theatre followed by weeks of previews.

It can be difficult to make plans for a lighting rig without most of this information. However, it may be some time before all these things become clear. Working with limited information is a problem we will look at again in later chapters, but for now let's assume that we are not in that position. So as lighting designer you have had several meetings with the director and the other members of the creative team, and now you know who the 'we' is. 'We' have had discussions about the world we are going to create and those discussions continue to be informed by research, both text-based and practical. 'We' know what the main elements of the set are, how they frame the performance, and the spatial relationship between audience and performers. (Generally, we know the shape of the stage and where the audience will be sitting.) 'We' (and actually this might be a different 'we' made up of the producer and production manager) have discussed practical matters including expectations, budget and such matters as time, equipment and personnel available at each stage in the realisation. As lighting designer you have a thorough knowledge of the script, and some ideas about how you might eventually realise the performance lighting on stage, and some answers to the question, 'What will lighting do for this production?' Time then to go into some detail, and start to make plans.

A lighting designer and their team will usually want to produce two distinct types of document. The first type includes the rig plan or lighting plot (the primary concern of the next chapter). The second type includes the cue synopsis — a document that will evolve throughout the production period and will ultimately contain important information about the purpose of each lighting state and how that purpose is achieved, the placement of the cue within the piece, and the nature of the transition from one state to the next.

Lighting score

Most performance lighting is made up of a number of different looks which we have called lighting states. Each lighting cue triggers a change to a new state. Like method-trained actors, lighting cues usually need a motivation. This might be something very obvious such

as a cue required to brighten a room setting when an actor turns on a light switch or the rapid increase in intensity at the end of a dance number in a traditional musical (known as a button cue). At other times we will need a cue to provide a subtle change in atmosphere over a number of minutes, motivated perhaps by the mention of a sunset or the intention to slowly change the feel of the performance from normal to threatening. The question, 'What will lighting do for this production?' needs to be asked for each moment of the production, each dramatic unit or scene, and each transition. 'What will light do for this scene?' For drama and many other production genres, a good way to begin to answer these questions is by producing a lighting score. This can then evolve into the first cue synopsis, and form the basis of our whole approach to creating the light for the piece.

What we are attempting to achieve with the lighting score is to record practical and artistic requirements for each major moment in the piece. At first, the lighting designer may only be able to make abstract responses to both the text and to concepts expressed by their fellow collaborators on the project — the director or producer, other designers, etc. Later, by watching the production get on its feet — usually in a rehearsal room — the lighting designer will be able to see more clearly which areas of the performance space require what kind of light at different moments during the piece. Often slowly, concrete ideas about the quantity, quality, colour and direction of light required to best serve each moment of the production emerge, and these turn into lantern choices at each of the lighting positions to be used for the production. Ideally, the novice lighting designer should not try to hurry this process, being prepared to go back over sections of the text and re-work ideas in the light of new discoveries from later sections of the text, from discussions with other members of the artistic team or from rehearsals.

As you will see, in the lighting score example the piece has been divided into dramatic units. Exactly what a unit is composed of should change to reflect the text and how detailed an approach is being taken. A unit is simply the smallest part of the text that can conveniently be considered in isolation. For a piece already made up of multiple acts and short scenes, each scene might constitute a unit. For a multi-character drama each entrance and exit might define a unit. For a musical theatre piece each song might be a unit, but might also usefully be split further into sub-units — verse, chorus, middle eight, etc. The beauty of using a computer to make this table is that you can split units up at will — the disadvantage is that you can't easily sketch or make marks on the lighting score until it is printed out[2]. Whether the lighting score is computer generated or hand drawn, when you decide on the layout, it will probably be most useful if the squares that ask for a visual response are not too small.

For most designers who use a tool like this, what works best is to record an emotional response that will be a step towards an understanding of the light required for each moment rather than a direct leap to specifics of lantern type, position, focus, colour, etc. For example, the colour section asks, 'If this scene was a colour what would that colour be?' rather than, 'What colour will I light this scene in?' And the Intensity section asks, 'What (emotional or psychological) intensity does this scene have?' rather than directly, 'How bright will I make this scene on stage?' This is not to say that impressions recorded in these sections of the lighting score will not eventually feed into my choice of colour or the overall intensity of a cue, but that the primary purpose of the document is to develop ideas.

This lighting score does have some sections that will provide practical information to feed directly into the placement of fixtures; direction of key light — that is the direction of the 'apparent' source of illumination, numbers and positions of performers and area of primary focus and details of any specials we might use, for example. Using this document we can begin to imagine the quality and quantity of light on stage at any particular moment — and from that we can begin to imagine what equipment placed where might achieve that.

A note of warning

If the aspiring lighting designer observes established practitioners at work, they are unlikely to find them producing a formal lighting score as extensive as the one shown here. By the time most practitioners can earn a living as lighting designers, much of this process has become instinctive. If it is documented at all it is in the form of a personal short-hand that helps the lighting designer to draw on their extensive technical and artistic experience. This method is offered as a kind of short cut to evolving a lighting design for the less experienced practitioner, but it cannot replace that experience.

In the performance space, the lighting designer will often have only minutes to work with the board operator or programmer to create the exact composition of each major cue state. Extensive preparation is often the only way to create lighting that truly serves the production in these circumstances.

Using the lighting score

If you decide to make a lighting score, remember that it is a tool with which to evolve a lighting design, not an end in itself. As such, it is more important that a general approach to the performance lighting emerges than that each square is completed.

The lighting score allows the lighting designer to evolve a visual language for the piece based on their response to the text, whatever that may be. It can be used to condense visual ideas and the practical requirements of the production onto a single, usually quite large, piece of paper. As such it can help to give a unity to a design by presenting the required elements in one place. It can help to reveal underlying rhythms and structures; between 'bright' and 'dark' scenes, between high and low contrast scenes, between open and confined scenes, and between scenes with different colour feels. From this we can begin to construct a cue synopsis, as we shall soon see.

[2]The increasing sophistication of computer software however begins to allow designers of all kinds to develop digital practices, which can include sketching, in two, three or even four dimensions (the fourth being time) quickly, within more conventional documents such as tables and spread-sheets. This is clearly a rapidly developing area which we will touch on again later.

Example of a lighting score (from R.H. Palmer, M.A. Jones, and others)

Production:	**Venue:**			**Act:**	
Lighting designer:	**Director:** **Set designer:**			**Scene:**	
	Unit/page number		*Unit 1*	*Unit 2*	*Unit 3*
Primarily from the text & discussions with artistic collaborators*	**Key idea/reason for the unit**		*Words*		
	Time & location		*Words*		
	Intensity (emotional/ psychological)		*Graph*		
	Colour (emotional/ psychological)		*Paint, gel sample or word?*		
	Mood (conflict/ aggression/passion etc.)		*Words*		
From rehearsals & scenic design/model box*	**Tempo of scene**		*Graph?*		
	Entrances/exits Use of stage area (blocking) Area(s) of focus & implied sources of light		*Sketch ground plan with arrows & notes Words?*		
Design decisions that will influence type and placing of equipment*	**Overall brightness**		*Graph?*		
	(comment)		*Words*		
	Openness/closure of space		*Words/graphics*		
	Key light		*Arrows?*		
	(comment)		*Words*		
	Amount of contrast		*Words or shading?*		
	Lighting specials		*Words/sketch*		
	Movement		*Sketch? Arrows?*		

* These divisions are for guidance only and may be quite different in some production's setups.

Working with music

So far the approach to breaking down the text into something we can use as an inspiration for design has largely assumed a written script. For a recorded text, such as a full recording of a musical or an opera, the process is much the same, though it helps enormously to have the libretto when it comes to trying to work out who is on stage and where each scene is set.

Musical training or knowledge can be very useful in making responses to music, but as long as you can respond to the music — allowing it to affect you in some way — you can find a way into it, and produce some design ideas. (If you don't feel anything on hearing the music, perhaps you should not be working on the piece.)

When working with music I find it useful to make a response to each song or musical number along the following lines to begin with:

- Who is involved? What are their roles in the piece?

- What is the number about? Is that important or is the number just a pretty filler?

- Size. Does this number 'look' big or small? Solo, duet, chorus? Is much movement likely in performance? Are there all-out dance sections?

- Shape. Does it start small and grow? Does it grow slowly or dramatically at a particular point? Are there changes in rhythm, in atmosphere or in musical key? What happens at the end — big finish or gentle fade?

- Texture of the music. Is there one simple melody or are there counter melodies and complex accompaniments?

- Emotional response. What feelings does the music evoke in me? Does the tune soar between powerful high notes leading the accompaniment and appealing to the heart of the audience, or maybe the words are most important, or the music is complex and the appeal is to the head?

- Colour response. Does the music make me think of a particular colour? Is it multi-coloured or mono-chrome? It is usually a bit early in the process to get

too tied into particular tints and hues, but more generally, does this feel like a 'blue' song, or maybe a pink and amber number.

- Brightness. Again, usually too early to be thinking about the intensity of individual lanterns, but does the number 'sound' bright or dark? You might consider placing each musical number in the piece on a scale of brightness, say 0 to 10, and see if this reveals something useful about the overall structure of the piece.

As with the table in the previous section, this list is clearly not exhaustive. I use some or all of these factors as a starting point to help record my immediate response to the music.

Just as with the written text, we now need to take out first response and develop it. Many designers for pop and rock music concerts use a similar approach to that outlined above when evolving a design — deciding what each song will look like. Is this a 'blue' and 'red' 'big' song with a bright chorus? Does it have a lot of quick cues or is the look based round one massive statement for lighting. Without the support or perhaps constraint, of a 'story' running through the whole evening, designers for live music concerts may need to find themes to tie individual numbers together, and to ensure that similar sounding numbers don't all look the same — so there is clearly more work to do for a rock and pop lighting designer just as for a music theatre lighting designer.

Collaboration

In music theatre, the music director is responsible for creating tonalities and textures with the music for the performance. If lighting is doing a 'brooding storm' atmosphere while the music is doing 'joys of spring' it is likely neither signifier will be read as the lighting designer or musical director intended. As we have said before, for lighting to be read as intended, it must work with all the other channels of communication in use. Even when there is no music as such on stage, the power of sound to evoke place and atmosphere should not be left out. Many multi-location plays have successfully used sound to identify 'place' while light does 'atmosphere'[3]. The point is that when thinking about the creation of most types of performance, the signification at any one moment will come from many different channels. No single channel of communication between stage and audience should usually try to do everything; whether that channel is lighting, sound, set or the many channels available to each performer. Almost all live performance requires the collaboration of all those responsible for these many channels in order to be successful.

Story-board

Another approach to evolving the general design and perhaps the blocking of a production is to story-board the piece. A story-board is common in the worlds of film and animation. At its simplest it is a series of sketch representations of the stage at different moments through the production. It can be drawn by hand, created through rendering a 3D model of the set on a computer, or by taking photographs of the lit model box. If at all possible, the lighting designer, set designer and director should sit down and create the story-board together. For many productions, the story-board becomes the focus for the evolution of the performance, acting as both initial inspiration for the staging of each scene and as a road-map for the whole production. For shows with large movable elements of set, story-boarding is almost essential to both plan and show how each different scene will be achieved on stage.

For other theatre practitioners, making a story-board at this stage in the process makes too much too concrete too soon, limiting the extent to which the production can grow and develop in rehearsal. If other members of the creative team are reluctant to get involved in creating a story-board, it will be of limited use. That said, some lighting designers use their own story-board to sell ideas to the director and set designer (and others) and to assist in the development of their own response to the piece.

From the point of view of the lighting designer, there are pros and cons to story-boards; the hand-drawn, the photographed and the computer rendered. A hand-drawn story-board can be based on photocopies of a single sketch of the performance space or even on copies of photos of the set model. Many lighting designers like to use black paper, drawing in the light with white or coloured chalk, and revealing form. Hand-drawn work can provide a quick response. It can also be shared with others in the room, since most people feel they can pick up a pencil and make a few marks. Rough sketches can seem friendly and organic and can be changed, which is usually appropriate for a stage in the design process still some weeks or months away from a time when the performers will be in the performance space.

The look of computer renders on the other hand can seem quite alien to anyone who has not grown up with computer gaming images, and can be intimidating if it appears that only a specialist can make changes to the render. They can, however, give a much clearer picture of what the finished result might look like (again providing the viewer can see past the technology) and can usually be set up to be viewed from a variety of audience positions. Most of the computer programmes used to produce renders take many hours to create an accurate set model, and some require the lighting rig to be more or less complete before an illuminated render can be produced. This is one of the limiting factors in the use of this technology at present.

Using a story-board
Where story-boards work best they are the joint work of everyone who is responsible for the look of the

---

[3]Consider a scene set just after dawn on the stage of a theatre in the round. If we do 'strong long shadow caused by low light from one direction — very little fill' at least half the audience will not see anything, and yet this is the nature of dawn light. If we use an evocative soundscape for dawn and concentrate on creating atmosphere with the lighting, the whole effect will probably be much more successful for more of the audience.

The musical score

The score is the written record of what each instrument or group of instruments (each 'part') is doing through the piece. Most music is divided into bars each containing a number of beats. Most pop music and a lot of other Western music, has four beats to the bar. Usually the musicians playing for opera, musicals and some dance are lead by a conductor. Each time the music begins a new bar, the conductor or band leader gives a down beat. This helps the musicians to play together. In a full score the notes are written out, bar by bar, with a line of bars for each part. In a orchestral number scored for many parts, each page of the score may have as little as five seconds of music written out on it — clearly a full score for such a piece will be a large book! Often the lighting designer (and others who need a written copy of the music) will use a piano score or a vocal score. This is a condensed version of the music, often used for rehearsals, written for piano so the many lines or parts are reduced to two for the piano (one for each on the pianist's hands) and a line or lines for the singer's music, and the words. This is more manageable, though for a long opera it may still be quite a size!

Every score is marked up with section markers, usually capital letters printed in bold or bar numbers. They allow musicians to identify a particular place in the music without having to count bars right from the beginning of the piece. In rehearsals, the conductor might ask everybody to begin at eight bars after figure G. Section markers are also useful to the lighting and stage management team when it comes to discussing where the lighting cues go.

Score reading is clearly a useful skill when working with opera and musicals and dance. In most large music theatre and dance productions there will be an assistant following the score so that the lighting designer can concentrate on looking at the stage. When it comes to placing cues with the music, this assistant can give a clear indication to others about where in the music each cue goes. Having the skill to do this well can be a good way to start working in larger scale music theatre.

Accurate score reading requires a good deal of practice, but with a rudimentary knowledge of written music it is possible to follow roughly what is going on. (Having the words in your score will clearly help for the sung passages at least.) Listening out for a particular musical phrase — maybe a flourish from the trumpets or for changes in an accompanying part, maybe a change in bass rhythm — can give clues to link what you are hearing to what you are reading. Some knowledge of music, preferably from playing an instrument, will help too, not only with reading the score but also in understanding some of the ways music works.

Finally, two cautions: first, make sure the section markers in your copy of the vocal or piano score are the same as everyone elses. Second, beware repeated sections of music that are not written out in full, and check with the music department which (if any) repeats will be played.

production. Problems can occur, however, when they are used by one department (either set and costume or lighting or dance or projection, etc) to share ideas with others. Inevitably the visual representation produced by only one department will contain information that implies choices made by the others. The closer the representation is to reality, the more those other departments are likely to focus on what they don't like about the bits of the world of performance that are 'theirs' rather than anything positive. This seems to be especially true for near photographic quality computer renders. For example, if the set design team present a render it will be lit in some way, and should have performers placed in the space.

However, the light may not be what the lighting designer wants or can achieve and the placement of the performers may not be what either director or choreographer want either. In these situations it will often fall to the lighting designer to negotiate possible practical solutions from initially conflicting ideas.

As we have already noted, some directors shy away from the formally planned approach implied by storyboarding (and to some, by the model box too). However, when the production situation or the working methods of the creative team incline towards this approach, it can be very helpful in leading the lighting designer towards both a cue synopsis and a rig plan.

If you really can't draw

Many successful lighting designers say they can't draw. Often what they mean is that compared to their ability to make pictures in living three dimensional space on stage, their ability on the two dimensional page is disappointing. I advise young designers to practice drawing and to find the media that they are most comfortable with, but many practitioners need other ways to record and develop their design ideas. One useful method is to sketch out in words the 'story of the light of the performance'. This is the preferred way of working for award winning British lighting designer Paule Constable. She reads the script, and the book if that is what the script is based on, and any other source material, and creates in writing a description of the light at each key point in the performance. This might be along the lines of 'the Mediterranean sunlight streaming in through the window' (*Don Carlos* by Frederic Schiller) or 'this man lives in a room with no daylight' (*Krapp's Last Tape* by Samuel Beckett)[4]. These descriptions become more detailed as the production evolves through rehearsal and becomes the basis for developing a detailed cue synopsis, rig plan and lighting design.

Whatever method is used by each lighting designer on each project, it is important to invest the time and intellectual effort to produce communicable ideas for the light at each key moment of performance, and to discuss these ideas with the other members of the creative team.

The set model box

It is common practice in many genres of performance for the set designer to produce a scale model of the proposed design. This is called the model box. For many set designers, the model box is an important part of their process. It is a tool with which to present the final design to the director, producer, cast and other collaborators, and one of the main guides to those who will make the set in workshops and build it in the performance space. But it is also a tool used to evolve the design — to move from two dimensional sketches and other initial inspirations towards a realisable three dimensional environment for the performance. Many set designers enjoy working with light in the spaces they are evolving and if the lighting designer is employed early enough in the process, a productive collaboration can take place to develop the design of a lit space in the model box.

It can be quite hard to reproduce accurate stage lighting at the usual model box scale of 1:25, but it is usually worth making the effort. All too often the model box is illuminated by a single desk work-light. To reproduce this effect at full scale would involve taking the roof off the performance space and hiring a large generator to power the single enormous lantern. Clearly this is not usually possible so the impression gained from a model box illuminated in this way can be quite different from the eventual realised outcome on stage. Careful positioning of sources, including perhaps a small torch for highlights, can produce much more effective lighting of the model. Ask if the model can be made with holes at the side to allow various angles of side lighting to be introduced. Model boxes for proscenium spaces can be made much easier to light

---

[4]Both these examples were quoted by Paule in an informal talk on the set of *Coram Boy* at the Royal National Theatre.

FIGURE 1A & B. THE MODEL BOX FOR *SWEENEY TODD*, DESIGNED AND BUILT BY KEITH ORTON. THE PICTURE ON THE RIGHT SHOWS HOW THE BOX CAN BE LIT WITH A COUPLE OF TASK LAMPS. BOTH PHOTOGRAPHS HAVE A BLUE CAST — THE CAMERA WAS SET FOR TUNGSTEN BUT THERE WAS A LOT OF DAYLIGHT IN THE ROOM TOO.

effectively if there is access from the sides. Try to use sources with a similar colour temperature to the lanterns that will eventually shine on the finished set — these are more likely to be found in task-light with small low-voltage lamps.

A small torch such as a Mag-lite can be used with samples from standard colour media swatch books. The standard Mag-lite has a bulb with a colour temperature close to that of theatre lanterns (when the batteries are fresh) so this can be a good way to find out how par-

FIGURE 2. THE SAME MODEL BOX LIT IN A MODEL LIGHTING STUDIO TO ILLUSTRATE THREE SEPARATED AREAS. THE COLOUR IS RENDERED BETTER HERE TOO, BECAUSE DAYLIGHT HAS BEEN EXCLUDED.

ticular colours will work with the set, and how different colours of light might work together. Focusable white light LED torches are similar enough in colour temperature to some moving lights to indicate how they might look on stage too.

Try to ensure that the box has figures, with some facial detail, in suitable places when the photographs are taken. This will usually produce much more satisfactory images, which will be more useful to director and designers alike.

For more subtle lighting effects you can use fixtures designed for shop windows and other display purposes while coloured light can be added using birdies (also known as PAR 16s). Many larger theatre organisations and specialist performance design schools have a model lighting studio with small scale specialist lanterns. This kind of facility can be useful for trying out effects and for taking photographs.

The lit model box should be viewed from similar angles to those from which the audience will eventually see the realised lit stage. It is of limited use to view the model box from above unless this is how the audience will see the space. As well as giving the director and the design team some idea about the evolving world that will be created for the performance, viewing the model box from the same perspective as the audience offers an opportunity to investigate what each section of the audience will or will not see. This in turn may well inform

decisions about blocking and masking arrangements and which lighting positions can be used — all information which will usually be key to the way the lighting design can evolve.

Working with the set and costume designer(s) and the director in the model box can be a very effective way to evolve truly integrated design solutions at a point in the production process when major changes to structures can still be made. Discovering, for example, that some small changes to the position or construction of a large set element will allow light from a new angle to highlight a strong performer location on the stage can be an exciting advance in the creation of the final performance. If it is made in the model box before that set element has been constructed and positioned, valuable time and money can be saved.

Generally, the more accurate the model is the more useful it will be. For example, if texture is reproduced accurately at scale and illuminated in a way that is achievable on the full size stage, then its impact in show conditions can be properly assessed. If this does not happen, if for example instead of correctly scaling down the ridges of a corrugated roof or the roughness of a brick wall, or a textured floor is lit from an angle that will not be achievable on stage, expectations are raised that cannot be met, and everyone is likely to be disappointed.

Photographs of the lit model box, with the set elements in their proposed position and with scale

Theatre masking

Masking refers to materials that hide potentially distracting elements of production infrastructure from the view of the audience and help to create a frame for the stage picture. It is also used to provide a hidden off-stage place from which performers can enter.

Masking at the sides of the performance space is often referred to as 'legs' (which are generally tall and narrow pieces). Masking pieces above a performance space are usually referred to as 'borders' and are often used to hide the lighting equipment from the audience.

Masking can be hard flats or soft drapes and can be general purpose black or specially designed as part of the overall look of the production design. Positioning masking can have a significant impact on what each lantern can do and on the overall effectiveness of the lighting design.

No lighting designer, especially when working on a proscenium stage, would want to be excluded from any discussion about the position of masking.

further permission to an active section of the audience to join in with the performance and the singer can see them joining in and feeds off that. Making this happen depends much more on the charisma of the lead singer and his ability to work the crowd than on the concert lighting designer. For the lighting designer, getting it right means understanding the needs of both lead singer and the audience, understanding how each will (subconsciously) read your work, and of course having the technical competence to make it all happen. And it has to be said that if the lighting designer does not get it right, the singer is not so likely to get the audience on their feet, and therefore not likely to have a good gig — with all the potential consequences that can bring.

Very often in live music concerts, on the drama stage, and elsewhere, the lighting designer is responsible for determining to a large degree the way the audience reads the show and this is clearly important. Will the performance area be kept defined and separate from the audience area, as is common in most proscenium theatres, or will one part of the audience be at times the backdrop to the performance for another part of the audience, as can happen in a traverse configuration? Will the audience see the show from a very dark auditorium, creating a quite isolated feeling, or will they remain in a semi-lit auditorium, more aware of each other's presence and perhaps less intensely focused on the stage? These choices are clearly not the sole decision of the lighting designer but light will influence how well they are received.

Framing can be thought as the key to a large scale structure of a performance, and as such considerations of framing will clearly inform the lighting design. How will the performance space be presented to the audience at key moments of the piece? Questions also need to be asked about what the kind of world is being presented to the audience: are we in a particular place at a particular time or are we in a more gener-

alised world, or perhaps inside someone's head? Is the world of the performance the same throughout the piece or does it change? How will the audience 'get' this? (In other words, what signifiers will be used?) A consideration of framing also asks questions about how the audience looks at the performance: is the audience to be passive observers of a dramatised but essentially objective representation of events which have a history outside the script, or perhaps we want the audience to become partisan, supporting one of two or more contradictory views of an event presented or talked about on stage, or perhaps what happens on stage has no direct relation to the reality of everyday life? To look at this in another way, will the production tend towards a Brechtian approach, continually reminding the audience they are watching 'theatre' not 'real life', or at the other extreme, an approach based on Stanislavski, where the actors will immerse themselves in the role and present 'verisimilitude underpinned by psychological truth' to the audience?[5] Most designers working in performance would agree that the answers to these (and other) framing questions will influence their work on the piece. An established practitioner is already likely to be aware of the implications on design elements of any framing choices, and especially any decision to follow (if only vaguely) the theory and practice of particular practitioners. A young designer may have to research the practice and writings of Brecht, Stanislavski or whoever in order to take an active part in discussions and for their work to be truly collaborative.

Initial cue synopsis

The cue synopsis is often the most important document for the lighting designer. It outlines how each lighting state is constructed, links each state to a particular piece of action and place in the script or music, and details how we get into and out of each state.

[5]Brecht, Stanislavski and others, continue to have a huge influence on performance. Anyone wishing to work with actors needs to be familiar with their key ideas.

Whether the first cue synopsis comes before the thinking about signification[6] and framing, or after, or at the same time is a mater of personal preference and probably changes from project to project. Many lighting designers working in text-based drama make notes in the script as their first cue synopsis. Most will usually end up with a document in a table shown opposite. Note the large amount of specialist 'shorthand' used.

A quick note on time in cues

Generally cue time is the time between the start of the cue and its completion. We don't need to use the same time for every change involved in establishing the new cue state. If we are just dealing with intensity, we can 'split' the time for a cue and have a different up time and down time. Up time refers to the time taken for intensity to build — generally associated with the new cue state developing on stage, and down time is the time it takes for the intensity of units reducing in intensity to fade. These will generally be units not required in the new scene (if they are fading to zero intensity) or required at a lower intensity than in the previous cue state.

For example, if we wished to shift the focus of audience attention from an area down stage left (DSL) to one down stage right (DSR), we could use a cue that increases the intensity of the lanterns focused DSR and reduces the intensity of those focused DSL. Often this kind of cue works best if the new area of audience focus establishes quite quickly while the old area returns to a background intensity more slowly, so that this is almost unnoticed by the audience. (After all, we want them to be looking at the new area of focus, and we know that our attention is drawn towards rapid changes in intensity — increases or decreases.) The cue might use an up time of say three seconds, and a down time of say 12 or 15 seconds, which would mean the units focused DSR would increase in intensity to their new levels in three seconds, while the units focused DSL would reduce in intensity over 12 or 15 seconds. This is called a split time fade, and is very useful in all kinds of situations.

But what if action in the old area continues for a line or two after the need to establish the new area? Even with a slow fade we could finish up with the performers in the old area only dimly lit for an important line at the end of their scene. Well, we can delay the start of the down fade, using what most lighting desks refer to as a delay time. In this case we might have a cue with a delay of say six seconds, so the down fade, i.e. the reduction in intensity of the units focused DSL, would not begin until six seconds after the 'go', which initiated the up fade of the units focused DSR.

Modern lighting control desks allow many more variations in cue time and we will touch on these again in coming chapters. Detailed discussion of cue time in relation to moving lights is best left to specialist texts on programming performance lighting. However, let us look briefly at how we might use cue times with moving lights:

Suppose we have some discharge CMY wash fixtures, such as MAC 600s or Studio Colors. One problem with these units is that when they are set to produce pale colours or white light, as soon as the dimmer shutter

[6]Whether we are talking about signification of a time and place on stage or merely noting what the stage directions state, designed performance signifies and performance designers make choices about what to signify and how. The terminology of semiotics may not be used, but what is being thought about and talked about is essentially establishing the system of signs that will be used on the project. The words may be different but what is happening is the same.

opens the light that comes out is quite bright — they don't fade up like incandescent lanterns. One way to combat this is to use a delay time and the fading colour to help control intensity of light coming from the units. Say we want to build from a dark stage to a final result of a brightly-lit stage using a combination of discharge wash units and incandescent units. We might begin the cue by raising the intensity of the incandescent units alone, having placed a delay on the fade time for the discharge wash lights. This allows some light to establish the beginnings of the lit state before the brashness of the discharge sources becomes apparent. Alternatively, we might preset the wash lights in a dark version of their final colour. As the intensity increases, at first the wash lights remain in their darker preset colour, after a suitable delay, they begin to change to the desired final colour. Again we achieve the initial build without obtrusive distractions from the discharge units.

To achieve either result we would need to be able to allocate different fade and delay times to different attributes of the moving lights in the rig, but for a modern moving light controller this should be relatively straightforward. We will come back to cue times later.

Example of a simple cue synopsis for a drama on a proscenium stage

Cue no[7]	Position/cue line	Timing	Purpose	Notes
	Preset[8]		Tab[9] warmers[10] & house lights[11]	Working light[12] US[13]?
	House out[14]	12/12[15]	House & tabs out. Preset for Act 1 behind tabs	Loose US working light
	Tabs up[16]	8/8	Scene 1 — evening interior[17]	Practical?[18] Fire?[19] No FoH[20]
	Tabs out[21] Visual cue[22]	5/5	Add FoH — warm	

[7]Cue numbers will not be defined until much later, but we usually include the column for reference.

[8]Preset is a common theatre term for anything put in place in readiness. In this case it refers to the lighting state which the audience will see as they walk in.

[9]Tabs is shorthand for the main stage curtain (also called front of house curtain) on a proscenium stage — this is what the audience normally sees when they walk into a play house.

[10]Tab warmers are lanterns focused on the tabs, to add interest and focus audience attention.

[11]House lights light up the auditorium for the audience. They may be controlled from the main lighting desk or by a separate system.

[12]Working light is any light provided for people to do a job, such as setting up the scene; checking props and furniture are all in place. At this stage we don't know if it will be needed, but experience tells us to include it here as a reminder.

[13]US in this context is short for up stage (i.e. the area behind the house tabs).

[14]House out is one way a DSM (deputy stage manager) or show caller asks for the lights in the auditorium to be dimmed ready to begin the show.

[15]Time is usually in seconds, and at this stage is a guess, perhaps based on reading the script, talking to the director and designer, and experience. A standard notation is to write up time/down time (in this case both 12 seconds).

Cue no	Position/cue line	Timing	Purpose	Notes
	Act 1 scene 1 Entrance of Dad	12/12	Raise level round Dad's chair ready for … Dad sits	
	Dad begins ghost story	60s? maybe much longer	Slow partial close down — create atmosphere for story telling — move away from 'normal' look	Highlight Dad: moonlight through window SL or from fire light SR?
	When the story turns nasty? (somewhere near first death?)	30s	Heighten supernatural atmosphere further. Big shadows on US wall?	Birdies on DS edge? Dim red wash over walls? (from fire?)
	Just before end of story	To complete on last word	Rapid close down to Dad & chair and big shadow	
	'but its only a story'	6/3 wait 3	Restore to close to opening look	Keep red from fire? or the Birdies from DS

What we have here is an outline of the role of lighting in how the play will begin. At this stage many things are a guess. For example, it may not even have been decided whether or not to have tabs yet. Even if this decision has been made, how fast they should go out will not usually be decided until the technical rehearsal. This early cue synopsis is as much a document for discussion as anything else.

Further into the script the cue synopsis might look something like this:

The idea here is that we begin with a normal look, the Father comes in and very soon begins to tell a ghost story. The lighting will begin by helping to establish the normality of the opening scene. It will then help to direct audience focus onto the father in his chair, retaining the normal look. As the father begins to tell his ghost story, we slowly change the look from normal to supernatural. Exactly how we will do this is yet to be decided, but we have a few ideas — we might try to hint that father is lit by a beam of moonlight coming through the nearby window or from the flickering light of the fire. Again, at this stage we have yet to define how either of these signs would be realised or which sign would be most appropriate to also signify something about say the father's character or the amount of credence the audience should give to his story. As the story becomes

---

[16]This cue will 'go' at the same time the DSM or show-caller gives the command for the house tabs to be raised.

[17]This brief description is likely to have come from the stage directions in the script.

[18]A practical is a term for anything which actually works on stage, in this case, probably a practical light fitting. As it is evening, it may be mentioned in the script or just assumed, or the set designer might have discussed putting a practical reading lamp or suspending a fitting as if it were hanging from an unseen ceiling. At this stage it is a reminder that we will need to find out more.

[19]May be mentioned in the script, or merely implied — in either case this will need to be discussed with set designer and director.

[20]A reminder that, since the tabs will still be part way in, we do not want any lanterns in the auditorium to be on.

[21]When the house tabs have cleared they are sufficiently out of the way for the front of house lanterns to be used without ugly beams striking the tabs.

[22]Means the lighting operator will take the cue using their own judgment of the best time to hit the GO button, rather than waiting for the DSM or show-caller to say go.

---

nasty, we want to further enhance the supernatural atmosphere, and the idea of over life-sized shadows on the up-stage wall is mentioned (it seems we are working on a melodrama!). Clearly the ghost story has a big ending, and we want a lighting cue to enhance that. In placing this cue, what will be important is when it ends, not when it starts, hence the note in the cue synopsis, 'To complete on last word'. After this dramatic ending, we require a restore to 'normal' but perhaps with a hint of 'supernatural' left in too — hence the note to 'Keep red from fire? or the Birdies from DS'. As the production develops through rehearsals, with luck the director and lighting designer will be able to talk through these ideas and make some choices; will the sign of 'supernatural' be moonlight or flickering fire-light? (The choice here may well revolve around does 'warm' firelight look better in the scene than 'cool' moonlight but discussions might also take in motifs from later in the play) If the denouement involves fire, can the 'firelight' be a precursor? If the father is eventually revealed as a villain, can we hint at this by what we reveal of him in the 'moonlight'? (Gaunt features and the pale skin of one who avoids sunlight.)

Don't work in isolation!

There is little point evolving a complex system of lighting signs in isolation from the rest of the creative team. Performance lighting cannot successfully be developed in isolation from the rest of the makers of signification and spectacle working on the production — director, other designers working on the set, costume, sound, projection, etc; the choreographer if there is dance involved, and the writer if the script is still evolving. The performers will normally be carrying the main burden of signification, and the production lighting team will turn the dreams of the lighting designer into a reality. All these people and more will have valuable contributions that impact on the evolution of the lighting design. Making performance is about collaboration, and anyone who forgets this important fact is in trouble.

Watching rehearsals

Watching the performers develop the performance in rehearsal is often the best place to develop ideas and make choices about the lighting design. If the space chosen is suitable, the director will usually want to experiment with the relative positions of performers, and how they will move in the performance space. This is known as blocking. It is important for the lighting designer who wants to do more than blanket illumination to know where each performer will be at each moment of the performance. There are several ways of noting blocking; perhaps the most common is to make sketch copies of the main features of the performance space and draw annotated arrows indicating movement. Each sketch needs to be linked to a particular scene or part of a scene in the performance and this is where the lighting score is useful. It is best to work in pencil, since blocking is rarely completely worked out even by the technical rehearsal. Many genre of theatre performance rehearse with a member of the stage management team in the room. One of the primary functions of this person will often be to note blocking, and keep a record of changes. Amongst other things, this enables the stage management team to introduce an understudy in the absence of the director. If the lighting designer establishes good relations with the stage managers (a must for almost all theatre based work) they can arrange to be kept informed of significant changes that happen in their absence.

But a lighting designer can learn much more than where each performer will stand by attending rehearsals. How is the piece developing? Are new themes emerging? Are initial assumptions from the lighting designer's own text analysis being challenged by the performers as they evolve their characters? Are sections of the text being cut or new sections being added? At what pace are different sections being taken? More directly: has the set design changed? Have the colours of the costumes changed? Don't assume that someone would tell the lighting designer if that happened. Many people who work in the rehearsal room — and this can unfortunately include directors — have little or no understanding of how changes to set and costume impact on lighting. Another shock the aspiring lighting designer may get in the rehearsal room is how often the director might say 'Don't worry about that, we will leave it to lighting to sort out!' Again, the lighting

Stage management departments

Professional stage management is a key part of UK and North American theatre. The role of stage management that is likely to be encountered most often by the lighting practitioner is looking after and managing the performers in the rehearsal room, and on stage, and as they call the show.

A stage management department will usually be formed as follows:

Stage Manager — the head of the department, often responsible for health and safety on stage and in the rehearsal room, this person is usually quite senior in the company and works closely with the director. In larger organisations and on many tours the department is lead by the company manager, who often also handles wages and many of the duties of the production manager.

Deputy stage manager (DSM) — not only no. 2 but also usually responsible for assembling the book — an up-to-date copy of the script with all the cues for each department noted in it. During performances, the DSM will usually be the show caller, also known as being on the book. It is usually considered vital that the lighting designer has a good working relationship with the show caller.

Assistant stage managers (ASMs) may fulfil a variety of roles including preparing the stage or rehearsal space for each performance or rehearsal by setting props and furniture, buying and making small props and assisting with performer quick-changes and costume maintenance when there is no wardrobe department. Some companies use ASMs as technical operators for sound automation and sometimes lighting.

At least one member of the team (usually the DSM) will be in the rehearsal room for every rehearsal, taking notes for the director and cast. These will include cuts or additions to the script, blocking and other essential details that will all go towards making the book (also known as the prompt copy.)

In performances by UK and North American theatre, dance and opera companies almost every cue in the show is called by the show caller from notes in the prompt script. The show caller gives standbys to the technical operators and performers. For example, they might say, 'Standby lighting cue 6, sound cue 3, fly cue 4 and performers at the up stage entrance'. Each stand by needs to be acknowledged by an operator (lighting sound and flys) or an ASM standing close to the performers (performers at the up-stage entrance). The show caller then gives the signal to go, by cue-light and voice: 'Lx cue 6, GO: sound 3 and flys 4, GO: up stage performers GO:' The precise position of each GO is recorded in the script or score. This way of working enables more flexibility of staffing while maintaining a consistency of performance, though it can limit the potential for creative response by the operators.

When the show caller says 'GO', unless you can see you will kill someone, you GO!

designer cannot assume that someone will let them know about the new or changed expectations of those in the rehearsal room. The only solution is to be there as much as possible, especially once the production gets on its feet, a term usually used to indicate the stage when the performers have learnt the script and begin to move around the space in the manner of their character.

Watching rehearsals is usually very educational for non-performers, and can be great fun, but some rehearsal rooms are very tense and edgy places. When things are not going well, and sometimes even when they are, performers and director often behave in ways they would not behave in public. For many, the rehearsal room is like a laboratory where a performance can be built, but sometimes this involves behaving in an extreme way to get results. Aspiring makers of performance need to understand the potential vulnerability of performers, and to respect the rehearsal room as their work-place. If things are going badly you may be asked to leave a rehearsal or to limit your attendance. It is in these situations that your relationship with the stage management team becomes even more important. Most professional stage management teams produce rehearsal notes on a regular basis. These can be a very useful link to what is going on in the rehearsal room. With the prevalence of e-mail, there is little excuse for a lighting designer not getting rehearsal notes, and even less excuse for having got them not reading them. Rehearsal notes are usually broken down into sections for each department. It is a good idea to read everything — as I said earlier, not everyone in the rehearsal room is conscious of the impact of changes across departments.

Most genre of performance rehearse the performers in a different space to the one they will end up performing in. This is usually down to economics. If the venue is being used as a rehearsal space it cannot be making money as a performance space. In this country there is very little tradition of taking performance lighting into the rehearsal space except in the live concert sector, where the practice is very common. In my view, the failure to make performance lighting available in the rehearsal room has limited our role in making live performance, and has lead to a generally poor understanding of the potential of performance lighting particularly among theatre directors, actors and set designers. Perhaps a new generation of lighting practitioners can be bolder in taking the tools of their trade into the rehearsal room so that in the later stages of the evolution of a performance, the potential of light in the performance can be fully explored[23].

Working with performers

When a director needs a performer to do something they are not used to, the director needs to gain the trust of the performer. It is the same for a lighting designer, though without the advantage of the natural hierarchy of relationships that exists between director and performer. If a particular lighting state relies for its effectiveness on the actions of a performer, then the lighting designer will usually need to work with the director and the performer to ensure that the effect happens. Let's go back to the father telling his ghost story. If we want to make the most of the shadow play on the wall, we will need the actor playing Dad to work with the effect, perhaps leaning into the light at key moments to increase the size of his shadow, or tuning his head to show only a profile at certain points. By engaging the director and the performer in the project, showing them how small changes in performance can enhance the effect, all these things are possible but they will not happen by magic (at least not reliably). Different productions will require the lighting designer to accomplish these types of negotiation in different ways. At times it will be possible and appropriate to appeal directly to performer, 'Do this here and we can make you look great!' At times the negotiation will be harder, and sometimes the lighting designer loses. Some good advice I had as an aspiring lighting designer was to stand in the place you want the actor to be and see what it feels like for yourself. This helps the lighting designer to explain to the actor what they should experience when the effect is working, and allows the actor to see what they look like in the right place — and in the 'wrong' place. It also allows the lighting designer to experience any discomfort involved, and perhaps be able to temper that to the benefit of everyone involved.

Moving towards realisation

By now, in many production set-ups, the production manager or the production electrician will be asking for some details about the lighting rig the lighting designer intends to use. Certainly the lighting designer should be informing whoever will be responsible for the installation of the lighting rig of any special requirements,

[23]This practice would not be as new as perhaps it sounds. Many theatre traditions protected from the commercial and other pressures of North American and British commercial theatre, are able to spend more than their last rehearsals in the performance space 'under lights'.

even if only for costing purposes. It is good practice for the lighting designer to keep everyone who needs to know informed as lighting design ideas evolve. There is frequently competition for hanging space above the stage and elsewhere, and the lighting designer needs to make sure that their needs are not forgotten when decisions are made about what will hang where. A successful lighting designer will establish ways of keeping themselves informed of changes in other areas of the production; changes to anything from the way the set is being built (which might, for example, change the way practical fixtures can be attached to it, or restrict access to potential lighting positions) to the colour of the costume, to the schedule of the fit-up, to the position of speakers and microphones to the choice of images to be projected. Any of these could have an impact on what can and cannot be achieved by the lighting designer.

The lighting design department will need an accurate ground plan and section of the performance space and the set, with enough information to determine where lanterns can and cannot be placed. In the next chapter we will look at approaches to deciding what equipment should go where, translating ideas about the 'feel' or 'atmosphere' required at each moment of the performance into a rig that will enable these effects to be realised.

To close this chapter I want to underline once more the need to have your lighting ideas on paper — as sketches in a story-board, as computer renders, as treated photographs, or as a written out scenario for the motivation of the light at key moments in the performance. A detailed cue synopsis is most often the best way to express your lighting ideas in readiness for making cues in the performance space. This document will continue to evolve with rehearsals, and be influenced by meetings with the director and the other designers. Most often, when you come to make your cues in the space, you will not have as much time as you would like, but if you have thought out ideas ready for each key moment, you will have a place to start discussion. The ideas may turn out to be perfect, or to be truly awful, or most likely something in between, but it is better to have something down on paper in order to get some light on stage to work from, than to begin lighting each new scene with nothing!

from concept to lighting plan

What kind of light do you want where?

Having followed the process outlined in the last two chapters the lighting designer should by now have some idea about the kind of light they want at key moments of the production. This may not be totally worked out — almost every lighting design evolves in the performance space with the real performers and the real set and costume — but there needs to be some foundations in place.

Of course other foundations need to be in place too. These will include a good understanding of how light works in performance, and of what the equipment will

FIGURE 1. A SCENE FROM *THE CAUCASIAN CHALK CIRCLE* STAGED AS A FINAL YEAR PRODUCTION AT CSSD. THE BACK WALL OF THE OPEN STAGE SET IS WASHED IN DEEP BLUE FROM DISCHARGE LAMPED MOVING LIGHTS EVOKING THE RICH SPLENDOUR OF THE PALACE (ABOUT TO BE ABANDONED). A STRONG TOP-LIGHT WASH REVEALS THE FORM OF THE HANGING COSTUME, CASTING SHADOWS OF THE 'WARDROBE' OF THE ESCAPING ARISTOCRATS ON THE STAGE FLOOR BEHIND THE SERVANTS, WHO ARE LIT SEPARATELY AS THE PRIMARY FOCUS OF THIS PART OF THE SCENE. MEANWHILE THE HEROINE IS SEEN ESCAPING ON STAGE LEFT (WITH THE UNWANTED BABY) — LIT IN A CROSS-LIGHT SPECIAL — WHILE THE DUCHESS (DOWN STAGE RIGHT) HAS A ¾ BACK LIGHT AS SHE WATCHES OVER HER SERVANTS. LIGHTING DESIGN AND PHOTOGRAPH BY MATT DAW.

actually do. If you are not familiar with the different types of lantern that are available and the effects they can produce on stage you will not be able to make intelligent choices. As a lighting designer, if you have the opportunity to go into the space you will be working in and try out the equipment, this should not be missed. Experienced lighting designers often say they work a lot by instinct but this cannot be strictly true since science tells us we are born with instincts. As far as I know, nobody is born with a knowledge of how many PAR64 CP61s you need to backlight a 10m by 6m stage from a truss at 8m! This is knowledge which has been learned, either formally in a school or college, or by extended working with the equipment. A lighting designer needs an understanding of the kit their design will employ, and of colour, angle, glare, reflection, and hundreds of other things that will inform their choices. If you are a relative novice at lighting design, dipping in and out of this book, please make sure you have read chapters 2 and 3 before continuing.

As ideas for a lighting rig develop, it is important to keep in mind the priorities of the production. In the opening chapter I wrote briefly about the need to provide visual acuity of the performer to the spectator; literally to allow the audience keen sight of the performer, to assist in enabling clear communication between performer and spectator. Even though it is likely that at some moments of performance, the creative team will decide that clear and unmediated communication between performer and audience is not the first priority of the lighting design, the role of the performance lighting designer is most often to present the spectator with as much visual information as is appropriate at each moment of the performance. This is especially true in genres of performance where the spoken word is important, because as I mentioned in Chapter 1, it is harder to understand someone whose face we can't see well. For a lighting designer working in drama, the first priority is usually making sure the faces of the performers will be lit. It is worth noting that even on a proscenium stage, in most drama productions the performers face into the stage not out to the audience, so light for faces will need to come from places other than just out front.

When the focus of the performance is not the spoken word priorities will change. Dance work needs the lighting designer to direct attention to revealing the form of the body in space. Opera, especially at large scale, needs a design approach with a primary focus that is in harmony with the music. The lighting designer for rock 'n' roll or live concerts is usually hired to provide a visual feast on stage — the faces are taken care of by follow spots and image magnification.[1] Each genre of performance has a generalised set of priorities, but it is important to establish what is expected of lighting in the particular production you are working on before the design process gets too far down the road.

Sketching on a ground plan

The choices made by the lighting designer relating to what kit goes where, will be constrained by the availability of lanterns and other equipment and by the theatre architecture before any considerations of the particular needs of the production. So before we can get much further with the design, we need accurate information about the space in which we are going to stage the production and about the kind of equipment we can use.

Information about the space traditionally comes as a scale ground plan and section. These days however, it might come as a two or three dimensional CAD[2] drawing, a scaled visualisation, a series of photographs or a virtual reality tour! What most lighting designers and every production lighting chief needs is an accurate ground plan and section showing the position of the set

---

[1]Image magnification or IMag is when live cameras take pictures of the performing artists and these are shown on large screens. This is a very common technique for arena and stadium rock shows.

[2]CAD stands for computer aided design, and is generally used as shorthand for anything drawn on a computer in whatever programme. This includes AutoCAD, WYSIWYG, Vector Works, and many others.

and all the available hanging positions. As a lighting practitioner, if you don't know anything else about CAD, it is a very good idea to know how to obtain a scaled plan and section from a CAD file.[3]

The list of equipment that is available can be as definite as an inventory from the venue or, if the rig is to be hired, as vague as a figure in a budget. I will assume for the moment that, in addition to our detailed cue synopsis, we have accurate scale drawings of ground plan and section, and a reasonably extensive inventory of lighting equipment to draw on.

Scaled plan view and section drawings

A **plan drawing** is a **scale** drawing of the space viewed from above, with all vertical surfaces squashed to lines. Just like a street map, it represents an idealised bird's eye view of the area. Using the plan and a suitable **scale rule**, we should be able to find the dimensions of horizontal features such as lighting bars (pipes in North America) or set trucks, and the horizontal distance between varioius places in the building (when combined with vertical distance obtained from the **section**, see below, this is useful for calculating lamp throws and cable lengths for example).

Plan drawings are used extensively in architecture and engineering as well by lighting and sound designers, set designers and set constructors, stage management and production management.

The plan view cannot be a full representation of any but the simplest space. For example, a ramp may be represented in plan view in the same way as a large table, a trap door, or a flat rostrum. Most plans show the outline of structures at a particular level, typically just above floor level (to avoid the need to show inconsequential bumps and humps in the foor, and feature such as skirting boards). The plan may not show overhanging features, such as water pipes or a technical gallery that may have an impact on, for example, the space available to suspend scenery or lighting equipment.

The key. Like a map a plan has a key to help the users understand it. For example, symbols that may represent particular lanterns of differnet types or give the meaning of each line type used (dotted lines for this, solid lines in red for that, etc). Usually the key is on the same piece of paper as the plan drawing, but even when it is, there may well be signs and symbols used that the maker of the plan expects all users to understand. These common line types and symbols are often part of a set of national or international standards, used by professional drafts people throughout an industry sector (e.g. architecture) or across a geo-political area (e.g. the EU). One example is the combination of short and long dashes used for all centre lines. If it is not clear to you what a line or symbol represents, it is as well to ask, and preferably to ask the person who drew the original.

A **section drawing** is usually a view of the space from the side. To create a section drawing think of the space sliced open down a particular line (in theatre this often the centre line of the stage and auditorium) and made into two parts. Next imagine picking up one half of the building, inking the newly severed walls, floors, ceilings, etc, and making a print of it — just as children might make a potato print — then shrinking the paper down to scale! This kind of section has big limitations — anything that is not actually on the particular line of the section will not be on the drawing. To make the section more useful, details of any structures of significance, even if they do not cross the section line, are usually included.

---

[3]You might give the file to a friend to do, but what will you do when that friend is not around?

Important uses of the section drawing include showing relative heights of objects, determining what the audience can and can't see (called sight lines), helping in the calculation of beam angles, and determining the position of top masking. Clearly, for the lighting designer, the section is just as important as the plan. It is usual for the lighting designer working on paper to produce several sections themselves, often using height information gathered at a site visit. These will be used to accurately determine the throw and required beam angle for lanterns from each position they intend to use.

To some extent, computer-aided drawing packages have reduced the need to draw multiple sections. Providing the performance space has been accurately modelled in three dimensions, any competent user of the better programmes can put themselves in a position to see — in the virtual world at least — the effect of any lantern from any position. The user can try out different beam angles and see what impact they have on the size of the beam on stage and what structures might get in the way of the beam. However, accurate modelling of a venue is time consuming and therefore costly and many lighting designers prefer to sketch sections as they need them.

This is often the phase of the lighting design process lighting designers try to postpone for as long as possible. Each decision seems so fixed and final, and usually has to be made at a time in the process when the piece is anything but fixed and final. Each decision made seems to remove more possibilities than it presents, but if you want to make bold statements with light whenever it is appropriate you must be bold in making choices. The better informed your choices, the more likely they are to be successful, so rigorous research into the piece, the space, and the equipment and detailed discussions with the director and the other designers needs to inform each choice.

The lighting score, story-board, written account or whatever has been used to produce the detailed cue synopsis will also have made some of the choices to be made clearer. It may not be clear, however, how these choices add up over the whole piece. With the help of detailed cue synopsis and/or the lighting score it is possible to distil the generalised lighting requirements of each section of the piece into a unified wish-list for the whole production. This can often be achieved in the

first instance by drawing coloured arrows onto a ground plan. Figure 2 is a sketch of what I might require to light the melodrama briefly mentioned in Chapter 5.

Looking at the sketch we can see the major elements that the rig will need to provide are a strong cool ¾ back light from up stage left, representing moonlight through the window; a generalised blue back light (probably over the whole stage), warm and cool ¾ front light, and a neutral straight in front light. There is also an indication of a top light colour wash over the whole stage in nine areas. I would almost certainly plan to make all the front light work in the same nine areas too. In addition there is some fire-light coming from mid/low stage right, and low open/white from the front edge of the stage. Notice that the position of this source is determined by where we want the shadow on the set. To make the most of the effect I have included a wash to animate the wall in a fire red, and something in blue to add contrast to the wall and fill the shadow, which will hopefully allow us to build the impact of the shadow.

I have included some notes on possible practicals and the fact that we will need units to light the backing flats[4]

[4]A example of a backing flat could be the scenic elements seen through the door or window of a naturalistic set. At times this may be simply the wall of the theatre painted black. In other situations it may be custom-built elements used to indicate the continuation of the world of performance beyond the space on stage.

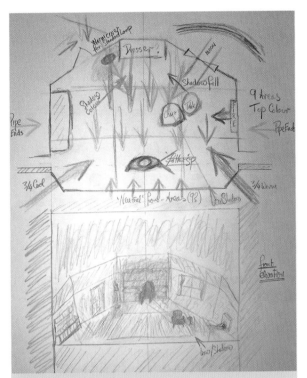

FIGURE 2. GROUND-PLAN AND ELEVATION WITH COLOURED ARROWS. GETTING A SENSE OF WHAT THE RIG WILL NEED TO DO. THE COLOUR AT THIS STAGE USUALLY JUST RELATES TO WARM/COOL/NEUTRAL AND THICKNESS OF THE ARROWS RELATE TO THE MAXIMUM STRENGTH OF LIGHT FROM THAT DIRECTION.

out of practical necessity that is what most lighting designers must do most of the time.

So with our very simple set of major requirements documented on a single piece of paper, the next step is to decide how each requirement will be achieved.

Washes and specials

What most people mean by a wash of light is the same quality over a relatively large area. In nature this usually means direct sunlight over all or part of the field of view. In film-making, a wash can often be achieved with a single very large fixture for example a 'daylight' Fresnel of 10kW or 12kW or even a 20kW. On most performance stages this is not possible; most washes in performance lighting are achieved by blending the output of several fixtures. This can be troublesome as it can be difficult to make the blending work well, but it also has advantages. Because our washes are made from multiple units we can highlight smaller areas within the wash by selectively raising the intensity of one or more of the units. We can even use individual units in a wash on their own, as specials.

What most lighting people mean by a lighting special is light in a particular area of a different quality to the general light of the rest of the space drawing attention to that particular area. It could be anything from a small display unit used to illuminate a painting on the wall of a gallery to the very intense white light used in many films to indicate alien abduction. What makes the special stand out could be higher intensity or different colour or beam quality. Often a special is just one unit, but it doesn't have to be. For example, in the sketch above there is an area marked 'cover for standard lamp'. This will be lanterns focused to enhance the effect of light from the practical fixture, probably creating a splash of light on the floor at the base of the lamp and also on the adjacent wall. Other specials implied on the sketch include something for the Father centre stage, and low o/w[5] that will throw shadows onto the back

outside the door and window in the sketch too, mainly so I don't forget to include these elements on the final plan.

The first limitation of this method is there is no easy way to show the difference between light from the same horizontal direction but from different heights. In an ideal world, this whole process of consolidating the lighting needs of the production into a wish list for the lighting rig would take place in the performance space. The designers and production chiefs would walk through the space discussing the balance between the aesthetic and the practical, between what design would like and what production can achieve. Without that luxury it can be hard to visualise the three dimensional space represented by the two dimensional drawing but

[5]o/w is a commonly used short hand for open white, i.e. no colour media.

wall. At this stage, the moonlight may be a single fixture shining through a window in the set, or less directly naturalistic, a more general wash over most of the stage producing strong shadows in front of the performers. This latter choice would probably require the rest of the creative team to buy-in to the potential symbolism of the shadows doing more for the show that a strong light through a window. If budget and time allowed, we might rig both solutions and see which worked best in the space.

Designing washes by thinking in boxes

To make the right choices about equipment and placement, a lighting designer needs to be able to think in three dimensions. This is especially true when it comes to choosing beam angle and hanging positions for units in a wash. Much of the time, we are lighting bodies in space and not the flat walls or floors around them. This is where we need to think about the usable box of light on stage produced by each unit and how we can seamlessly merge each one with its neighbours. The height of the box will depend to an extent on the height of the performers and whether they jump, but a safe general rule would be about 2.5m.

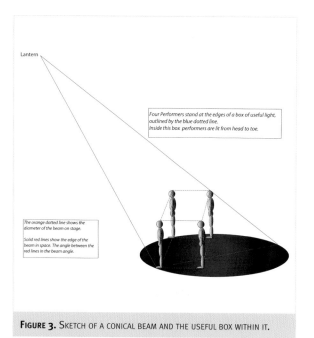

The orange dotted line shows the diameter of the beam on stage.

Solid red lines show the edge of the beam in space. The angle between the red lines in the beam angle.

Lantern

Four Performers stand at the edges of a box of useful light, outlined by the blue dotted line.
Inside this box performers are lit from head to toe.

FIGURE 3. Sketch of a conical beam and the useful box within it.

The whole box must be within the cone of the beam for it to be useful for lighting performers. Outside the box and up-stage in the drawing (but with their feet still in the beam on stage) the performer's head will be unlit. As the performer moves down stage out of the box, we will lose first the feet, then the legs, torso and neck until eventually their head disappears.

The size of the beam at the top surface of the box will give us a measurement of the diagonal across the top (and bottom) of the box. There is quite a tricky bit of geometry involved in working this out mathematically, but fortunately there is an easier way.

You will need a ruler and a protractor for measuring angles, a pencil and a scale rule, a lantern data book (or suitable trusted website) to find the beam angle of the lanterns you want to use, a good, fine tipped permanent marker, a scale drawing of the ground plan and section of the performance space and some clear gel or acetate a little smaller in size than the section drawing. The section should be of the whole performance space, preferably taken down the centre line.

1 Look up the beam angle(s) of the lanterns you have available. If you are using zoom lanterns there will be two angles quoted. Use an angle half way between the two. Let's assume you have ETC Source 4 profiles with 26 degree and 36 degree lens tubes.

2 Draw a line on the clear gel from the centre of one edge to an opposite corner. The start point in the centre of one side we will call the origin.

3 Working from the origin, carefully measure off the required angles from this line; for our Source 4s this will be 26 and 36 degrees

4 Carefully draw lines from the origin at 26 and 36 degrees to the first line. You have now produced one of the most useful tools in lighting design!

5 On the section drawing, measure 2.5m (at scale) up from the performance level and draw a pencil line at this level and parallel to performance level.

6 Again with the section drawing, place the origin on a hanging position you know exists in the centre of the performance space with the first line touching the nearest edge of the stage.

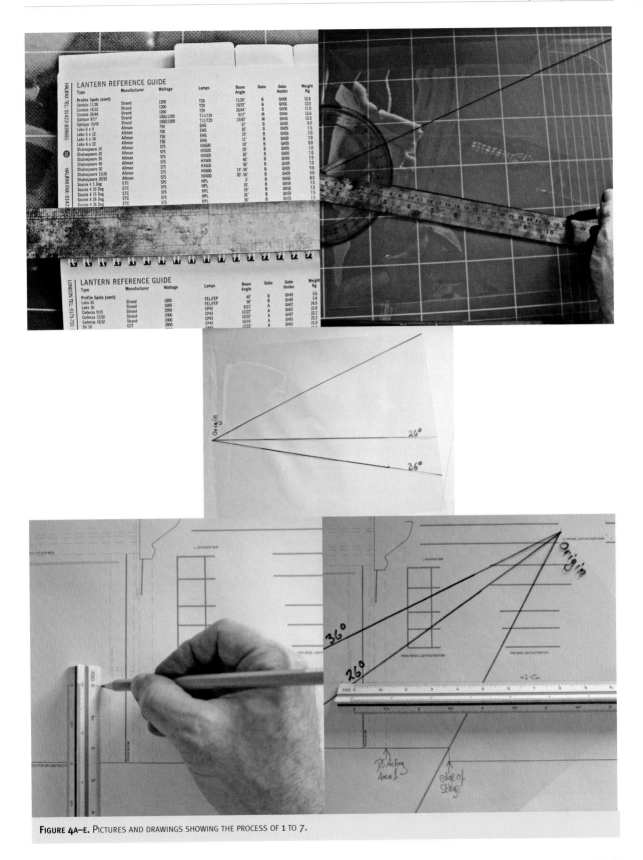

Figure 4A–E. Pictures and drawings showing the process of 1 to 7.

7 Using the scale rule, at the point where the 2.5m pencil line crosses the lines on your new tool, measure the distance between the first drawn line and each of the other two lines. This is the diagonal of your box for a 26 degree and a 36 degree lantern hanging at the chosen point of origin and focused towards the nearest part of the stage.

If you want to, you can mark up the ground plan with circles that will represent the size of the beams from that hanging position hitting that part of the stage. Halve the distance you measured in 7 above, and set a drawing compass to that radius, and carefully draw in the beam circles on the ground plan. You will need to make sure you drawing the right sized circles by checking each throw (i.e. each distance from hanging position to stage) on the section. Remember these circles represent the edge of the beam at 2.5m above stage height, so you will need to overlap them a bit.

In many performance spaces the section will not give an accurate measurement of the throw because the hanging position and the target are not in the same plane. If the hanging position is fixed to a side wall for example, and you want a unit from that position to illuminate centre stage, the throw will not be the scale distance measured from the hanging position to centre stage on the section. To gain a reasonable idea of what the size of beam you will have from this unit at centre stage we will have to do a bit more practical geometry.

1 Using the correct scale, measure the height of the side wall hanging position above the stage. Cut a strip of stiff card to this length in the scale of the *ground plan*.[6] It is a good idea if the card is thick enough to take a dress-maker's pin through the edge.

2 This time working with a scale ground plan of the whole performance space, draw a faint pencil line from the hanging position on the side wall to the target centre stage.

3 Put the base of the strip on the ground plan at the point representing the position of the unit you wish to hang.

4 Put the origin of your tool at the top of the strip. If you have a pin handy, put this through the origin of the tool and use it to attach the origin to the top of the strip of card.

5 Point the tool's beam at centre stage (or where ever you want the target for that unit to be) and you will get a good idea of what size the beam will be on stage.

You can repeat this process for each hanging position, producing a height strip, and pointing the beam where you want it to go. This approach can give you a reasonable idea of what to expect when you eventually get to the real performance space. It can give you information about the angle of incidence on the performer, the amount of spill you will get outside the usefully illuminated area. (Again, check back to Chapter 3 for more on what these terms mean to your design.) However, when using this method you will need to remember two things:

1 Look out for obstructions! It can be very easy to think you have found the ideal position for a unit only to discover that in the real space there is something in the way and the light will not get to where you want it to go. The obstruction may be part of the set, or the structure of the performance space, or speakers, or even lighting units you have already put on the plan. In traditional theatres the proscenium arch gets in the way of lots of things! Ink over any lines on the ground plan that represent structures that might get in the way.

2 When we measured the height for the scale height strip, we measured the height from stage level, not from 1.7m to 2m above stage level — the approxi-

---

[6]Usually the ground plan and section are drawn at the same scale, so you could measure the distance and the length of the strip of card with a standard ruler. Just occasionally though, for all kinds of reasons, the section and plan are drawn at different scales! In any event you should always check both the scale of whatever drawing you are working with and the ruler you are using.

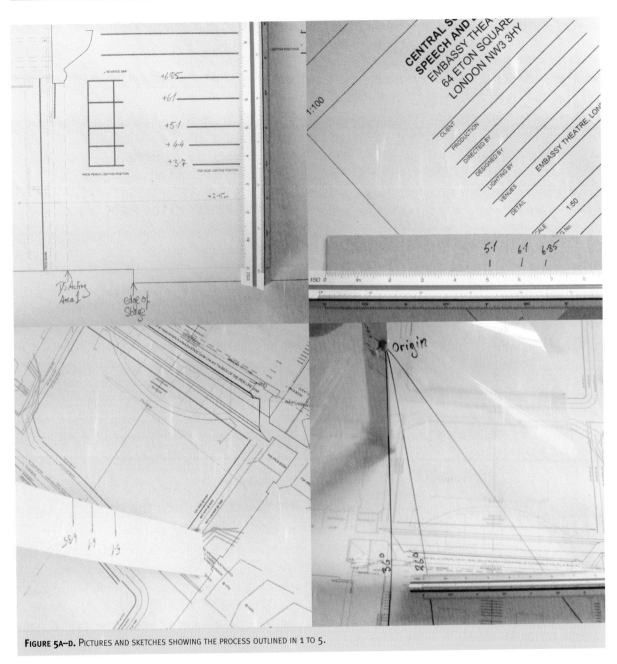

FIGURE 5A–D. PICTURES AND SKETCHES SHOWING THE PROCESS OUTLINED IN 1 TO 5.

mate position of the face of a standing performer. This is fine if we are planning to light the floor, but if we want to light people, we have to take their height into account too. You may wish to reduce the scale height of your strips to compensate, or perhaps to use a suitable scale model of a person as your target.

This approach can help you determine how many units of a particular beam angle you will need to make up a wash over a particular area, and what beam angle you will need for a special of a particular size on stage.

Do lighting designers do this for every lantern on every rig? No, of course not. It is possible to train yourself to be pretty good at guessing how many 26 degree lanterns will be needed to do a particular job. But almost every lighting designer I have talked to does some checking of beam angles and throws in the process of designing their lighting rig.

115

There are alternatives to the practical geometry approach too. There are tables and software that can be used to calculate beam size for a particular beam angle from a given throw. Software includes LD Calculator and Beamwright.

Most of the CAD packages for performance lighting will give a reasonable approximation of what the beam of a particular lantern will look like on stage, but to do this involves creating the performance area in 3D virtual space, which will not be a short process. However, if you have the computer model of your performance space, this is undoubtedly a good way to try ideas out.

Making choices and drawing the plan

Let us assume that as lighting designer you have gained a good knowledge of the space in which the performance will take place, whether by visiting the venue or from a careful study of the ground-plan and section drawings, or from study of the virtual space created within a lighting design package such as Vector Works or WYSIWYG. You should have a grasp of the potential angles of incidence and throw available from each hanging position to each part of the stage, and be aware of any part of the stage that units hung in a particular position will not be able to illuminate. You should ideally also have a good knowledge of what equipment you have available and what it will be able to do. And remember this is on top of your detailed understanding of the piece gained from extensive research and discussion with the other members of the creative team. You have already made some decisions about what kind of light should be coming from where at the key moments of the piece, and now we have to start drawing the lighting plan.

CAD or hand drawn?

We have already touched on the pros and cons of these two different ways of presenting the information. In the next chapter there is more information on what should be included in a full production lighting plan, and how that information can be best laid out to enable unambiguous assembly of the lighting rig by the production chief and their crew, perhaps without any further information from the lighting designer. That process is about communicating information to others. What we need to do now, though, is to enable the lighting designer to make the choices required to assemble the rig and afterwards light the show. The lighting plan we produce at this point can be quite sketchy. It is going to be used to help us advance the design ideas and make choices, and not yet to realise the lighting system.

Get your basics in the right place

By this point in the process, the lighting designer should be fairly clear about what are going to be the basic elements of the rig. For most drama, for example, this will include light for the actors' faces. For anything with a big cyclorama, getting that lit right will also be important. For almost any piece involving dance of any kind, the rig will need to contain elements that can be used to enhance the three dimensional form of the body. For productions that enable or require the lighting to make grand statements, it will be important to get the elements that do this in the right positions. Whatever the priorities are for your production, the units that enable this will usually be the ones you want to place on the plan first.

Top masking to hide the rig — borders

The conventions of most European and North American theatre dictate that the majority of performance light will come from a rig above the performance space more or less hidden in the auditorium. For this kind of play, it is likely that we will want to hide as much of the rig as possible with borders above the stage. Very often the first thing we have to do in preparing the rig plan is position these borders. We will need to get a section drawing, which includes the sight-line from the front row of the audience. The sight-line on a plan or section indicates what a particular viewer can and cannot see. In figure 6, a person sitting in the front row stalls can see everything upstage of the borders *below* the red sight lines. Anything behind a border and above the sight line for that border is hidden for that audience member.

It is quite usual for the production manager to tell the lighting designer which bars can be used for lanterns

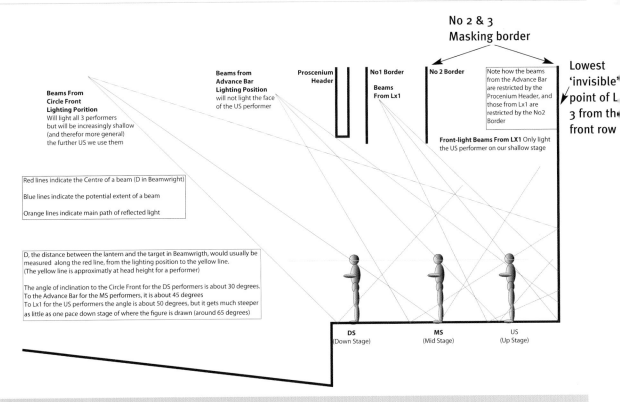

No 2 & 3 Masking border

Beams from
Advance Bar
Lighting Position
will not light the face
of the US performer

Proscenium
Header

No1 Border

Beams
From Lx1

No 2 Border

Note how the beams
from the Advance Bar
are restricted by the
Procenium Header, and
those from Lx1 are
restricted by the No2
Border

Lowest 'invisible' point of L 3 from the front row

Beams From
Circle Front
Lighting Porition
Will light all 3 performers
but will be increasingly shallow
(and therefor more general)
the further US we use them

Front-light Beams From LX1 Only light
the US performer on our shallow stage

Red lines indicate the Centre of a beam (D in Beamwright)

Blue lines indicate the potential extent of a beam

Orange lines indicate main path of reflected light

D, the distance between the lantern and the target in Beamwrigth, would usually be
measured along the red line, from the lighting position to the yellow line.
(The yellow line is approximately at head height for a performer)

The angle of inclination to the Circle Front for the DS performers is about 30 degrees.
To the Advance Bar for the MS performers, it is about 45 degrees
To Lx1 for the US performers the angle is about 50 degrees, but it gets much steeper
as little as one pace down stage of where the figure is drawn (around 65 degrees)

DS
(Down Stage)

MS
(Mid Stage)

US
(Up Stage)

FIGURE 6. SKETCH SECTION. THE RED LINES SHOW THE SIGHT LINE FROM THE FRONT ROW STALLS TO THE BORDER MASKING. CLEARLY THIS SECTION HAS BEEN USED FOR MORE THAN JUST ASSESSING OVERHEAD SIGHT LINES AND TRIM HEIGHT.

and which will be used for masking. Whenever there is a particular need to have a lighting bar in a particular place, the lighting designer needs to let everyone know that as early in the process as possible. Down stage of each lighting bar is a masking border. There will need to be a suitable gap between the two to make sure the hot lanterns do not burn the masking. The borders hide the lanterns and provide a clean finishing line to the top of the frame of the stage picture. It can be difficult to place a back light and front light on the same bar if borders are used to mask the rig. It is not always necessary or desirable to use borders to mask the lighting rig — sometimes we want to expose the rig.

Now the positions of the Lx bars and borders have been determined, we can start to consider what lanterns should go where.

Key light

In lighting for camera, the key light is the main source on the main subject. In lighting for live performance, the phrase is less well defined. In the first place, the camera has by definition a single point of view on its subject. Each member of an audience for a live performance has their own point of view and these can be radically different from each other. Think about a performance in the round where one audience member's perception of back light is another's front light. Generally in lighting design for live performance what we mean by key light is the light which provides the apparent main source of illumination for the subject or the space. That is not a very tight definition; can there successfully be several different keys in the same space at the same time? Well yes, but it depends what you mean by the same space. Often, on a performance stage where different 'performance worlds' are represented side by side, their boundaries are defined by different keys.

Going back to the world of lighting for camera, the key light is not necessarily the strongest source on the subject, but it is usually the one that is most responsible for getting useable visual information into the camera. This means that almost always as it strikes the main

FIGURE 7. CAST OF A STUDENT PRODUCTION LOOKING UP-STAGE TOWARDS A STRONG LIGHT SOURCE. LIGHTING BY SABR HEMMING, DIRECTED BY PETER MCALLISTER, SET AND COSTUME DESIGN BY YASUKO HASEGAWA

Using the live performance meaning of key light, we want to key the daylight and moonlight scenes using ¾ back-light from up stage right. For the day time scenes, this key might be in a daylight colour — say Lee 201, which the manufacturer tells us corrects tungsten light to daylight, 5700 degrees Kelvin. For the moonlight we might get away with dimming this down and using the decrease in colour temperature along with the decrease in intensity to signify moonlight.

For the evening scenes when the apparent light source is the standard lamp, we want a more or less ¾ back light from up stage left. This needs to be coloured to signify light from a domestic light — comparatively low in colour temperature compared to the 3200 degrees Kelvin of most tungsten filament stage light. We could use something like Lee 204; designed to shift daylight down in colour temperature to stage light, it can sometimes work to shift stage light down in colour temperature to domestic lighting. Alternatively we can use high wattage sources and run them at no more than 70% of full, which will have a similar effect.

So, what types of lanterns will we need and where will we place them? One way to start is to use the tool we made earlier in the chapter. According to the section we used to position and set the trim of the borders, the bottom of the lanterns on the up stage lighting bars — Lx2 & Lx3 — is around 6.5m. If we make a height strip around 7m at scale (the centre of the lanterns will be at least 40cm above the lowest point) we can look at the effect of various beam angles from different positions. (But remember we are interested in lighting people not the floor, so we are most interested in what is happening around performer head height, that is between 1.5 and 1.75m above stage floor.) A beam imitating light from the window clearly needs from come from that direction, say near the end of Lx3. We can make a reasonable guess that the beam of a lantern from this position is unlikely to successfully light the heads of performers all the way down stage. If we were to try that, the beam would continue into the eyes of the front rows of audience, resulting in distracting glare. In this case the border will get in the way. We can construct a simple section along the line we are interested in (say a line from the centre of the window to down stage centre)

subject, camera key light has a major front light component. A strong back light source would not be called a key light for camera. Key light for camera usually attempts to re-create naturalism and limit distractions, especially in close up. To make sure there are no distracting double shadows on actors' faces, there is generally only one key light in each camera set-up. On the stage, however, we frequently refer to keying a scene from behind the actors, and very often have to use multiple sources to do the job of a camera key light, to satisfy the visual demands of multiple audience points of view, performers who move in the space, and the limitations of both equipment and hanging positions.

Looking back to the sketch of lighting ideas for the melodrama at the beginning of this chapter, apparent sources of light come from up stage, behind the performers; during the day, light from the window, and at night too with the moonlight, in the evening, light from the fire and from the standard lamp up stage left. These then will provide our key light sources in the rig, also referred to as the motivational sources. They will not provide much in the way of useful face light, however, so we will have to make sure that the face light can do its important job without overwhelming the effect of the keys.

and use that to find out where the cut off due to the border will be. With experience this becomes less necessary. We could also argue that, since in the natural world — the world we are imitating on stage — the effect of the light from the window will decrease as we move down stage, the beam we are planning should not reach to the down stage edge anyway. The same argument holds for the light appearing to come from the standard lamp up stage right.

The imitation of light from a single source (sun, moon or standard lamp) will work best if like these natural sources, there is only one shadow. That means only one source if at all possible. We can see that the beam angle required to cover a suitable portion of the stage is well within the range of most Fresnel/PC lanterns and many theatre profiles. Something between 35 degrees and 45 degrees will do the job. (We will want something more controllable than a flood light here.) Deciding between these different types of unit sometimes depends on availability, but let's assume we have a wide choice available, and look at some of the factors that will influence the final decision:

- Profiles provide the most control with their shutters, but are generally not as bright, watt for watt, as Fresnels, which in turn generally loose out to PCs.

- The edge of the beams of each unit type is different. Generally, profiles have the most defined edge, Fresnels the least, with PC somewhere in between. Diffusion material can help to further soften the edge of a profile's beam, but again we loose light output when we use diffusion.

- The evenness of the light distribution across the beam also varies with unit type. Although not true of every profile, most can be tweaked to produce a flat beam, more or less even in intensity from edge to edge. Fresnel units usually have a hot central section

to the beam which gently falls off in intensity towards the edge. PCs generally have a more defined peak in the centre of the beam, which then falls off evenly towards the edge, but more rapidly than happens in the beam of a Fresnel unit.

So let's think about what we want from each of these two keys. Direct light through windows is ultimately coming from distant sources — the sun (or the moon). It will usually be even in intensity across the beam, which will have a well-defined edge.[7] However, along with the direct sunlight, during the day there is also more diffuse light reflected from the sky and nearby structures. This has a much softer quality, gently falling off in intensity towards a loosely defined edge. If we want to imitate direct sunlight we might choose the defined edge of the beam from a profile, while indirect sunlight might be better imitated by the beam from a Fresnel. But how closely do we want to imitate reality? If this were a film set, it could be lit through the window, with the camera placed to make sure the lantern (which might be a 12 or 20 kW Fresnel) was not seen. On stage we can rarely do this. If we used the profile, the sharply-defined edge to the beam may well become distracting as performers move in and out of it.[8] The Fresnel may create an effect less similar to direct sunlight in a real room, but will often be more appropriate on stage than the more technically accurate profile beam. (We will come back to the effect of direct moonlight through the window later.)

Moving to the other side of our room, the key from up stage right is imitating the light from a standard lamp. This might be better mimicked by the 'peaky' beam of a PC unit, flooded to fill as much of the stage as the production needs. The peakyness of the beam can be used to help create the impression of dark corners in a room with a bright centre, focusing audience attention, and working with the underlying dramaturgy of the piece. The end result might not be totally accurate to the

---

[7]Next time you see direct sunlight coming into a room through a window check this out.

[8]Remember the attention of the human eye is drawn to the sharp edge of a beam — the rapid change in intensity — much more than soft edges. A performer moving through the sharp edges of beams of light looks immediately unnatural and this can easily be distracting.

natural world — a room with more walls, a ceiling and at a more natural scale might not look like this — but we need to work with the reality of what we have. That is a cottage with an 8m wide living room, 5m high walls and an auditorium where the fourth wall should be!

In both these cases, we need to concern ourselves with the needs of the production whilst bearing in mind what natural world effect we are attempting to imitate. The stage is not a direct and true imitation of the natural world, even in genres where this is apparently what is happening. First, we have created this world on stage for a bunch of people to be spectators of an event, and in doing that we have generally removed at least one wall and often much more. By placing the event before an audience we have raised the potential significance of everything that audience sees and hears (and increasingly smells, touches and even tastes). As a member of the creative team that will develop and present this event, the lighting designer must keep their primary focus on what makes sense to the audience, rather than slavishly sticking to the attempt to accurately reproduce a version of the natural world.

The first two units in our rig have almost been decided upon. We know where they will go, what type of unit they will be and probably what colour they will use. All that remains is to decide the wattage — how much power they should draw — which affects how bright the stage will be. If we use a unit that is too bright at or near full intensity, and we have to use it at a lower intensity, the colour will not be what we designed, due to the drop in colour temperature of the cooler filament running at less than 100%. Also many Fresnel and PC units lose definition and beam size at lower intensities. If we choose a unit with insufficient intensity to do the job, we may have to bring down the intensity of every other unit in the scene to allow the chosen unit to show through. Again there will be problems with colour temperature, but there may also be problems with intensity — we will not be able to reduce below a certain intensity level or the audience will not be able to see.

Tradition says that large auditoria require more light on stage so the people at the back can see well, and large casts on stage require more power because bodies soak up light. As with most traditions there is

some truth in both statements. If you are lighting a show in an unfamiliar space, find out what size of units previous lighting designers have used. In recent times there has been a move towards smaller, more energy-efficient units. The ETC Source 4 at 575 watts produces a similar intensity to a traditional 1000 watt lantern. These improvements in optical efficiency will continue, and that means the rule-book on what power lanterns go where will change too.

This show is likely to be relatively dark — the single setting is a cottage interior — and it is in a medium-sized auditorium, using, as we shall see, Source 4 profiles front of house. We need the stage left key to be quite bright however, so we might go for a 2kW Fresnel. The PC on the other hand is only going to be used for night-time scenes, so a 1.2kW unit might be appropriate here.

One other factor that we might have to take into account is the relative size of units with different power consumption; generally the higher the wattage the bigger the unit. This can mean units with different power hang from the same bar at different heights. We could find that the 2kW Fresnel is longer than the 1.2kW units that fill the rest of the Lx3. If we have to trim the border a little lower in order to mask the 2kW, the 1.2kW will not be able to see as far down stage as we (may be) planned. This is an area where the advice of an experienced chief electrician or production electrician can be extremely useful. They are likely to know the relative sizes of units and be able to tell you if a particular combination will create problems.

Planning front light washes

This is a piece where the spoken word is important, so an important element of the lighting rig is light for the actors' faces. We should note that face light does not have to come from the front, even on a proscenium stage. Actors spend most of the time looking into the stage rather than looking out from it towards the audience. The best place for face light to come from for two actors talking to each other across the stage will often be from the side of the stage each one is facing. However, on this stage the walls of the set get in the way, so our major sources of face light will be from the front.

We can divide the stage area into nine areas, three wide and three deep, as shown below. We can name them using the conventions of British and North American stage practice. This will provide enough flexibility within the lighting system to focus the attention of the audience on the sections of the stage where the artistic team decide it should be.

Up stage right (USR)	Up stage centre (USC)	Up stage left (USL)
Mid-stage right (MSR)	Mid-stage centre (MSC)	Mid-stage left (MSL)
Down stage right (DSR)	Down stage centre (DSC)	Down stage left (DSL)

Audience

Nine is not a magic number for us — on a larger stage or with a different shape or configuration of stage we might chose a different number of areas. Generally speaking in a conventional end on performance space, odd numbers work better in dividing up the stage if for no other reason than they give us centre stage areas. Performers and directors very often like to do important stuff centre stage.[9] In many situations, a lighting designer needs to be able to bring up the intensity of centre stage relative to the rest of the stage. If we have an even number of equally-sized areas across a roughly symmetrical stage, there will be no single area in the centre, and consequently the lighting design will not be as able to concentrate audience attention centre stage. The size of each area will usually be slightly larger than the space occupied by a performer with outstretched arms, say between 2.5 to 3m wide. Any smaller and the areas become harder to blend into a unified wash. Much larger and we loose too much control over the differences in the light at different places on the stage. Other factors can override these considerations at times, for example you may be limited by the number of lanterns or dimmers available, or the number of suitable hanging positions, or by the amount of time you have to focus the rig. (The more lanterns you have the longer the focus takes and the less time is left for creating cues and evolving the performance.)

Back on the set of the melodrama, each of the nine areas is just over 2.5m wide by 2m deep on our 8m wide by 6m deep stage area. By drawing out one face of the box at scale I find that the diagonal of each box will be about 3.5m so this is the size of beam I am looking for to fill my nine boxes and make my washes.

I might start by placing three profiles on a convenient straight-in position front of house for the beginnings of the neutral wash. Such a position is the upper circle front, which according to the plan and section is about 8m from the front edge of the stage and 8m higher than the stage. Using LD Calculator Lite,[10] I can find out what the throw will be to the centre of the down stage 3 boxes (~10m) and from that the required beam angle (about 15 degrees for a 2.5 to 3m wide beam at about 2m above stage). Placing three 19 degree Source 4 lanterns on the upper circle front, evenly spaced, should fill the most down stage three areas with front face light. The angle of incidence is a little shallower than I would like, meaning (amongst other things) that the spill outside the useful area will be larger, extending well into the three mid-stage areas. I may need to have an alternative if I need really tight definition of one or more of these down stage areas. However, the slightly shallower angle will help get light under heavy brows and into the eyes of the performers.

I want some modelling light from front of house too, and I will need something to facilitate both warm and cool looks across the whole acting area. The traditional

---

[9] The point about centre stage is that it is very often the natural focus point of the performance space, the area from which the performer can most easily become the centre of audience attention. This is especially true for stages in conventional proscenium theatres. For all configurations of performance space, one of the major factors influencing the decisions of designers and director will be the position of the natural focus of audience attention on the stage. For now we will assume that this is centre stage.

[10] LD Calculator Lite is a very useful resource which (at the time of writing) you can find and down-load from the world wide web for free!

45 degree positions will do this well — on the ground plan for this theatre they are called gallery sides. We can use the same techniques applied above to determine the required beam angles for lanterns from these positions focused to our down stage areas, DSL, DSC and DSR. Depending on your assessment of the needs of the production, we might place a single set of three lanterns each side, and plan to colour one side cool and the other warm. Alternatively, to provide greater flexibility for the lighting design we might want a warm and a cool set of lanterns at each side, and perhaps a neutral set, too. (Of course this assumes we have the budget/ dimmer circuits/space at the hanging position for the additional lanterns.)

In many theatres in the UK and elsewhere, it is likely that the venue will supply zoom profile lanterns specifically for these positions. The advantage of zoom lanterns is that the beam angle can be adjusted to suit the role required of the lantern. In this particular case for example, the throw for a lantern focused from the gallery side house right position to DSL will be shorter than that for a lantern focused to DSR from the same position. Consequently the beam angle required for the first lantern will be larger than that required for the second. Zooming a profile lantern is not the same as reducing the beam size with an iris — as you zoom the beam down (making it smaller) the beam gets brighter — roughly the amount of light is getting more concentrated into a smaller beam. We also know that as we move away from any light source the intensity reduces according to the inverse square law — move twice as far away and the intensity reduces by a quarter. With luck, the reduction in intensity due to the extra throw will be compensated for by the increase in intensity due to the zoomed down beam angle. This appears to work out

most of the time which is great. If the design has to incorporate fixed beam lanterns from these positions, it will often be necessary to proportionally reduce the intensity of the lanterns with the shorter throws in order to achieve an even intensity from that angle across the whole stage. However, since incandescent lanterns at different intensities produce light of different colours (due to the difference in colour temperature of the filament at different intensities; see Chapter 2) this is not always an acceptable solution.[11]

Having addressed the most downstage areas, we now need to consider the rest of the stage. The whole idea behind creating an even wash of light is usually to give the audience the impression that the area is a single unified space — that performers at rest or moving through the lit space are all in the same world — same time, same location, same feel. To do this the audience should not be aware that, as a performer is moving through the space, they are lit by different units. We know already that light from different angles of incidence lights the body differently — indeed we will use this as a signifier in the design. So we need to try to match the angle of incidence of each unit within our wash group.

You may have realised that we have already failed to do this with the 45 degree wash from the gallery sides. The angle of incidence from these positions will be greater for the units focused to their own sides (the ones with the shortest throws) than for the units focused to the far side. This gradual change in angle across stage is not usually significant enough to cause problems.[12] What will create noticeable changes in 'feel', however, are sharp and significant differences in angle of incidence on the performers as they move between lighting areas. We need to ensure that the next

---

[11]This problem can be addressed by using neutral density filters on the lanterns with shorter throws. These filters — more often used when lighting for camera than for the eye — are designed to reduce the intensity without altering the colour temperature. This can be very useful if you have to use the same dimmer for two lanterns, one of which has a much shorter throw to the target than the other.

[12]Having said that, many contemporary lighting designers working in Europe make much less use of these positions than the previous generation of practitioners. Working in a style with fewer sources does tend to show the weakness of some traditional techniques, including extensive use of 45 degree front light systems. If you are attentive to the work of contemporary lighting designers, you will see many alternative solutions to the problem of providing illumination for faces.

sets of lanterns placed on the plan to light the mid- and up-stage areas will blend with those already in place to light the down stage areas.

The straight-in system that began from the upper circle front could be continued from the advance bar. The angle of incidence to the centre of the mid-stage areas from this position is about 40 degrees — slightly steeper than the 35 degree angle we have from the upper circle front to the centre of the down stage areas. These angles of incidence are probably sufficiently close to work for the design and blend into a single wash. The slightly increasing angle will help us in that it will decrease the spill area up stage and give better control of these mid-stage areas. However, this same increased angle of incidence will also tend to create shadows over the eyes of some performers. Helping out here though is bounce light. The amount of bounce light will depend on a number of factors, including the colour and texture of the walls and floor of the set. What will almost always be true, however, is that there will be more bounce from front lights the further up-stage you go, simply because as the performer moves further up stage there are more lit surfaces down stage of them for light be reflected off. So generally speaking we can use steeper angles for front light the further up stage we go. In my rough sketch you can see that by the time we get to lighting the up-stage areas from Lx 1 the angle of incidence is about 50 degrees. This increasing angle also helps to reduce the length of potentially distracting shadows on the back wall.

Again using LD Calculator Lite, we can determine that the throw from the advance bar to mid-stage is about 7.5m and the beam angle required to produce a beam 3m wide from that distance is just over 18 degrees. This presents us with a tricky problem. Many ranges of fixed beam angle lanterns come in 19 degree, 26 degree and

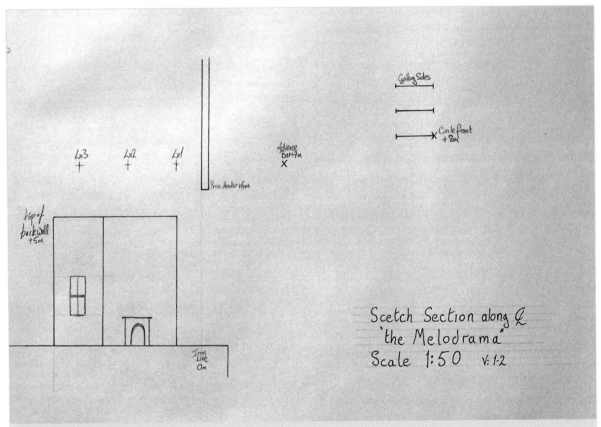

FIGURE 8. SKETCH SECTION OF THE MELODRAMA. AS A LIGHTING DIRECTOR YOU WON'T ALWAYS GET A SECTION DRAWING GIVEN TO YOU BY THE SET DESIGNER OR PRODUCTION MANAGER. SOMETIMES YOU NEED TO DRAW ONE FOR YOURSELF FROM INFORMATION.

36 degree, including the popular ETC Source 4 range. Do we choose a 19 and hope our calculations are correct, or play safe and go for a 26, but live with less light on stage (the 26 degree lantern will be less bright because the same amount of light is spread over a larger area)? The decision depends on several factors, including the amount of confidence you have in the measurements provided to you, the time available to rectify any mistakes, availability of equipment and how much you intend to shape the beams using shutters. All other things being equal, this last is often the key one for me. To be able to use the shutters of a profile lantern, there has to be spare beam to get rid of. In most situations, I would play safe and go for the 26 degree lantern to be sure I had enough spare beam to shape.

Using the same techniques as before we can establish that to continue the straight-in wash into the up stage areas from Lx1, the throw will be about 6.5m and the required angle will be 21 degrees. The set gets narrower up stage so we will have no problem choosing 26 degree units to complete this straight-in wash or system.

Completing the 45 degree front light wash raises more questions. We could attempt to cover the whole stage from the gallery sides. Yes, the angle of incidence will change as the performers move on stage, but because all the light really does come from more or less the same place, blending the discrete sources into each other is much less of a problem. If these units are to be used primarily to fill shadow and aid perception of depth then the differences in angle of incidence will probably not be registered. If, however, they are to provide the apparent source of illumination, it could be difficult to maintain the similarity of feel across the whole stage.

There are several other problems to be looked at if we are going to try to use a position like this to site a full stage wash. First we may not be able to see the whole stage from this position, especially in a proscenium

theatre. If the set has walls, as ours does, this might not be too much of a problem as bounce light may well help out in the hard to reach up-stage corners on the near sides.[13]

Sketching a ground plan to scale can be a good place to try out ideas. Supposing we decide to light as much of the stage as possible from the gallery sides; using LD Calculator and the sketch ground plan we can estimate how much the angle of incidence changes across our set. I have measured the horizontal distance on the sketch ground plan (H in LD Calc) and we know from the theatre's information pack or from our own measurements that there are bars at 8m, 9m, and 10m above stage level at both the gallery side positions. We can usefully focus on only six of the nine areas from each of these positions. From house left these will be: DSL, DSC, DSR, MSL, MSC and possibly USL. From house right the six are: DSL, DSC, DSR, MSC, MSR and possibly USR. The up-stage areas are probably the ones least usefully lit from these positions; they have the lowest angle of incidence and therefore create the longest shadows and the largest spill area (and that spill will create potentially distracting shadows all over the corners of the set — something we are unlikely to want). We will leave placing these units for now.

The beam size here will be the distance across the diagonal of each area since the light is striking the area from the diagonal rather than from straight on as in the first examples. This means the beam size (X in LD Calc) needs to be about 3.25m rather than the 2.5 to 3m used previously. Some quick calculation using LD Calc gives us a range of required beam angles between 10 and 15 degrees, well within the working range of most long-throw zoom profile lanterns.

If we have nine available hanging positions (see the sketch), we need to decide where to place the units that will light each of the six areas. To achieve our aim of a smooth even wash, we need to minimise the change in

[13]These corners are in any case unlikely to be important areas of the performance space, especially if some sections of the audience don't have a perfect view of them.

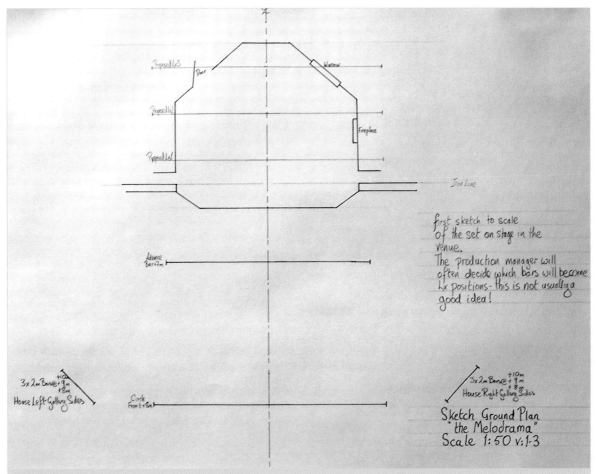

first sketch to scale of the set on stage in the venue.
The production manager will often decide which bars will become Lx positions- this is not usually a good idea!

Sketch Ground Plan "the Melodrama"
Scale 1:50 v:1·3

FIGURE 9. SKETCH GROUND PLAN FOR THE MELODRAMA, SHOWING ONLY THE BARE ESSENTIALS; THE PROSCENIUM, THE OUTLINE OF THE SET AND THE MAIN LIGHTING POSITIONS. THIS MIGHT BE SKETCHED FROM THE FULL PRODUCTION GROUND PLAN OR FROM INFORMATION PROVIDED BY THE VENUE AND THE SET DESIGNER/PRODUCTION MANAGER.

angle of incidence between any two adjacent areas. In practice this means don't cross the beams.

Let's take this opportunity to place our first specials. We know from reading the play and talking to the director that we need to be able to isolate the chair and there will be a dramatic moment when a character comes in through the door and stands there. We already have a plan to light the chair from birdies at the front of stage,[14] and the entrance special is probably going to work better from a steeper angle. Provided you have the budget and the dimmers, it is often best to hang and focus extras as a back up. You can be more or less sure that units from these positions will light the performers' faces — it may help key cue states to have just a touch from front of house to add a sparkle to the performers' eyes, for example. Also, units in these positions can usually be re-focused quite quickly, so if the position of the chair changes I can still light it without

[14]Look back at the cue synopsis p. 99.

125

having to clear the stage and access the overhead lanterns[15].

Before we leave the gallery side positions, we have space to hang another few units. How about some colour fill from here? We can work out that a 25 degree beam angle would create a wash from a single lantern that would fill the whole of the stage that is visible from the gallery side, taking some account of shuttering. It could be really useful to have, say, a deep blue wash to fill the shadows at certain moments, or perhaps to 'fake' darkness.

The alternative to continuing the 45 degree wash from front of house is to use lanterns from the overhead rig on the advance bar and on stage. Again using a sketch ground plan and LD Calc, we can determine that the throw to mid stage from the advance bar for this system would be about 8.5m requiring a unit with a beam angle of around 16 degrees but that we will probably only be able to see two of the three mid-stage areas from each side. The angle of incidence from the horizontal will be about 40 degrees, which should be close enough to the angle of incidence from front of house to allow smooth blending between these areas. From Lx1 the angle to the up stage areas will be steeper — around 55 degrees — and the required beam angle will be about 22 degrees, indicating Source 4 26 degree units. Once more the stage left area will only be lit from stage right and the stage right area only from stage left.

Pipe-ends

Because of the set walls, the only light from the sides we can get into the mid- and up-stage areas will be from the overhead rig (rather than from booms). As we have already seen, whenever the actors are facing each other across the set, light from these positions is likely to be of more use for faces than light from the front. One very useful way to do side light from overhead is referred to as pipe-end lighting.[16] Two (or more) units from near the end of the overhead lighting bar are focused across stage. These units can also be used to provide modelling and colour. The usual way to focus them is for one unit to cover each half of the stage — this determines the required beam angle. On more open stages PAR 64s are often used, though here we might want a bit more control to be able to light the set sensitively. If we want to keep this (potentially) coloured light off some of the set we will need barn doors and the flexible beam angle offered by Fresnel lanterns. We shall need to sketch another section to work out beam angles and positions, this time across stage. The same drawing will serve for placing lanterns on Lx1 and Lx2.

From the sketch we can see that we will need units with a beam angle of between 25 and 40 degrees; almost any Fresnel unit will do this, so the choice is wide. For extra control we could use profiles. It is also clear from the sketch that light from these units will have a small front light component for the mid stage and up stage areas. It will probably be useful to continue this high side light into the down stage areas by placing a pair of fixtures at each end of the advance bar. This would usually restrict the choice of unit to profiles, because any other kind of unit would produce too much distracting stray light on the proscenium.

There will be a large difference between the angle of incidence on, for example, two performers both lit from stage left, one on stage left and one on stage right. However, the change is gradual across the stage, and it is unlikely that pipe-end systems will be used as the apparent source of illumination or key in this piece.

---

[15]If I still want to use lanterns from the overhead rig I can re-focus them at the next suitable break and then re-plot the cue. In the meantime the rehearsal can continue — there is still a special on the chair, there is still a meaningful cue to time, place and respond to, and the piece can continue to develop.

[16]Clearly this name comes from the North American practice of calling lighting bars pipes, and has nothing to do with smoking.

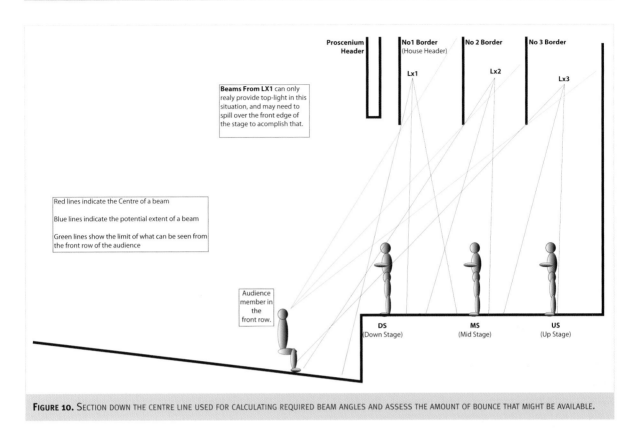

Proscenium Header

No1 Border (House Header)

No 2 Border

No 3 Border

Lx1

Lx2

Lx3

Beams From LX1 can only realy provide top-light in this situation, and may need to spill over the front edge of the stage to acomplish that.

Red lines indicate the Centre of a beam

Blue lines indicate the potential extent of a beam

Green lines show the limit of what can be seen from the front row of the audience

Audience member in the front row.

DS (Down Stage)

MS (Mid Stage)

US (Up Stage)

FIGURE 10. SECTION DOWN THE CENTRE LINE USED FOR CALCULATING REQUIRED BEAM ANGLES AND ASSESS THE AMOUNT OF BOUNCE THAT MIGHT BE AVAILABLE.

This position is frequently used to add texture to the lighting design in the form of a gobo wash. If this is the intention we would normally base all the calculations on the size of the beam at stage level, not at performer head level.

Other apparent sources of light

In the first sketches we identified several other sources of light. First, let's look at the low source from down stage that will cast a shadow of the father in the chair. The original sketch had a position on the down stage edge for a birdie. The line passing through the centre of the birdie and the chair gives us an approximate position for the unit. However, experience tells us that this is probably something that will need to be worked out on the performance stage to make sure we get the best possible result. A note on the plan is usually enough to indicate that this unit has yet to have a defined final position.

The fire will need to glow and that might come from a source built into the set, but we might be able to add extra glow from the rig — shining a narrow beam of suit-

ably coloured light from, say, Lx2 to mimic the light from a fire. There are various effects that could be used with the lantern providing this light, including a static gobo, a slowly rotating gobo, or a gobo and an effects wheel in front of the unit. Either of these latter two could provide some subtle movement within the beam, again imitating light from a fire. However, since we are projecting this light onto the fire rather than making it actually come from the fire, we will have to be extra careful, first to make sure the effect we create really does look to be coming from the fireplace, and second to make sure it will not hit any of the performers and give away its true source.

The sky outside the window will need to show (at different times) late afternoon, sunset, and evening. This will need the appearance of light from above the horizon, a warm glow on the horizon, and perhaps even stars for evening. The sky is visible behind the stage action for almost all the audience and will be our best way of indicating time of day through the play. Clearly the lighting on it will have an important dramaturgical impact on the piece. We will need to talk to the set designer and others to make sure the material used for the sky cloth will be suitable for taking light, and that there will be enough room to place our lanterns, top and bottom.

One important consideration is will we be able to light the sky from behind. Some materials can usefully spread out light for us when lit from behind, turning the light from several individual floods into a smooth even wash. However, if there are structural elements of the frame that supports the sky across the back of it, these will create ugly shadows. Squeezing in sufficient equipment to provide the number of different looks required by the script can be tough, especially if we are restricted to lighting the sky from the small area between the back of the window flat and the sky frame. Two or three colours of flood light from above and below would be nice — a sky blue for day time, some warm sunset colour, and perhaps a night-time blue for evening (since this is likely to look better than leaving the sky un-lit in the evening scenes — un-lit often looks dead on stage).

If LED equipment is available, perhaps this would be an ideal place for it. LED strip lights generally have clusters of three or four different coloured LEDs and offer control of colour and overall intensity by mixing the light from each colour. They don't need dimmer channels, just a few dmx 512[17] control channels. LED batons are relatively compact, can be used very close to scenery, since they don't get as hot as conventional units, and generally come with a range of diffusers to spread their light as required. Some units are available with a suitable range of colours and smoothness of dimming but it would be wise to try out whatever you are offered before committing a substantial proportion of budget to this solution.

Lighting sky cloths and cycs (cyclorama) can be enormously rewarding. When it is done well, a simple piece of cloth turns into the infinite and variable heavens, able to signify not just time and place, but whatever dramaturgical qualities are called for by the production. When it is done poorly, the simple piece of cloth remains a piece of cloth, with no potential other than to disappoint.

Apart from the sky, we want moonlight through the window. If there is enough space, this might just be possible to achieve by placing a lantern so that its beam shines through the window and casts a beam framed by the shadow of the window frame, just where we want it. This will often be the ideal solution, a large Fresnel — perhaps even a discharge source such as an HMI — rigged so no audience member can see it, and in such a way as to create the shadow of the window frame where its dramatic significance can be most clearly read by the audience. It's not going to happen here though, because the back wall of our little theatre gets in the way. What can be done, however, is to use a suitable gobo in a profile lantern on Lx3 to 'fake' the moonlight shadow where we need it. This will need to be supported by suitable lighting of the window frame to simulate light coming through it (perhaps by birdies just out of sight of the audience, attached to the back of the set). Just as with the faking of firelight, however, we will need to be sure that no performer is going to disrupt the trick by, for example, standing at the window and not being in the shadow cast on stage! Ensuring this trick works for the play could involve a series of conversations with the director and set designer where the lighting designer has to speak both for what is dramaturgically desirable and what is practically achievable. In these situations it is often useful to remember that a well presented illusion can

---

[17]dmx 512 is the most widely used control protocol in performance lighting today. It allows us to send up to 512 separate pieces of information 24 times every second. Each separate piece of information can be the level of a dimmer or the position of a gobo wheel or colour wheel in a moving light, or almost anything else that can be defined by a number between 0 and 255 (also known technically as an 8-bit word). For more details on dmx 512 you should consult specialist technical literature or the USITT web site www.usitt.org. For a simple introduction go to www.whitelight.ltd.uk/resource

---

be stronger than a poorly supported simulation of reality.

On the opposite side of the set is the doorway. The direction the door opens has been chosen to allow a performer to enter, opening the door and standing framed in the doorway, without the door blocking sight of them for any of the audience, and without having to stand back as they would if the door opened towards them. This allows us to place a suitable lantern off stage and above head height, backlighting this position and making it stronger still. This lantern will create a beam that casts a shadow of the opening door in the doorway. Working with a suitable section, we can make a reasonable estimate of where the shadow will fall for different achievable hanging positions. From a height of around 3m, say on a lighting stand at the off stage end of the backing flats, the beam could fall across the chair! If the lantern hangs higher, the beam will not spread so far across stage, and the shadow cast by anyone standing in the doorway will be smaller.

We put in a front light special for the doorway from the gallery side house right. I would want to add a steeper (and therefore more selective) light, say from the far end of Lx1, in the same cool colour as the ¾ wash from stage left. This gives us alternatives for the entrance.

We will also need to light the backing flats themselves. If they represent another room, light in that room will at some times be daylight, at other times lamp light, so we will need different sources to show this. We will also need to think about the shadows cast on the flats by performers entering or exiting. If we cast long shadows here, the audience may see the shadow of a performer about to make an entrance before they see that performer, or they may continue to see the shadow of a performer for a little while after they have left the stage. The impact and desir-ability of this will need to be discussed by the artistic team.

Practical units on stage[18]

Finally we have a standard lamp on stage. For the evening scenes this will be the apparent source of light (along with the fire). As well as the key light wash the colour of a domestic tungsten lamp from up stage left (the PC on Lx3 we have already mentioned) we will need something to enhance the effect of the practical fixture on the walls and floor.

If the performance space is small, and the show lighting is not too bright, the un-modified practical itself may create a suitable effect on walls and floor. In larger venues the amount of light required on stage increases, just to provide enough visual acuity for more distant spectators. Even in a medium-sized studio theatre it is likely that most practical fixtures will need some help from the lighting rig to look natural. This can come in two ways. Traditionally, lanterns from the overheard rig are used to mimic the splash of light created by the practical fixture. What can work better sometimes is modifying the practical fixture to create its own splash at a suitably increased intensity. Care needs to be taken to make sure that the practical does not become a source of glare for the audience, and that the increased heat that often comes with higher intensity sources does not create its own problems. That said, if the 'effect' of the practical is actually coming from the practical, then no one can disrupt the illusion. What we can do for the melodrama is to replace the domestic lamp-holder and shade of the standard lamp with a thicker fireproofed shade and stronger lamps. For example, a new shade can be built round a central disc; mounted on the disc, above and below, a number of fittings to take the MR16 lamps found in birdies, and suitable transformers. The MR16 lamps come in a range of beam

---

[18]The term practical in this context refers to light fittings that are part of the setting. In our show this is just the standard lamp, but it could be desk lamps, chandeliers, wall lights, or even a torch. Usually the actors will at least appear to switch them on and/or off, though to make things more reliable light switches on stage are usually dummies, and the lamp(s) are controlled directly from the lighting console.

angles and wattage so the size of the splash can be determined by the number and type of lamps used. Provided the shade is tall enough and thick enough to hide the direct sources from the audience, this can be a successful solution.

Choosing colour

Many professional lighting designers stick to their base of favourite colours through the years. They might try out one or two new ones each show (or for the more cautious, each year) and slowly over time change or broaden their palette. The reason behind this may be innate conservatism, but it may also tell us something about just how hard it can be to get colour right in performance lighting design. Once you have a few colours that you know work well together on most faces and with most costumes, why throw that away and start afresh every show? We have already mentioned several times how dimming tungsten lamps changes the colour of the light on stage, and understanding how this works for your favourite colours is important too.

Drama lighting — especially for faces — generally uses tints and subtle colours close to the white light we are used to seeing in nature. We know that responses to colour are subjective from person to person, and to some extent from culture to culture, so it can be counter-productive to rely on coloured light for too much signification. Also, whenever any one element of the performance design tries to do too much, things generally go wrong. If the set designer and director have agreed with the painters or costume makers on the colours of costume and set, what purpose does the lighting designer serve by flooding the stage with coloured light, changing these carefully chosen colours?[19]

In some circumstances, the design team may agree on the use of strongly coloured light, and when this happens it can be the signal to go into parts of the colour swatch-book you have previously not explored. Choosing colour for a lighting rig is often a really big deal. If you get it wrong, even on a relatively small scale, replacing colour can eat up budget and take time away from potentially more useful work. Getting it wrong on a large scale show can be a nightmare! But this knowledge should not stop experimentation, indeed it should encourage you to try out colours and colour combinations before deciding on what colours to use in your rig.

Samples and swatch books

Back in Chapter 3, we discussed some of the implications of using coloured light on stage, mixing complimentary colours from each side of stage to create something close to a neutral white light where the sources overlap for example. We would use this idea when it comes to choosing colours for the ¾ front light for the melodrama, and for the pipe-ends too. We need to make sure that whatever choices we make the resulting colours will work with the colour choices of the set and costume, of the performers' faces, and of any special make-up that is proposed. Try to get hold of samples of the materials to be used and shine your chosen coloured light on them in an otherwise darkened space. (It does not have to be a dark room, but beware of direct sunlight and fluorescent fixtures, as both of these can affect colour perception). Make sure you use a source close to the same colour temperature as the fixtures you will be using on stage. For example, a mini Mag-lite torch is suitable since it has a QI lamp, but a standard angle poise or study light is probably not, since it is likely to have a lamp with a much lower colour temperature. Do not use LED torches for sampling colour unless you propose to light that material with LED light.

If you have access to the model-box, try out a few different colours in that using a couple of torches and samples from a lighting filter swatch book. If you can get to the costume workshop, take down your QI torches

---

[19] Of course, sometimes when elements of the set or costume appear on stage the colours don't work for the production team and it falls to the lighting designer to do something about it. But that is a different situation.

---

and the lighting filter swatch book. Better still, take a small lantern and a power adaptor so you can plug it in at the workshop. You will need slightly larger gel samples, but you can often get hold of off-cuts from a theatre workshop or a hire shop. You can then try out different colours of light on the fabric used for the stage costumes, which will help you to choose colours that everyone is going to be happy with. You can (and should) do the same thing if you can get to the space where the set is being painted, where large props are being made, or where special effects are being created. Apart from the knowledge you will gain about how the coloured light will affect stuff on stage, you will be meeting with some of the other people who will contribute to making the performance and perhaps getting new ideas on the piece (and making new friends). The more stuff you try out before you get into the performance space, the more likely you are to be able to realise your creative dreams.

Scrollers vs. CMY[20]

It is possible to delay the choice of colour for some lanterns, for example by asking for colour change equipment instead of deciding on a specific gel. This is not really the best use of colour change kit. The money spent on it (and time invested in getting it working and keeping it effective) is only really justified if the design needs several different colours at different times from the same location. If this is the case, however, there is a choice of equipment types; the discrete colour frames of a scroller, or the continuous variation offered by a colour mixing device, often referred to as CMY devices. Scrollers are programmed from the lighting desk to present a frame of gel in front of the unit to which they are attached. CMY devices use a combination of subtractive filters to produce a much larger range of colours. To get from colour 1 to colour 12 on a scroller requires the unit to go through colours 2 through 11 too;

clearly, planning the order of gels on the roll will be important if we want to use the effect of a light source changing colour during a piece. CMY changers can theoretically change from any one colour to any other colour, and at present are relatively expensive. In practice, lighting designers working in drama very often sacrifice this apparent flexibility in favour of having the exact colours they know and love in their lighting rig, especially in the face light. 'The less that can go wrong the better' is how many view it. That said, there are many professional lighting designs based around colour change equipment. For any aspiring lighting designer, getting to know how to make the best use colour changers is time well spent.

Concert rigs — structure as part of the visual design

The expectation of lighting for live music concerts and festivals is quite different from that of our little melodrama. As we noted earlier in this section, the expectation for the melodrama is usually that the lighting rig will be hidden from view. For many live music concerts, the lighting rig is not only not hidden, often it forms a major part of the structural scenography on stage — the lighting rig itself as set. But how much does this change the process of deciding what units go where? There will be the same considerations of how to make the washes, and where to place the specials, the same calculations concerning beam angles. Even if the majority of units in the lighting rig are moving lights, these calculations will still be needed: How many of the particular moving lights will be needed to wash the whole stage? What beam angle of front-light unit will work as a special for (say) the backing vocals or the drummer? Will the moving lights give that beam angle?

Two things are very different. The first, the shape of the lighting rig and the impact it has on a structure, is

---

[20]CMY stands for cyan, magenta and yellow, the three secondary colours for light, which are usually used to mix colour into the light beam in both moving lights and static colour change units. These devices are often referred to in ways that suggest they add colour to a white beam — we know that colouring white light is always a subtractive process.

important and has already been covered. This often means that the lighting designer and set designer work closely together to come up with a visual concept that defines the space of performance. These days there will usually be a media designer involved too, who will need screens or other display surfaces incorporated into the look. Just as with the melodrama, only after a shape has been agreed on does any work begin on placing lanterns. The difference is that it is much more likely that the lighting designer will have had a major say in what that shape is.

The second difference is that almost all design for live music has to take into consideration touring. It is quite normal for several large trucks to turn up at 8am outside an empty concert hall, for those trucks to be unloaded, the equipment assembled, flown, powered up, focused, and sound checked in the following 7 to 8 hours, for the concert to happen at 8pm, and for the hall to be empty once more by midnight, all the equipment back in the trucks and on the way to the next venue. This has an impact on what can and cannot be part of the lighting design. Everything has to be modular, from the truss structures that support the lights, to the set elements, to the cabling and dimmer systems. And every focused unit has to be able to be ready in time for the show — no long hours spent getting each wash perfect — this is big brush stuff, with the minimum of subtle hard to achieve effects.

Both practices have something to teach the other. The few practitioners who move comfortably between the two ways of working produce some of the most visually stimulating work around, for example Patrick Woodruffe, lighting designer for the Rolling Stones amongst others, and Durham Marenghi. If drama lighting is often about attention to detail, rarely demanding overt signification by light, concert lighting is often about scale and ambition and big statements, with lighting as major signifier, providing overt content.

The lighting plan — an evolving document

Back thinking about the stage of our melodrama, the first draft of the plan is just about complete. We have

our big keys — one for the daytime scenes and one for the lamp-lit evening scenes. We have several systems of face light, and through experiment in the wardrobe department, and at the set painter's workshop, we have chosen the colours for these. We have other systems and specials and practical fixtures being made in our workshop for the fire place and the standard lamp. In short we have enough information to allow the chief electrician (Lx) or production electrician to assemble the bits that will go into making our rig. Each decision that has had to be made has involved combining information from several sources: dramaturgical information concerning the effects we want to create on stage; technical information, for example concerning what different lanterns will do; and practical information, for example the relative positions of Lx bars and the set. We have had to do several scale drawings, and we have made a new tool. At times it has been hard to resolve conflicting demands, but we have produced a lighting plan!

Then the production manager tells you that the position of the number 3 lighting bar they gave you was wrong, or the budget is not big enough to hire all the lanterns you want, but that the theatre has found some (old) ones in the cellar! It won't always be like that but sometimes it will and changes will happen. As lighting designer you need to stay on top of them, keep your team informed, and try your hardest to keep the plan up-to-date. All this at the same time as you are going to rehearsals, talking to the director and other designers, establishing relationships with the stage management team and the performers, and keeping your cue synopsis up-to-date. Well, nobody said it would be easy!

It is most unusual for the lighting plan to remain unchanged from its initial inception through to the opening of the show in front of an audience, whatever the genre and whatever the scale. As lighting designer, your work depends on this document, and you need to make every effort to ensure the current version is accurate and that everybody is working to the current version. But you will need more than just a lighting plan to get your rig up and your design on stage.

7

plans, paperwork and patching

Good documentation aids good lighting design

Getting the equipment in the right place, connected to the right dimmers and desk channels, with the right colours and other accessories, is what enables the lighting designer to create performance lighting. Achieving this happy state as quickly and as accurately as possible requires planning and communication, even for relatively small lighting systems. For larger systems involving several people in their realisation, good paperwork becomes an essential tool. Who produces the paperwork, and keeps it up to date, is different in different production situations. Sometimes the lighting designer will produce it all, at other times, the production electrician, master electrician, or design associate will produce much of it. Getting it right, and that includes making it easy for all concerned to use it, is a vital part of getting the lighting rig in place and working on time. Doing that creates more time on stage for the lighting designer to create cues, and for the production as a whole to evolve, which in the end is what it is all about.

To keep this chapter to a manageable length, I am making the distinction between the documentation required to get the lighting system in place and working, and that required to focus or point the instruments and to build the cues that make up the design. I will come back to these later documents in the next chapters.

The lighting plan or plot

To realise most lighting designs, somebody draws a lighting plan.[1] It may be drawn on a computer using two-dimensional plotting programmes or a full 3D computer drawing package, or a drawing board with pencil, stencils and ink, or on the back of a cigarette packet with a ball point pen. It may be drawn by the lighting designer, by an assistant or associate, by the production electrician, by staff from the lighting hire company, or by the chief electrician (Lx) or lighting manager in a repertory theatre. There is no generally accepted correct format, though it is clear that some layouts work better than others, and different situations require different types of lighting plan, with different levels of detail. The lighting plan or plot, however, is *not* the lighting design; it is one of several tools required to get that lighting design realised. It should be about the efficient unambiguous communication of information, but that is not to say it can't look good.

---

[1]European practice tends to use the words lighting plan (in English and some other languages) while North American practice uses light plot. Both usually refer to an idealised or schematic view of the lighting rig from overhead. The generally understood meaning of lighting plot in UK theatre is some kind of record of the lighting cues.

In the build period of a production there are at least three distinct users of the information on a lighting plan:

- On productions with a substantial lighting system there will normally be one person in charge of the realisation of the performance lighting system. That person may have a different title in different situations; chief Lx, head of lighting or the production electrician for example. This person will want to have speedy access to all the patch information, weights, colour materials and gobos used, fixture addresses and many other details of the rig. Much of this may well be displayed and recorded on a lighting plan.

- On all but the simplest of fit-ups, the people hanging the luminaries will need information to help them get each unit in the correct place, plugged to the correct socket, and with all the correct ancillary equipment properly in place.

- When focusing or creating cues, the lighting designer may use the lighting plan to inform themself of the channel and fixture numbers, group names and other information needed to access the lanterns.

Three different user types, working in different ways and needing different information from the lighting plan.

What goes on a lighting plan?

In the heat of the moment, and when working with close colleagues, it is occasionally possible to communicate sufficient information with a hastily drawn sketch lighting plan. However, in many more situations it is necessary to be much clearer, both to communicate to those who will prepare the equipment to be used, and those who will hang it and make it work. Versions of the lighting plan may also be required as part of the documentation of the show, for touring, for maintenance during an extended run, and for possible future representation. It is usual to include an obligation to produce an accurate plan as part of the contract of a professional lighting designer. With this in mind, here are some features that should appear on every lighting plan.

A border

The continuous line framing the plan, about 2cm inside the edge of the paper. This may sound odd, but it is essential for those who are using the plan to be sure they have it all and that a section has not been lost or removed. Many computer-generated plans can be printed on multiple smaller sheets intended to be taped together for use, and borders not only help ensure all sheets are present, but can help to make it easier to line multiple sheets up.

Titles

What is the show? Is this the drawing for a particular version of the show, e.g. the US tour, or the London opening? If the drawing relates to a specific venue, this should be clearly stated.

Drawing type

Does the drawing include everything, or are there more drawings of detail from lighting inside a scenic truck or practical fittings on the set, or fixtures rigged on the ground, for example, that if these were included on the plot would make it less intelligible.

Date and version number

This is very important, especially when working on a production that is still changing. Everyone involved needs to know they are working from the same, up-to-date information, and this is one of the best ways to make sure they can check that. Anyone who makes alterations to a drawing will need to alter these information fields too. If a drawing is based on a ground plan it is a good idea to make the ground plan date and version number used clear.

Whose plan is it?

It is important that intellectual property, in this case the lighting design which is, in part, represented by the drawing, is acknowledged and protected. All drawings that are part of a design need to acknowledge the designer. A performance lighting design is part of a larger thing — the production — so the other intellectual property holders also need to be acknowledged, the director, the other designers, and perhaps the writer and producer.

The venue

The whole production will be constrained by the walls, doorways and other architectural features of the venue. The edges of the performance space, the extent of any spaces off stage and hidden from the audience, and where the audience will be, all have an impact on the implementation of the lighting design. In a proscenium theatre, the location of the proscenium arch is clearly important too. For a show that uses the production infrastructure of the venue; hanging positions, follow spot booths etc, these should also all be clearly marked.

Main features of the set

The position of the lighting fixtures will to a large extent be determined by the position of the set. The set often also defines where the performers will be and so further determines the position of lighting fixtures. A ground plan showing the set will often be the base on which the lighting plan is drawn. However, it will normally be necessary to show the set in the background to the main content of the lighting plan — the lighting rig. This can be done in a number of ways; by using thinner lines or paler colour, for example. For productions with more than one set the lines indicating set positions at different moments during the piece will need to be clearly labelled.

Heights

In an ideal world, any plan drawing should be accompanied by a section drawing. In a plan view there is no difference between the line representing a lighting bar 3m above stage level and the line representing a lighting bar 12m above stage level, unless we label them. Convention uses the stage floor as a reference height of zero, so an object 10 metres above stage level would be labelled +10m, an object or area one metre below stage level would be labelled −1m, and so on.

Contact information

This does not need to be explicit, but it does need to be there. As someone using the plan, who do I contact if any information is unclear or something needs to be changed? The lighting designer's name is already on the plan. The person who drew the plan needs to put their name on it too, and for a large show so might the production electrician or any other front line person responsible for the realisation of the lighting design.

A key and legend

Luminaires and other units are usually represented by symbols on a lighting plan. The key allows users to know precisely what each symbol represents. The legend should also make clear the meaning of each of the many numbers that appear on most lighting plans.

Scale

This defines how much linear distance on the stage is represented by each unit of measurement on the plan. European plans are generally in metric scales, 1:25 (one centimetre on the plan represents 25 centimetres on stage), 1:50, and 1:100 and so on. US plans are usually in imperial scales, 1:24 (one inch to two feet) or 1:48. Measuring distance on a plan of any kind is best done with a scale rule. This is a ruler marked with the dimensions in real space for a particular scale. For example, a 1:25 scale rule will have metres marked off every 4 centimetres along its length. Most scale rules have more than one scale, for example, a flat scale rule will have at least one scale on each edge and usually this will be repeated on the underside. Always check the scale you are using is correct for that drawing.

Some plans include detail drawings in a different scale, for example, drawings of an unconventional hanging position. These parts should have a definite border and be clearly marked with their own scale.

If you are not sure how your plans will be copied, it is a good idea to include a scale bar in the drawing. This can then be measured by the user to check the scale is correct, and to compensate if it is not.

Load-in date/Focus date

Those preparing the equipment need to know when it has to be ready; those working at the venue need to know when they have to be ready. Any other important dates in the production schedule should also be included.

Software title and version number

For computer generated drawings only, this is particu-

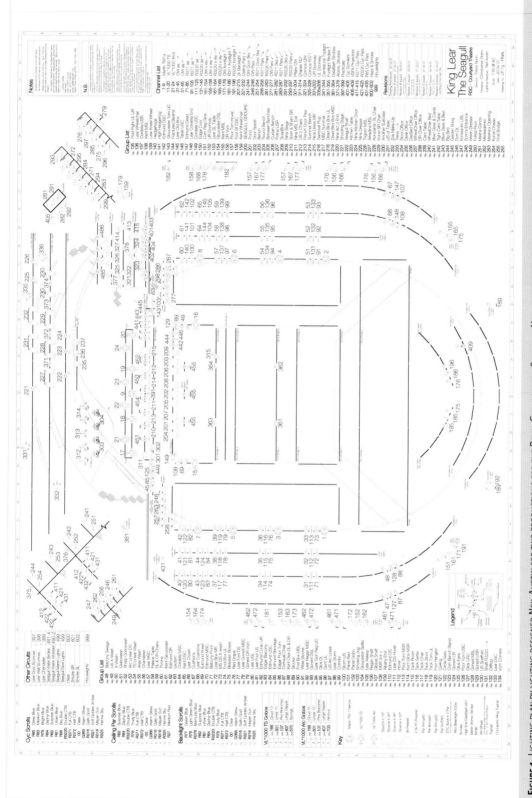

FIGURE 1. LIGHTING PLAN BY LIGHTING DESIGNER NEIL AUSTIN FOR TWO PRODUCTIONS FOR THE ROYAL SHAKESPEARE COMPANY. NEIL HAS INCLUDED ADDITIONAL INFORMATION THAT WILL HELP HIM ACCESS WHAT HE NEEDS WHILE LIGHTING THE SHOW, INCLUDING GROUP LISTS AND SCROLLER COLOURS, AND EXTENSIVE NOTES THAT WILL HELP THE CREW GET THE RIG IN THE RIGHT PLACE AND WORKING. A PLAN FOR A RIG ON THIS SCALE WOULD NORMALLY BE PRINTED AT A MUCH LARGER SIZE. THIS ONE CAN BE PRINTED AT A1 OR EVEN AT A0. IT WAS PRODUCED USING THE VECTOR WORKS DRAFTING PACKAGE. NOTE THE WAY THAT THE VERTICAL LIGHTING POSITIONS (E.G. THE BOOM THAT INCLUDES CHANNELS 251 & 241 ON STAGE RIGHT) IS REPRESENTED — SOLID SHAPES INDICATE WHERE THE FIXTURES ARE RIGGED WHILE THE DETAIL IS SHOWN AS IF THE BOOM WERE LYING DOWN WITH ITS BASE POINTING TOWARDS THE STAGE IN A CONVENIENT ADJACENT SPACE.

larly important when plans are sent electronically. It is possible to open some lighting plan files in programs other than the ones they were created in. This may result in information from the original drawing being lost, however. The same can happen when opening a file in a different version of the program, or when two users have different ways of creating or printing a drawing. By far the safest way to ensure that what is sent by one person is what is printed off by another is to use the portable document format (.pdf) from Adobe Inc. when sending plans electronically. Even though this loses associated information, and leaves the receiver with an uneditable file, do not assume any other method works until tested several times.

The lighting rig

A schematic representation of the luminaires, the structures they are rigged on, and other items of equipment that will be needed to realise the lighting design. Each hanging position needs to have a trim height[2] label as previously discussed, and as we shall shortly see, a name.

The set ground plan

In previous chapters, I wrote that the set ground plan is an important starting point for the lighting designer when they come to deciding where to place the lighting instruments that will make up the lighting rig. Almost all lighting plans are based on a set ground plan. There are very good reasons for this, such as:

- The set most often defines the space of performance and therefore the space that needs performance lighting.

- The set ground plan and section(s) indicate potential playing areas, locations of audience focus, boundaries, and potential obstacles — all of which will need to be considered when deciding where the lighting instruments need to be placed.

- Lighting instruments and equipment cannot occupy the same space as elements of the set. Basing the lighting plan on the set ground plan helps to ensure everything gets its own space.

The set ground plan often does not include the whole of the performance space — for example the auditorium of a theatre. It is likely that the lighting designer will want to place equipment outside the area on the set ground plan so a plan that shows the set and the whole space, with all the potential hanging positions and production infrastructure, will be needed by the lighting designer and the team.

Deciding the level of detail

Exactly what kinds of detail are included will depend on who the drawing is intended for. For example, the hire company is unlikely to need to know the same information as the lighting designer, or the production electrician, or the local authority licensing officer. No doubt each user could work from the same basic plan, highlighting the information they need, and ignoring anything they do not. The better computer drafting programs, however, allow several different drawings to be made from the same information, each one tailored to the needs of specific users.

Take as an example a medium-sized live music tour — say a two or three truck tour playing one night stands in large theatres and sports halls. The lighting plan is likely to have been produced using a computer drafting package. There could be several drawings of the lighting plan, each showing a different level of detail for different users. The rigger, responsible for suspending the trusses that will hold the lighting equipment, will require a plan that gives the weight of each truss, the load exerted on each of the suspension points, and the location of each suspension point relative to a known datum point (often the centre stage point at the front edge of the stage).

---

[2]Trim height is usually the distance from the stage floor to the bar or pipe holding the lanterns etc. For trusses, trim is usually to the lowest 'chord' — or load bearing member — of the truss.

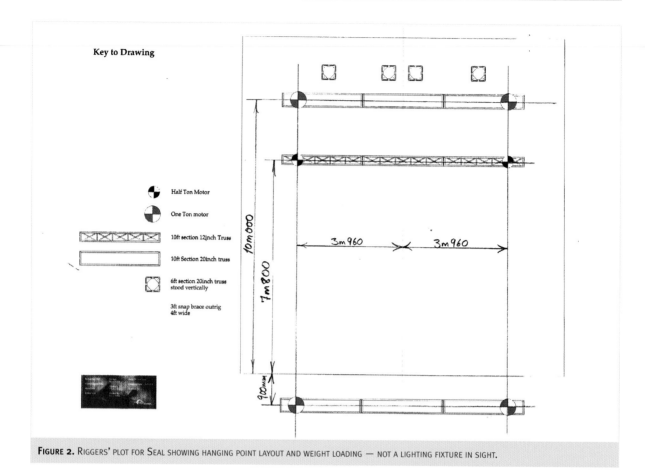

Key to Drawing

Half Ton Motor

One Ton motor

10ft section 12inch Truss

10ft Section 20inch truss

6ft section 20inch truss
stood vertically

3ft snap brace outrig
4ft wide

10m 800

7m 800

900mm

3m 960

3m 960

FIGURE 2. RIGGERS' PLOT FOR SEAL SHOWING HANGING POINT LAYOUT AND WEIGHT LOADING — NOT A LIGHTING FIXTURE IN SIGHT.

The person responsible for planning dimming and distributing power will need a drawing showing all the lighting fixtures, and providing enough detail to allow cable lengths to be calculated. This drawing will show the circuit details and the address of each unit, to enable full preparation of the system, and to help with locating and fixing faults. It should also show the trim height of all bars or trusses, and the intended route for cables connecting the luminaires in the rig to the dimmers and power distribution. This drawing is usually the one with the most information, and can be hard to read at first. Often the information is more useable when presented as a table.

The production manager, responsible for fitting the show into each venue on the tour, will need to know overall dimensions of the production. They will also need other information including the total power draw

equipment schedule, but they will not expect to have to get that from a plan. The production manager will want information in an appropriate form for their use; the dimensions in graphical form and the rest in an easily accessible spreadsheet; total power draw so the tour venues can be informed, and numbers of each category of unit, so a bid for equipment hire can be compiled.

The lighting designer and the lighting programmer require a drawing that shows the schematic location of each unit, any colour filter used, and its channel number, that is the number that when typed into the lighting desk will activate the unit. They need to be able to access each fixture as easily as possible. Though they may quickly become familiar with the layout of the lighting rig, at first they need rapid access to control numbers. Their drawing should have little or no additional information.

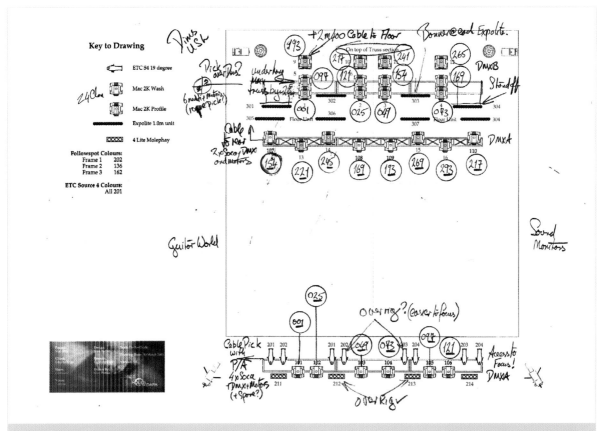

FIGURE 3. LIGHTING PLOT SHOWING SOME OF THE ADDITIONAL INFORMATION NEEDED TO MAKE THE LIGHTING SYSTEM WORK INCLUDING DMX 512 AND CHANNEL NUMBERS, CABLE ROUTES AND DIMMER POSITION.

Hanging positions and unit numbers[3]

It is useful in any lighting rig to have an unambiguous name for each unit in the rig — a unique identifier. The most commonly used system is to name each hanging position, and then number each instrument in that hanging position from an agreed starting point, say the stage left end of overhead bars[4] and trusses, and from the top of vertical bars and trusses (booms)

Conventionally in theatres, the bars used for lighting are numbered in from the proscenium arch towards up stage, i.e. Lx 1 upstage of and nearest to the proscenium. Moving out over the audience (down stage from the proscenium) lighting positions often have names peculiar to the space. Closest to the proscenium is usually called the advance bar. Concert touring systems tend to follow these conventions, with the most down stage cross stage trusses being number 1, and a position over the front of the audience being an advance truss.

Vertical rigging positions at the side of the stage, in theatres called boom positions, are usually numbered using the same conventions, lowest numbers nearest the proscenium. They also take a name from the side of the stage they are on, stage right or stage left. Thus the

---

[3]Also know as fixture numbers.

[4]Known as pipes in North America, and consequently in several drafting programs for lighting.

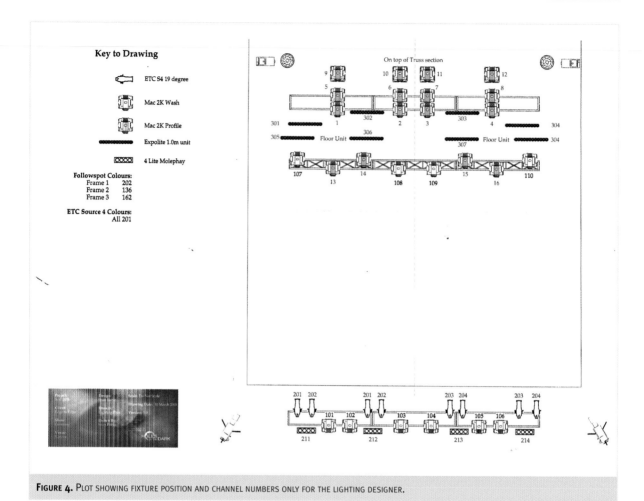

FIGURE 4. PLOT SHOWING FIXTURE POSITION AND CHANNEL NUMBERS ONLY FOR THE LIGHTING DESIGNER.

No1 SL boom is the most down stage on stage left. One frequent exception is the proscenium boom. Many theatres a have built-in position usually attached to the up-stage wall of the proscenium, and called the prosc boom. This may also be called the No1 boom.[5] Also to be found immediately behind some proscenium arches are perches. These can vary from stubby remnants of an ancient installation to purpose-built platforms that include on-stage follow spot positions. In many theatres outside the UK, these positions are very well equipped.

Some theatre front of house positions have already been mentioned, box booms and gallery booms — the high side positions that have been a vital part of many theatre lighting designs over the past 50 years — and circle fronts, good for getting light into the eyes of a performer, but problematic in other ways. Some theatre spaces have many others with names particular to that space.

Some more modern theatres and concert halls have lighting bridges front of house. These are usually numbered starting with the bridge closest to the down stage edge of the performance space and increasing towards the back or the audience space.

Outside proscenium spaces, naming lighting positions becomes less certain. Many studio spaces, capable of being set up in a number of audience/per-

------

[5]Occasionally the prosc boom is on the audience's side of the proscenium, so it is worth checking.

------

former configurations, simply begin numbering from one wall and try to keep as logical as possible. Spaces used in the round sometimes use compass points and levels as position names (top west, mid south east, etc.) or the names of adjacent roads or local landmarks to designate positions. The system matters less than agreement on its use.

Once each hanging position has a name, no matter how arbitrary, each unit hung in that position can have a unit number — again staring at one for each position and ideally using the same convention throughout the space. Each lantern now has a unique identifier — a hanging position and a unit number — and can then be handled more efficiently in a spreadsheet or database, and referred to unambiguously by the whole lighting crew.

Ways to make plans more readable

Returning to the lighting plan, let us look at some established ways of making it work well for each user. It is common practice in the UK for a theatre lighting designer to sit at a production desk in the auditorium to plot the lighting cues. This may be done during scheduled plotting sessions, or more commonly during technical or other rehearsals on stage, presenting the lighting designer with an opportunity to light the bodies of the performers rather than an empty stage space. We will discuss the pros and cons of each approach in later chapters. What we are concerned with now is enabling the lighting designer to access the elements of their rig as efficiently as possible in the middle of a dark auditorium.

The lighting designer will have to be looking at the stage for as much of the time as possible, so needs to be able to read channel numbers from the plan as quickly as possible. The auditorium will generally be dark, and the production desk will often have dim blue work lights to minimise distractions. The most important pieces of information on the plan are usually the location of the luminaires in relation to the stage, and channel or fixture numbers needed for the lighting desk to change the value of attributes and make cues. Next comes the colour, gobo, or other information that will affect the colour or quality of the light reaching the stage. Only when there is a fault discovered and a lantern does not respond to the lighting desk, will it be necessary to know details of multicore and way number, dimmer number, dmx 512 address etc.

Except when the lighting system is of such a small scale that the lighting designer is working without other technical support, patch information is best left off the lighting designer's plan.[6]

So the lighting designer using a lighting plan to help to create cues needs to be able to read channel information for each fixture quickly, under dim blue light, whilst possibly looking at a bright stage and the screen of a computer monitor at the same time! It is clear that in this case the outline and fixture number of each luminaire needs to almost pop out of the plan.

Computer drafting vs. the drawing board

Computer-generated plans rarely look as good as a well executed hand-drawn plan, but they do have one great advantage when they are linked or linkable to a spreadsheet or database program. This means that changes made by computer on the drawing are automatically made on the paperwork too, and vice versa.

Computer-generated plans have a few other advantages too. Chief among these are the ease with which copies can be made, the relatively low cost of using colour, the ability to send computer plans great distances by e-mail, and the ease with which different versions of the same plan can be produced from the same base information, as we shall see. Colour can be especially useful in making a plan more readable. For example, multiple set positions can be drawn in blue or

---

[6]Many lighting designers follow North American practice and use cheat sheets rather than a plan, and we will discuss the pros and cons of this approach too in later chapters.

cyan; the lines will be clear enough under white light, but will disappear under the blue light of the production desk (when they become the same colour as the now blue paper) leaving other information more clearly displayed.

Computer drafting programmes use a concept called layers. Imagine a drawing board with three sheets of transparent drawing material on top of each other. If the venue is drawn on the bottom layer, the set on the next layer up, and the lighting rig on the final layer, alterations can be made to each layer with no danger of affecting the other two. Also, we can remove the set drawing or the

lighting drawing to make the remaining drawings clearer. This is what programs like AutoCAD enable us to do, except that we can have almost as many layers as we like. We can select the combination of layers appropriate to each version of the drawing we require.

There are formal and informal standards for computer drawings, dictating for example line weights and line colour for the representation of various different objects. Layer names are also defined. In the UK, the Association of British Theatre Technicians (ABTT) has issued the following standards relating to the layers on lighting plans:

ABTT layer name	Outline description of layer content
5 LX	Building infrastructure, e.g. control room, installed dimmers etc.
5a Fixed Lx positions	e.g. bars etc used only as lighting positions
5a Temp Lx positions	Temp = temporary
5b Lx outlets	Socket outlets connected to the building's permanent dimmers
5c Lanterns	Or fixtures — and including accessories such as scrollers, barn doors etc.
5d Text	e.g. trim height
5e Attributes	Undefined lantern information
5e Channel att.	Desk channel or fixture number
5e Circuit att.	Dimmer or dmx 512 channel number
5e Colour att.	Gel colour

The lighting designer's lighting plan would be printed with only the layers in red, while the production electrician's version would have all ten layers and quite possibly more.

Using standards makes it easier for a wider circle of users to read and use plans and other drawings.

However, we must not lose sight of the needs of the immediate user of any paperwork produced. The ABTT standards say Lx layers should be cyan but this is clearly impractical in most cases.[7] These and other standards were developed primarily for building drawings rather than for production drawings, and should be used with

---

[7] It should be said that the ABTT standards in this form were set when colour printing was expensive and the colours were chosen primarily for their appearance on the computer screen. Now that colour printing is often cheaper than large format black and white copying (such as dyeline) there is a need to revise the standard and I am sure in time that will happen.

---

this in mind. Here are my personal rules for line weight and colour on lighting plans.

Line weight

Unless there is a really good reason not to, lanterns and their channel or fixture numbers should be printed or drawn in black, with a line weight of at least 0.35mm, and if possible 0.50mm with channel numbers *at least* 4mm high (i.e. a font size of *at least* 12pt). This helps to make the lanterns the subject of the drawing, and the primary attribute used to control them from the lighting desk clear.

Symbol vs. picture

I prefer to use simple outline symbols for lanterns, with the unit number discretely *inside* the symbol, the colour in front of the symbol (in front being the side where the light comes out) and the channel or fixture number behind the symbol, close enough to the lantern to be unambiguous. This last is not always easy with CAD drawings, especially when representing vertical structures. It is often necessary to play around with the way the attributes are laid out in the default symbols of CAD libraries to make the drawing work. This is one area where hand drafting definitely scores over CAD — it is much easier to lay out attributes neatly by hand than with most CAD programs; software writers are, however, addressing this.

Lay-out — real or idealised

There are several ways of representing vertical lighting positions on a lighting plan. Lighting plans for UK theatre usually aim to show the boom or other structure as if it were lying down flat with its base on its correct position. If this takes more space than is available, sections of the boom where there are no units may be missed out (using the standard missing section line type). In any case, the height from stage of all fixtures should be clearly shown using the same units throughout the plan.

Other ways of representing vertical positions include boxed drawings of appropriate parts of the section to each side of the overhead plan drawing, or not including them in the plan at all, and instead using separate section drawings. In either case, it is usually necessary to include an indication of the horizontal position of all vertical lighting positions, and any other vertical features.

Many performance spaces include features that make them difficult to represent on a flat piece of paper of a manageable size. In some large theatres, front of house positions are a long way from the stage. If the plan was made to show this accurately, there would be a big empty space in the middle of the plan, and we would need to use very large paper or use a smaller scale. The solution is usually to truncate the horizontal distance to these positions to avoid a large empty central area of the paper. However, this means that we can no longer use the plan to draw our simple section. If this practice is adopted, it must be made evident to the user. Imagine a visiting lighting designer using a scale rule to measure from down stage to the upper circle front position on a plan with a middle part of the auditorium cut out for convenience. The plan has the height above stage level of this position, so the designer can sketch a section. Lanterns with a beam size that appears to work based on the distance from stage to the position *on the plan* are chosen and installed. When the lighting designer turns up and discovers the mistake it may be too late to change the lanterns for more appropriate units with a narrower beam. There may not even be enough cable to get power to these too wide lanterns. If the visiting production lighting person has not spotted the truncation on the auditorium space on the plan, they may arrive with cable lengths suitable for lighting positions much closer to the stage than they actually are.

Another problem arises when we want to represent two lighting bars that sit above one another. If they were drawn above one another clearly there would be confusion at best or an unreadable mess at worst. Common practice is to take the least important position and draw it in a box with arrows pointing to where it sits in the space.

Anyone who needs to alter the representation of real space on paper should be aware of these kinds of problem. Most users would prefer a plan to a recognised scale, printable on paper we can actually buy

145

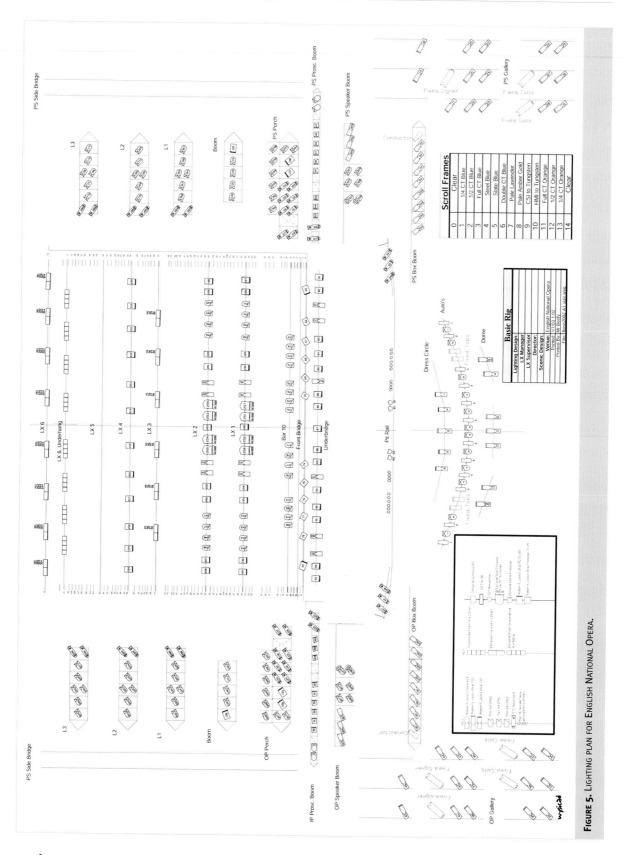

Figure 5. Lighting plan for English National Opera.

which fits into a standard plotter or printer. Sometimes to achieve this, distances are shrunk and positions are altered. All potential users need to be made aware of this.

These issues are much more common in large scale work. Plans for this scale of work are usually at least 1m wide, even when printed at 1:50 scale, and so difficult to reproduce in a book. Figure 5 is a schematic of the lighting system at the London Coliseum. All the side hanging positions are represented lying down as if they had fallen on their backs away from the stage. The front of house positions are shown much closer than they should be, in order not to have a large wasted area of white paper and to try to keep the plot down to a reasonable size. To be able to see enough detail to light or maintain a show, this plot prints at A1.

As has already been suggested, the lighting plan is rarely the only document needed to realise a lighting rig; here are some others.

Instrument schedule/equipment list

Instrument schedule and equipment list are the North American and UK version of more or less the same thing — a list of everything the production will use to realise the lighting design, hopefully arranged logically. The list may be presented to the lighting designer, giving them the total equipment they have to work with, or it may come from the lighting designer, as a request to hire for the production, or it may be a combination of both. In the last situation, it will often be important to be clear which equipment is hired and which is from the venue, to calculate costs and maintain an inventory for both venue and hire company. The sort function of computer spreadsheet programs is useful here. Below is an example of an equipment list as it might be laid out by a production electrician or chief LX going through a plan for the first time to put together a shopping list for a production.

Equipment list 1
First response to the Lx plan

Unit type	Hanging position	Unit no	Lamp type	Watts	Colour	Frame size
A clear description of the luminaire, including beam angle required and manufacture if specified by the LD	*Helps with identifying each fixture in the rig, and to decide what additional equipment may be needed to rig the unit; e.g. hook clamp, boom arm etc*	*No 1 is SL end of horizontal bars/trusses, and the top of vertical booms*	*Many modern fixtures come with several lamp options so it is important to note this. Also the watts column can be added up later to find out how much power might be required*		*These columns will give an experienced prod Lx a feel for how much colour needs to be ordered* *Later, information from these two columns will help the prod Lx to assemble an accurate colour call (see p. 155)*	
ETC Source 4 profile 36° c/w gobo holder	**Lx 1**	**1**	**Standard life HPL**	**575 Watts**	**L202**	**170mm²**
Harmony Fresnel & barn door	**Lx 1**	**2**	**T11**	**1000 Watts**	**#53**	**180mm²**

Patching the rig

Once the total number and type of luminaires required is known, the next task will help define the type and quantity of other equipment required to realise the lighting rig, including cables, dimmers, and power distribution. This is the process of patching the rig. The allocation of a unit or units to each dimmer or circuit breaker is know as hard patching, while the allocation of control channel numbers[8] to each dimmer or group of dimmers is called the soft patch. Most lighting systems use multicore cables — large cables carrying multiple circuits. Power or dimming for each unit is allocated to a particular way on a particular multicore. This means we have at least five numbers associated with providing power and control to each unit:

- ■ **Unit number** and hanging position provide a unique identifier for each unit.

- ■ **Hard patch** the dimmer or circuit breaker allocated to each unit.

- ■ **Soft patch** the control channel allocated to each unit, the number which when typed into the desk, will enable control of the unit.

- ■ **Multicore** the large cable feeding several units, usually all in close proximity to each other.

- ■ **Multicore way** the plug and socket number within the larger multicore

It is easy to become confused about which of these numbers we are talking about in relation to which unit, at any one time. Add to this potential confusion the possibility that allocations may need to change, due to equipment failure, errors in plugging, or the lighting designer changing their mind, and it becomes clear that good record keeping is the only way a large lighting system can be kept working. Below is an example of a lay out for an equipment list to show patch information.

So far we have looked at lists or tables with just a few column headings. These tables present us with the information we need to perform particular tasks. The

Equipment list 2
A simple patch sheet

Hanging position	Unit no	Unit type	Multicore/way	Dimmer/breaker no	dmx 512 address	Desk channel no
A unique identifier for every unit in the lighting rig			*AKA plugging information; which socket in which cable spider or stage box is each unit plugged to*	*Incandescent units need dimmers, moving lights need hard power. One unit per breaker is the ideal — more secure protection and easier to reset rogue moving lights*	*The digital address used by the lighting control system to access each dimmer or moving light[9]*	*The number used to make the unit respond from the desk*
Lx1	1	S4 pro 36°	Lx1A / 1	Rack 1 dim 27	1/027	101
Lx1	2	Harmony F	Lx1A / 2	Rack 3 dim 14	1/114	31

[8]Also known as handle number in some circles; this practice is taken from manual preset desks where each control channel had its own slider or handle.

[9]Larger systems will have multiple universes of dmx 512, or even Ethernet addresses, meaning another set of numbers to record for each unit.

Example 3
Table showing some equipment on Lx bar 1

Unit type	Hanging position	Unit no	Suspension accessory?	Other accessory?	Lamp type	Watts	Weight (kg)	Colour	Frame size (mm)	Gobo inc. size	Multi/way	Dimmer/breaker no	dmx 512 address	No channels req.	Desk ch no (fixture number)
ETC Source 4 36 degree profile	Lx 1	1	Hook clamp / Rated safety bond	Non	HPL/575	575W	7.5	L202	170	B size DHA 238-221	Lx1 A/1	Dim 27	1/27	1	101
Strand Harmony F	Lx 1	2	Hook clamp / Rated safety bond	B/D	T11	1kW	6.1 + B/D	SG53	180		Lx1A/2	Dim 114	1/114	1	31
Strand Harmony F	Lx 1	3	Hook clamp / Rated safety bond	non	T11	1kW	6.1 + B/D	Scroller	180		Lx1A/3	Dim 115	1/115	1	41
Scroller for Strand Harmony F	Lx1	3a	180mm back plate / Rated safety bond	B/D	NA	NA	2.2	Stage Scroll	180		NA	NA	2/301	2	41/colour
Scroller Power Supply	Lx1	4	Hook clamp / Rated safety bond		NA	50W	3	NA			Lx1M/6	Breaker 12	NA	0	NA
ETC Source 4 Junior Zoom	Lx1	5	Hook clamp / Rated safety bond	non	HPL/750	750W	7.6	SG 375	190	non	Lx1A/4	Dim 28	1/28	1	51
PAR 64 Standard	Lx1	6	Hook clamp / Rated safety bond	Top Hat	CP62	1kW	3.3	L180	255		Lx1A/5	Dim 116	1/116	1	71
Martin MAC500	Lx1	7	2 clamps / 50kg safety bond	Non	MSR575	~600W	33	Standard	NA	Custom 1 see sheet	Lx1M/1	Breaker 01	2/001	16	1

first might be used to hire equipment for a production, while the second might be used to ensure each unit in the rig is correctly plugged up.

The column headings for a full equipment list might look something like those shown in example 3 on p.149.

This table shows information for just six luminaires and one scroller, perhaps less than a quarter of the equipment on just one lighting bar for a medium-sized theatre show. The column headings should not be seen as definitive, but as an example of what might be required. There are many circumstances where more information is needed.

Notes on Example 3

Suspension accessory?
What extra equipment is needed to get the unit to stay where the lighting designer wants it? If the unit is a standard luminaire designed for theatre use, and the hanging position is a horizontal 48mm or 50mm diameter bar or pipe, then this will be a clamp of some kind. If the hanging position is a vertical boom, the luminaire will need a boom arm or equivalent piece of hardware. If the lantern is to be mounted on the floor, a floor stand or floor plate will normally be required.

Industry standard practice in the UK, North America and elsewhere, requires all suspended fixtures and their accessories to have a secondary means of suspension that will prevent further damage or injury should the main suspension equipment fail. This secondary suspension is usually a rated safety bond, that is a bonded length of steel wire rope with a securable clip and a safe working load limit stamped or otherwise attached to it. Safety chains used to be common, but are no longer recommended unless they come with an authorised safe working load limit. In the countries of the EU it is a legal obligation to use only secondary suspension that is clearly marked to be rated for the full weight of the unit, and for the clip to be used according to the maker's instructions. Notice that the scroller also has a safety bond specified for it. This is normal practice.

Other accessory?
B/D stands for the barn doors used to shape the beam of a Fresnel or PC unit. It too should come with a safety bond. A top hat looks very much as the name suggests, except there is no top to it! Top hats are used to reduce flare on lanterns which are either in view of the audience or close to elements of the set or the building. Flare is the unwanted light at the edge of the beam of any unit with a soft edge, including PARs, Fresnels and even profiles when they are not hard focused. Top hats are also used to shield the audience from direct sight of a light source, which might otherwise cause distraction.

FIGURE 6. FROM THE LEFT, A VARI*LITE VL5 ™ WITH A TOP HAT TO REDUCE FLARE ON ADJACENT SURFACES, A FRESNEL WITH A COLOUR SCROLLER AND BARN DOORS, AND A PROFILE LANTERN WITH AN ANIMATION WHEEL. ALL THE LANTERNS AND THE ACCESSORIES HAVE SECONDARY SAFETY FIXINGS, AS WELL AS THEIR PRIMARY SUPPORT.

Watts

If the table is to be used to work out total electrical loading, the entries in this column need to be consistent. They should be entered either as a number of watts *or* kilowatts (kW). If this is not done, you or your software will not be able to accurately sum the column. The column may be divided into sub columns, one for each individual supply or phase.

Colour

We have used some common conventions here. L stands for the Lee range of gel, SG for Rosco's Super Gel range. Other conventions include # for Super-Gel, and HT for Lee's High Temperature range, and GAM for the Great American Market range.

The scroller on unit 3 has a number of colours on a roll. Any colour on the roll can be remotely positioned to be in the beam of the lantern to which the scroller is attached. In this case, the exact colours used in each frame of the scroll and their order on the roll are specified on a separate list. The implication of the label stage scroll is that there is more than one set of colours. Perhaps there is one set for lanterns over stage and another for those used front of house.

The MAC 500 is a hard edged moving light with an internal colour wheel rather than continuously fading colour (sometimes fading colour is referred to as CYM or CMY colour, see footnote on p. 131). It is possible to have special colours added to the colour wheels and to change the gobos of some moving lights. This production has a standard colour wheel.

Frame size

This refers to the size of the colour frame, and therefore the size of colour that needs to be cut. It is normal to cut all the colour for the rig to size as part of the preparation process, to save valuable time in the performance space. The table specifying every cut of colour for a production is called the 'colour call'.

Gobo

Gobos come in a range of sizes, and it is as well to be sure which size is required for each unit in the rig. Some lanterns (for example ETC Source 4 profiles) have two gobo slots each of which is a different size, and gobo holders of different sizes, too.

Our Mac 500 has a custom selection of gobos, that is a different set from those supplied by the manufacturer. Like the colours on the scrolls, these too will be documented elsewhere.

Multi/Way

Many lighting systems use multicore to simplify plugging the lanterns in and powering them up. Labelling each multicore and recording which lantern is plugged into which way makes it possible to get the system working quickly, and to find and repair faults. It can be helpful to use multicore labels that mean something. In the example, the 5 multicore cables feeding the No1 lighting bar are labelled Lx1A to Lx1D connecting dimmers to conventional lanterns, and Lx1M connecting the moving lights to circuit breakers. The multicore feeding the second lighting bar would be named with the prefixed Lx2, those on the third Lx3 and so on. Multicore feeding the stage right booms might be prefixed SRB1, SRB2, etc, where the number indicates which boom the cable is connected to. Current practice in London's West End is to use short labels with at most two digits or letters. For example, the five multicore cables feeding Lx1 might be labelled 11, 12, 13, 14, M1. Lx2's cables would be marked up 21, 22, 23, 24 and M2. Lx3's would be 31, 32, 33 etc. The point is there needs to be an agreed system, and of course, both ends of each cable need the same label!

FIGURE 7. A SHORT SOCAPEX MULTICORE, ABLE TO CARRY SIX INDIVIDUAL CIRCUITS EACH UP TO 10 AMPS.

Socapex multicore protocols

What is Socapex?

It is a trade name for the 19 pole round multicore connector used for production lighting in Europe and North America. It is usually connected to 18 core cable, three cores per circuit, one for live, one for neutral and one for ground, making six complete circuits per multicore.

Although the connector is robust, it should always be treated with some care. If a connector or cable is damaged during the build period of a production, it can cause great inconvenience, and may lead to increased risk of electric shock. Avoid connecting or disconnecting Socapex plugs and sockets live — they are NOT designed for this and repeatedly doing it will damage the pins, which may then cause the connector to no longer work or to work badly, which in turn may lead to equipment failure, or cause fire due to the damaged pins overheating.

Socapex and three phase electricity

Many Socapex connectors used in the performance lighting industry are not constructed to carry more than 250V. In Europe (including the UK) when two or more phases of electricity are present, potentials of 380V or 415V exist. For this reason and others, **multiple phases should not be allowed down a single multicore.**

Plugging moving lights

Connecting the power supply for the motors and electronics of a moving light to a dimmer can damage the moving light and the dimmer. It is normal practice to have separate multicore for moving light power and for dimmers. This reduces the risk of damaging either. However, many modern dimmers can be set up to provide hard power (this is a commonly used term for circuits set up to power moving lights). Clearly to make safe use of this new feature will require good planning and paperwork, and accurate plugging.

One further word of warning — some PA hire shops also use Socapex connectors! Not every Socapex is a lighting cable, some come from audio amplifiers and feed speakers.

Dimmer and dmx 512 address

To make the lighting system work, it is necessary to know which dimmer is controlling which lantern or lanterns in order to patch those lanterns to a desk channel, to enable optimum use to be made of the available dimmers, and to enable the crew to quickly switch off the power to any unit that presents a problem. If a unit has been damaged or is in danger of burning a drape the surest way will be to remove the fuse or trip the breaker of the dimmer controlling it.

In the dmx 512 column, the number in front of the slash indicates the universe of dmx 512 and the number after the slash is the address in that universe. For any unit that uses more than one channel, the address is the first channel used by that unit, also know as the 'start address'.[10]

---

[10]dmx 512 may soon be superseded by other control protocols, including RDM (remote device management) and Ethernet based systems. Even if this does happen, the basic principals will remain the same — a unit will require an address to enable the control system to control it.

Many dimmer systems allow the user to address each individual dimmer with a different dmx 512 address. In many complex systems with multiple dimmer locations this is a very useful feature, however it introduces yet another number into the necessary description of each lantern and you might ask just how necessary this extra number is.

It is usual to separate the power information (hard patch) from the control information (soft patch).[11] In a well-organised production build, all the patch information can be worked out and made available before the fit-up. This should mean that all the electrical and software connections for each unit are made correctly first time, and the lighting system is ready for the lighting designer to use in the shortest possible time, saving valuable stage time for more interesting work of actually lighting the production.

Channel number and fixture number

Conventional lanterns with no remotely controlled accessories require a single dmx 512 channel for their control. This can be soft patched to a single desk channel number. A lantern with a scroller will require two separate dmx 512 control channels, one for the intensity of the lantern, and one for the position of the scroller — that is the colour. A moving light will require many channels of control. In example 3, the MAC 500 requires 16 dmx 512 channels, but does that mean 16 desk channels? Well, it might do, but it is much easier for most users to think in terms of one luminaire, one number at the desk, and any good moving light desk will allow the user to do this. To avoid too much ambiguity, once we are dealing with one desk number controlling a luminaire with more than one property or attribute we use the term fixture.[12]

In example 3, channel 41, or more correctly fixture 41, is the Harmony Fresnel with a scroller, so entering 41 at the lighting desk will allow us to control it. Ideally, once 41 has been selected at the lighting desk, there should be one controller for intensity and another for colour available to the user without further fixture selection being necessary. The lighting desk should handle control of the dimmer (dim 115 at dmx 512 address 1/115) and control of the colour (at dmx 512 address 2/301) as if both were part of the same entity — a single fixture with two attributes; intensity and colour.

The same goes for our MAC 500 (desk channel 1) but even more so. Now when channel 1 is entered, the user of the lighting desk should be able to access all the functions of the luminaire, intensity, pan and tilt (focus), colour, beam, and special functions, without any need to know which function is controlled by which dmx 512 address or addresses: one luminaire — one desk fixture number (or name[13]). This time the fixture has many attributes and it will usually be necessary to press other buttons to access all of these. The important thing is that the lighting desk should behave as if all these different attributes are part of a single fixture. So when a desk user types in fixture 1 they should be presented with a set of controllers for each property of that MAC 500 luminaire. The lighting desk should be able to display the state of each property as a part of the information for fixture 1.

The mapping of dmx 512 control channels to fixture attributes — hopefully in a user friendly way — is accomplished by the fixture personality file in the desk. Each fixture type needs its own personality file. How well that personality file is written, by the desk's soft-

---

[11]As we said earlier hard patch refers to the physical electrical connections, and soft patch and refers to the connections made in the control software, usually in the lighting desk, but sometimes elsewhere.

[12]Attributes are not the same as control channels. For example, most moving lights use two control channels for the single attribute pan and another two for the attribute tilt. This is done to enable better resolution. On the other hand some moving lights control more than one attribute with a single control channel. An attribute is what appears in the display of the moving light desk — colour wheel position or gobo rotation speed — while the control channel is one of the 8-bit words used to communicate from the desk to the luminaire or fixture.

[13]Some moving light desks are moving away from numbers as a way to access luminaires. Instead user definable names enable the programmer to select units in a variety of different ways.

ware engineers or by the user, will determine how well the fixture responds to the desk.

In lighting systems using dmx 512, which only allows information to travel in one direction from desk to fixtures, the fixture personality resides in the desk. It is considered the responsibility of the desk manufacturer to make it work. In the near future, systems that allow communication back from any fixture to any suitable lighting desk, may enable the lanterns themselves to tell the desk how they need to be controlled.[14]

Pairing units

Pairing is the term for connecting two or more lighting units to the same dimmer. When reliable electronic dimming was first used in theatres it was expensive. The tendency was to use large capacity dimmers to control two, three or even more units all plugged together, and so all going up and down in intensity at the same time. This presented the lighting designer with a choice — use a few units and have control over each one individually or use many units but lose individual control — large parts of the stage therefore going dark or becoming light at the same time. Dimmers are no longer so expensive, and most production lighting staff will attempt to give each unit its own dimmer, for electrical as well as aesthetic reasons. There are limits though, and it is frequently necessary to pair units together, for example cyclorama units that are all in the same colour on the same cyc are frequently paired. Other pairings may be made to cut down on the numbers of multicore cables required to feed a particular lighting bar, truss or structure, especially if that structure moves during the show.

Pairing fixtures together can free up dimmers or cable ways for other uses, including more fixtures, but it can also limit the selectivity possible with the lighting design, and can result in small failures having a larger impact on the lighting. (When the lamp in a fixture fails, it is quite usual for the protective device at the dimmer — the fuse or trip — to fail also. If that dimmer controls more than one fixture, then more than one light goes out on stage.) Clearly decisions on pairing lanterns need to be made with a technical and an aesthetic perspective.

Pairing can also present problems on lighting plans and in paperwork. Hand-drawn plans traditionally represent pairing by linking units with lines. This form of notation, where it is still used, usually denotes that the units should be paired on the bar, using some form of two into one connector, such as a Grelco, Snapper, raygun, or two-fer.[15]

In the past, some CAD and lighting paperwork programs have made it difficult to show pairing, but things are getting better. In any case, there are lots of ways to annotate both plans and paperwork, by hand or by computer, to make things clear, including using coloured highlighter pens to draw attention to paired units, drawing in pairing lines, either by hand or on a layer of the computer drawing, or adding notes to the plan, again either by hand or on a layer of the drawing.

When deciding which units can be paired and how, there are also electrical considerations. These include ensuring that the combined load of the paired units does not exceed the design load of either the dimmer or any of the circuit cables and connectors. As a designer, if you are in any doubt about these issues you will need to consult with a professional chief Lx or an experienced production lighting practitioner.

---

[14]Two-way communication between lighting desk and lighting fixture is on the horizon. RDM or remote device management uses the same cables as dmx 512. ACN or advanced control network uses Ethernet protocols and cables. Both are nearing release at the time of writing.

[15]All names for electrical kit that have one plug and two (or more) socket outlets on the same circuit. Grelco and Snapper are both trade names for UK 15amp style devices, ray-gun is slang for a particular type of 16amp splitter, and two-fer is US slang for anything that gets you two for one. Some of these devices have their own internal overload protection or trip. This can be helpful at times, but more often it leads to frustration, especially when re-setting the trip requires climbing a ladder.

Lighting spreadsheets

Some practitioners hardly use the lighting plan, preferring spreadsheets on paper or in electronic form. Even those who do make full use of the lighting plan will still be producing some information as spreadsheets. Electronic spreadsheets on a computer, whether generated by a drafting program or compiled independently in Excel for example, allow rapid access to data from a number of different entry points. Electronic data can be sorted by many different criteria, and in the right package, many different useful documents can be produced. These will include:

Colour call

This is the list showing the required gel colours and the sizes they need to be cut to.

Including the hanging position means the cut colour can easily be distributed to each area in which it is required. If the information is in a computer spreadsheet, the data can be re-arranged. It might be sorted by colour to find out how many sheets of each type are needed, or by lantern size so that all the cuts of a particular size can be made at one time. A similar document can be produced for gobos.

Hanging position	Gel colour	Cut size	Number required
FoH balcony left	L201	8' × 8'	4
	#04	180 × 180mm	8
	L200	10' × 10'	4
FoH balcony right	L202	8' × 8'	4
	#03	180 × 180mm	6
	L200	10' × 10'	4

Shop order

When a production needs to hire some or all of the lighting equipment, a shop order must be assembled. The order for luminaires will be one part of this, but there will be other parts, including the cable call, the accessories list, and the sales order (which will include everything from tape and string to colour, gobo holders and gobos). The table in example 1 in this chapter is one possible layout for a lantern order, but it could be time-consuming to check through this layout as the equipment is loaded onto a truck. A good spreadsheet package can produce a much more useable layout like the one shown below.

Lantern type	Hanging?	No	Present?
ETC Source 4 36 degree	Hook clamp	20	
ETC Source 4 36 degree	Floor mount	12	
ETC Source 4 26 degree	Boom arm	24	
PAR 64 CP61	Hook clamp	36	
PAR 64 CP62	Hook clamp	36	

The Present? column is there to have a tick entered once the successful count has been made. There will be a need to produce a similar check list for accessories, including colour frames.

Patch sheets

Using a computer spreadsheet can make it easy to view the patch in a variety of different ways. The data can be searched to find the answer to any number of questions concerning individual control channels, fixtures, or dimmers, or whole areas of the lighting system. For example, the data can reveal which dimmer should be connected to a particular fixture, what should be the start address a particular fixture, the next available dmx 512 address or the total electrical load of any particular part of the system. Once patch sheets are printed out, they can be carried round more easily, but will be less easy to search, and the data they contain may quickly become out of date. Many lighting engineers no longer use paper patch sheets, preferring instead to use an electronic version on a PDA or similar device. Increasingly this hand-held device can be networked (for example, using WiFi or Bluetooth) to access up-to-date information from either the CAD or spreadsheet package used by the production, or directly from the lighting desk.

Even with the most integrated drawing and data packages, some documents will need to be derived from a careful study of the plan, and a good knowledge of the venue, for example the cable call.

Cable call

This is the list of multicore and other electrical cable required to realise the lighting rig. Working out the amount of cable required for any particular individual element of the rig is relatively easy — just measure off on the lighting plan the length between each unit and the multicore it will plug to using a scale rule. However, working out the required length of multicore to feed each element usually requires a detailed knowledge of the show and the venue. Where are the dimmers to be placed? What route will the multicore and other cables take? What might be in the way — set elements, band equipment, quick change rooms? Will the element move in the show? Will it need to move for maintenance? The

master electrician will need to answer all these questions and more before they can determine cable lengths. Once all this is known however, using a table similar to the one shown here is a quick way of totalling up how much cable is required.

Most production situations are best served by a combination of plans and spreadsheets. Large complex productions require good data management and this is usually best accomplished with the help of computer programs such as LightWrite or WYSIWYG. Smaller productions may not be able to justify the expense of computer programs and PDAs. However, data still needs to be retrievable, for reproducing the event and for fault finding if for no other reason, and therefore it needs to be recorded somewhere. The preference of the individuals involved, and the particulars of the production will usually dictate what data is recorded where and how.

The show bible

All the documents we have talked about so far, with others, need to be gathered together and kept current, to help to get the lighting system working and to keep it working. This collection of essential paperwork is frequently referred to as the electrics bible for the show. It might be a large file containing sheets of paper or it may be a computer file or it may be both. Whatever the format, the electrics bible needs to be accessible to lighting designer, chief and crew alike, and needs to be reliably up-to-date. If it is kept on paper, documents need to be dated, and a system agreed upon to replace out-of-date documents with current ones every time a change is made. If the electrics bible is a collection of computer files, these too will need to be managed, perhaps using version numbers or timed update stamps.[16] Users will need to make suitable provision to back-up the files too, since it is all too easy to accidentally change or corrupt vital information on a computer, or spill coffee on a paper file.

---

[16] I strongly recommend putting date last printed in the document header or as a footer wherever possible.

	20m multi	15m multi	Stage box[17]	Short TRS[18]	Medium TRS	20m dmx 512	Short dmx 512
Advance bar	3	0	3	9	0	1	5
Lx 1	2	3	5	12	4	1	8
Lx 2	1	2	3	8	2	0	0
Lx 3	2	1	3	9	6	0	0
Booms	0	2	2	10	0	0	0
Totals	8	8	16	48	12	2	13
Order[19]	10	10	18	60	20	4	20

Well-designed software packages have the advantage of linking the various formats of document, and some can even link directly to a lighting control system, feeding, for example, changes in the patch directly into other spreadsheets and the plan. Ethernet, especially wireless Ethernet, offers some potentially powerful solutions here, keeping records up-to-date and safely backed up, allowing communication between lighting desk, handheld PDAs, laptop computers, and perhaps even dimmers and moving lights. This will radically alter the way we think about the electrics bible in the near future.

However the electrics bible is created and kept current, it provides all the information needed to make, maintain and if necessary re-make the lighting for the show. As such it becomes an integral part of the lighting design, and therefore part of the intellectual property of the lighting designer. **It is very important to get this part of the process right.** For many lighting designers, producing the production paperwork is the boring bit best left to someone else while we get on with design. This approach only works if someone competent and responsible is making that electrics bible. On most medium- to large-scale shows, and for many professional lighting designers, this is exactly what does happen. If you are (or want to be) a lighting designer it is worth remembering two things:

■ Giving a venue poor paperwork for your future lighting rig is much more likely to result in your disappointment when you arrive to make cues than giving them a clear and complete package of lighting paperwork.

■ That boring paperwork forms part of your lighting design, indeed if it is prepared in a thorough and professional way, the lighting design should be able to be reproduced without further reference to the

---

[17]A standard stage box has six circuit outlets (electrical sockets) and plugs into a multicore cable. Mounted on the lighting bar, it is used to plug in the lanterns. Other ways to get individual circuits from a multicore cable include fan outs or spiders where each circuit has a short cable linking the multicore connector and the socket outlet.

[18]TRS stands for toughened rubber sheath, and designates the cable type used most commonly for individual circuit cables in production lighting in the UK and most of Europe.

[19]The order includes spares. The proportion of spares ordered will vary, for example, with the distance between venue and hire company (if the company is next door you need fewer spares than if it is several hours drive away!), the time available to install the rig, and how close to a finished product the lighting designer feels the design is at the point when an order has to be placed.

lighting designer.[20] As such it is part of what you are paid to produce, and a proportion of your fee may be withheld if you don't produce it. Similarly, if you are not paid in full, you may be entitled to withhold the paperwork but be careful and take professional advice first.

As a lighting designer, taking an interest in the paperwork helps to ensure you get the system you asked for and that it will work, whilst at the same time safeguarding your intellectual property rights, and therefore your living.

If you have the time to design your lighting on site as the show is developing, and you have someone willing and able to follow on recording everything so that anything that breaks can be fixed quickly — great. Some fine site-specific work happens just like this. If you don't need to worry that your hard work is being used by someone who is not paying you for it, please don't encourage this practice because the rest of us need those fees! Otherwise protect your intellectual property and take an interest in the paperwork and make sure it does what you and the show need it to do.

---

[20]In reality this is rarely done, not least because productions evolve and the other members of the creative will usually want the lighting designer around to evolve the lighting too.

8

working in the performance space — I

In this chapter we will look at the process of getting the lighting rig ready to start lighting. Chapter 9 goes on to look at actually making lighting cues — the real business of lighting design.

In almost all productions the aim is to allow as much time as possible for the creation of the performance on stage, and that of course includes creating lighting cues. Preparation is key to all this, and time spent preparing before the fit up should release more time for useful creative work in the venue, for everybody including the lighting department.

The fit up

Here are two very different situations in which a lighting designer might find themselves:

■ Working in a fully blackout-able space with hanging positions and suspension points for additional hanging positions, and little else. The expectation might well be that the lighting designer and their team will specify not only all the performance lighting equipment, but also the house lighting and secondary/emergency lighting, suspension kit including pipes, trusses, rigging hardware and motors, all the dimmers and cables, and the power distribution equipment, not only for the performance lighting system but perhaps for dressing rooms, workshops, offices, catering and toilets. They might even be responsible for providing mobile electricity generators for the power.

■ Working in a fully equipped repertory theatre with a fixed rig of lighting equipment that cannot be re-focused, re-coloured or re-patched, with perhaps one assistant from the house who can program cues into the lighting console.

Both may well appear daunting for different reasons, and neither should not be taken on lightly. The first because of the range of knowledge and experience required to plan and then realise such a scenario, not least because it will be an extensive project and require person management skills. How much time and mental space will this leave the lighting designer to make a creative response to the piece and design some performance lighting? The second because in this kind of situation the work is often more about managing the expectations of other members of the creative team, and of yourself, than creative lighting design.

However, between these two extremes lie most of the situations encountered by a designer of performance lighting. For a well-organised production, staged in a working theatre, we can hope for good production infrastructure including a range of suitable hanging positions, dimmers and communication systems. Some or all of any equipment supplied by the venue will be able to be adjusted to suit the current production, and some budget will be available to augment the resources of the venue as necessary. Most importantly, there will be skilled and knowledgeable staff to assist in realising the dreams of the lighting designer and the other members of the creative team, and part of their job will be to fit up the space. This term covers the installation of set, lighting and sound rigs, and much more in some situations. So, in this chapter we will take a look at the role of the lighting designer during this phase of the production process.

Scale determines how much you do

There is probably no such thing as the average fit-up. Each one, in each different space, presents a different set of problems to be solved (or challenges to be addressed, depending on your preferred wording.) The fit up of a one night stand, typical of many live music touring shows and other genre of performance, will be a very different thing to the extended build/rehearsal/preview process of a West End, Broadway or Casino show. Likewise, the numbers of staff and the skills required to fit up a rig of 40 lanterns in a club or fringe theatre will be quite different to that for 400 in a mid-scale touring venue, or 4000 for an open air spectacular such as an Olympic opening or closing ceremony. In a club or fringe venue, there is normally an expectation that the lighting designer will get their hands dirty and at least assist if not lead the rigging and plugging of the lighting equipment. On a very large show, even focusing and some cue making may well be delegated by the lighting designer to assistants and associates. The sheer number of lights and scale of the site would make it impossible for a single lighting designer to do it all.

In most production situations, the lighting designer will normally lead the focus. Just how much involvement they have in getting the lighting rig to a state where it can be focused will vary. Generally, the more conventional the lighting rig is, for whatever performance genre, the less need for the lighting designer to lead actions during the fit-up. In most genres of performance lighting, methods of documenting conventional lighting rigs have evolved that are widely understood by the professional crew who build the shows. In such situations, the plans and paperwork are sufficiently unambiguous to allow skilled production lighting workers to mount all the lighting equipment and to make it ready to focus without much further input from the lighting designer.

In situations where the lighting design requires unusual hanging positions, unconventional equipment or conventional equipment used in unconventional ways, the lighting designer (or a trusted associate) will need to be on site during the fit-up to ensure things go according to plan. An on site presence will also be useful when other production elements, such as set or sound equipment, need to be rigged where lights appear on the plan. Since the placement of lighting fixtures will often impact on what can or cannot be achieved by the lighting design, the involvement of the lighting designer in negotiating a compromise is usually considered a good idea.

All of this can present the lighting designer with difficult choices. At the time when the fit-up is happening, the final off site rehearsals will usually be happening too. For theatre shows of all kinds, this is often the time when decisions about where, when and how areas of the stage will be used are made, about the dynamics and the emotion of the piece. The conscientious lighting designer will wish to be at least aware of these decisions, and preferably be involved in making them. If rehearsals are not happening close to the production venue, the lighting designer will often have to choose where to spend their time — in the venue or at rehearsals. The choice will often be influenced by the amount of time available to put right things that, during the fit-up, have not worked out as planned. Sometimes there is so little time available to fix problems that anything not fully accomplished by the focus session will not happen!

Even in the most ordinary and well-organised of fit-ups, the lighting designer will often visit to ensure that all is going according to plan and to attend to any small changes or miscommunications in person. This is good practice and should be followed when ever possible. However, in most production situations there will be a production electrician, chief, or other person in charge of the lighting fit-up. It is important that, on visits, the lighting designer respects this and communicates directly with that person, rather than bypass them and give new orders to the crew. The chief will often know more about the needs of the wider production and the venue at that point than the lighting designer does, and if the lighting designer wants to have the continuing support of the chief through the rest of the production period, it is a good idea to respect that.

As already noted, in much small-scale work the lighting designer will be expected to lead the lighting fit-up. The temptation here is to skimp on planning because it can be fixed on site. I would strongly advise against this tendency. Small-scale venues often have limited equipment and it frequently becomes important to make the best use of every working piece of kit the lighting department can lay their hands on. Finding out that the two cables you now desperately need were used to feed lanterns that it turns out are behind a piece of set and so won't work, can be frustrating. Good planning and preparation can usually prevent this.

Lighting designers can gain valuable experience working on production lighting and lighting design in small venues — often they will need to do both at the same time. It is important to remember, however, that as the scale of productions you work on gets bigger, so the complexity of both these roles increases. At some point it will become necessary for the person used to being both lighting designer and chief to decide which single role they are best suited for; deciding which lights should be where, and when they should be switched on, or managing how to get those lights there safely and on time, and with all the necessary cables feeding them. Ideally, lighting designer and chief should have a good understanding of the other's job, and a respect for the challenges each needs to overcome. Many lighting designers have a strong professional bond with one or two chiefs or master electricians or production electricians, and will by choice only work with these people. Other lighting designers have the ability to bond quickly with any competent performance lighting crew and can communicate almost instantly on an appropriate level with each new chief in each new venue. This is a valuable skill; except at the smallest scale no lighting designer creates their work without the help of other lighting people.

Preparation is the key to success

There are large variations in expectations and working environment over the range of genre and scale of pro-

duction encountered by the professional performance lighting practitioner. However, some things remain constant and the foremost of these is the need to plan in order to achieve the best results. We have already spent several chapters looking at the type and range of paperwork required to prepare and mount a performance lighting rig. The lighting team which has taken this route will have a lighting plan and (at least one) section, extensive equipment lists detailing exactly what equipment will be mounted where, what accessories, etc, it will have, what it will be plugged into and how it will be controlled. The shop order will have been placed with the venue or with a lighting hire company, so too the sales order, which will include colour (hopefully cut to size and separated into packets for each hanging position or area) gobos, Lx tape and gaffer tape, string and Black Wrap™. Black Wrap is black aluminium foil — thicker than the stuff you might use when cooking but still easily flexible — that is one of the best cure-all to have up your sleeve during a fit-up and focus. It is heat resistant enough to use on all but the hottest lanterns, and it stops light going where you don't want it to go. It can be used to provide an extra barn door, to block light leaking from ventilation holes in lanterns, or from between the front of a lantern and the back of an accessory such as a scroller, and for many other uses too.

The need for spares

Productions, especially new productions, are rarely unchangeable as they first move into the venue. Performers and director respond to the difference between rehearsal rooms and the real set. Changes are made during the final rehearsals in the venue, and frequently after that too, and these changes may well require changes to be made to the lighting rig. Also it has to be said that performance lighting equipment does not always do what we expect it to do. It may not quite work as expected from the data sheet, or as it appeared to work in the visualisation program, or it may just plain not work. In whatever case it will need to be changed, either for a different piece of equipment or for a working model of the same piece.

So changes to the piece, faulty or incorrectly specified equipment, and developing design ideas may all call for additional lighting equipment — spares. And every new piece of lighting equipment rigged will require cables and other accessories. The lighting team will have assessed their need for spares of all kinds, based on factors such as:

■ How much of what types of equipment are available in house?

■ How far through the rehearsals was the show when the shop order had to be placed? If the answer is 'not very' you should expect changes in the lighting rig to accommodate changes in the show.

So the next few questions are . . .

■ How close is the venue to the hire company?

■ What are opening hours of the hire company?

■ How much time is there in the venue for rehearsals and further development of the show?

■ How much time in the venue is there is likely to be to make changes to the lighting rig?

All these factors influence how much spare lighting equipment needs to be on site. Clearly if the rehearsals are still at an early stage when the shop order goes in there is likely to be a lot of guess work in the lighting designer's rig plan. Some of those guesses may turn out to be wrong and changes will have to be made to the rig. However, there is little point in providing spare equipment if there is not going to be any time to rig it! In this case it is likely that the spares would be incorporated into the lighting rig — from the beginning.

FIGURE 1. RIGGING MR16 FIXTURES ON AN INTERNALLY WIRED BAR IN A COUNTER-WEIGHT THEATRE. PHOTO ANA VILAR-BERGUE

There will be other factors for the chief to consider, such as whether the production is to tour, and if so, what is the likely availability of specialist lamps and other items that might fail. Even if the production is to remain in one venue, it is likely that some spare lamps will be required to replace ones that fail during the fit-up, focus and final rehearsals, and a few extra bits and pieces will be required 'just in case'. Another factor could well be the size of the production's budget for lighting equipment and the generosity of the lighting hire company. Getting the spares order right is another skill required of the good production electrician or chief — too many spares and budget that could be used elsewhere (and valuable space too) is tied up in stuff that never gets used. Too few spares and valuable time is lost while someone brings spare lamps from the hire company, which could have been on site.

Getting the rig hung

The main activity of the lighting department during a fit-up will almost always be hanging lanterns. It is common practice to winch, fly or otherwise lower the bars or trusses used as hanging positions to a suitable working height, usually between 1m and 2m from the working floor. Wherever this is possible, it speeds up hanging enormously. Where it is not, every piece of equipment and every cable has to be raised to the hanging position, where a crew member secures it, often working at the top of a ladder or similar piece of access equipment. This is often a longwinded and tedious process, and if it can be avoided, or limited, it should be.

The crew should always endeavour to get the equipment as close to where it is indicated on the lighting plan as possible. This usually involves measuring the position of each unit from a common datum point, and this is most often the intersection of the centre line and the setting line. (In a proscenium theatre, the setting line is usually the back of the iron fire curtain.)

Over the stage, each lighting bar (or pipe) truss or other hanging position is located by measuring its distance from the datum point(s) on the plan, and the scaling that distance up. Each unit on that hanging position is then placed to match its position on the plan, again scaling up measurements from a common point such as the centre line.[1] Whenever possible the rig should be positioned to the same datum point that the set construction team is using. This gives the best chance of everything being as on the plan.

Plugging up

As discussed in previous chapters, the lighting designer or a delegated member of the lighting team will have a scheme for the plug-up; that is, a power or dimmer outlet and a control channel for every unit. It is important that this information is available to the crew hanging and plugging up the equipment. This may sound self evident but I have seen too many lighting fit-ups where an inexperienced chief has kept all the plugging and patch information to themselves and then wondered why the crew are plugging lanterns into the wrong socket outlets.

If there has been sufficient time and space to prepare, all the cables for each bar or truss can be taped together into looms. The idea is that the socket outlet for each unit is suitably labelled and sits neatly above or close to that unit. Using cable looms can save time taken to plug up, and flash out a lighting rig.

Once the individual cables have been connected and attached securely to the bar or truss, the multicore can be attached and secured so as not to put undue strain on the connectors. If the bar or truss is to be flown out, it will be necessary to ensure the cables will not tangle or snag on anything else.

Flashing out

It is a good idea to ensure that all the lanterns are working and connected to the right dimmers, power

---

[1] It is usually not a good idea to measure from a point on the hanging position itself, since there is no real guarantee that the lighting designer has drawn the bar or truss to exactly the same length as is it is on the stage. This is especially true in theatres where for all kinds of reasons the hanging bars are often shorter, longer, or offset from their idealised position on the venue ground plan.

Working with counter-weight flying systems

Although slowly being replaced by motorised systems, many theatre and other venues suspend scenery, lanterns and drapes from bars connected to counter-weight flying systems. The basic principle of these systems is that the weight lifted from the stage is balanced by slabs of iron or lead weight in a cradle somewhere else, usually on the side wall of the stage space. These cradles are accessed by gantries, from which operators can load and unload weights from the cradle until the load on the bar over the stage is balanced by the weight in the cradle. Once balance has been achieved, a single operator can move quite large loads up and down over the stage using a rope line, connected to the cradle via a system of pulleys.

These systems have been in use for over 100 years and, providing a few simple procedures are followed, they are safe. It is important that each bar is balanced — if there is more weight in the cradle than on the bar, the bar may move upwards with uncontrolled speed. Likewise, if there is more weight on the bar than in the cradle the bar may move downwards with uncontrolled speed. Either way it is easy to see that the consequences could be severe. Here are some dos and don'ts when hanging lighting equipment on bars controlled by a counter-weight system:

■ The person in charge of all loading and unloading is *not* the lighting chief, but the head of the flying crew (traditionally referred to in the UK as the head flyman).

■ The head flyman must be informed of all intentions to hang or unhang equipment from counter-weight fly bars.

■ Only when the head flyman says it's OK to do so can anything be taken off or added to a counter-weight fly bar.

■ NEVER remove units from a counter-weight fly bar without the explicit say so of the head flyman. Failure to follow this guidance may result in the bar becoming lighter than the cradle, and so moving very quickly into the grid. It is almost certain that this will cause damage to lanterns and to the flying system.

■ Don't step over or lean over counter-weight fly bars. If the bar should move you will be injured.

■ As lighting bars fly out, i.e. move up to trim height, make sure someone is paying out the cables.

■ DO NOT go onto a working gantry of a counter-weight system without specific permission.

■ When lighting bars need to be lowered to the stage (we say 'brought in' in the UK) make sure that cable will not impede movement.

■ As a bar is brought in the fly operators should shout a warning such as 'Heads up!' or 'Bar coming in!' If you can't see which bar is coming in, move to the wings or to another space outside the area of the counterweight bars.

outlets, and control channels. In my view, this is best done by getting as close to the show set-up as possible. This means plugging the cables from the lanterns into the dimmers and power distribution equipment that will be used in the show, and bringing up each control channel on the lighting console to make sure it brings up the correct unit(s) — and only the correct unit(s).

This is known as flashing out — each channel is flashed on to ensure that the lantern(s) work and that all the connections have been made correctly. It is not always possible to flash out from the console. However, since it is generally much easier to fix problems with lanterns at ground level than it is when they are at trim height, it is standard practice, even when show dimmers or console are not available, to flash out as much of the rig as possible while it is at ground level. An increasing number of dmx 512 test devices are now on the market and these can be set to imitate the control output of the lighting console. When the console is not available, a suitable dmx 512 test device can be used to check the function of moving lights and other technology. It is much kinder to the filaments of incandescent lamps to fade them in (over about ½ a second), or at least flash them out at a reduced intensity (say 75 or 80%) — this will help to reduce the number of lamps blown during the flash out.

Flash out is also a good time to check the fixed lanterns — that the colour in the frame matches that indicated on the plan or the paperwork, that all necessary accessories are in place and secured, that lock off and focus controls are working correctly, and that the lanterns are pointed roughly in the direction they will be set in (if that is known) and cables are not too close to equipment that will get hot and burn them. It is a good idea to check that fixed lanterns have sufficient slack cable to allow them to be set in a different position if necessary, and that cables near moving lights will not get in the way of those lights. Many lighting professionals like to pre-set zoom lanterns to their narrowest beam setting, ready for the focus. All profiles should have their shutters in the furthest out position, and all barn doors should be open. Not only does this help the flash out (because you can see light coming out of the front of the lanterns) but this too is good preparation for the focus.

During the flash out, the crew may discover cable faults. Getting round these may well involve making changes to the plugging on the bar or in the truss. It is important that any changes required are noted and recorded in the appropriate paper or computer file.

Once the flash out is complete, and all the instruments have been shown to function properly from the correct control channel, the flown hanging positions — the fly bars and/or trusses — can be set at trim.[2] The next job for the lighting crew will normally be to prepare for the focus, but that does not usually happen straight away. For example, normally it will be necessary to get all the masking and the major set elements in place and for other departments to have got to a point in their fit-up when they can work outside the space or with very little light or with local working light. If the show is outside, it will normally need to be dark.

This wait can be very frustrating for the lighting designer, who is eager to get their rig set and ready to make some cues. Often there are useful things that can be done while other departments are still working on the stage. The lighting programmer can make colour and beam palettes for any moving lights, and sometimes make approximate position palettes too, and the lighting designer may find small sections of the rig can be focused during a meal break of the other departments; making the best use of time here will often pay dividends later.

The focus

Clearly, getting the lights pointing in the right place, illuminating what they are designed to illuminate and leaving everything else dark is important. Most lighting designers, especially those working in theatre, consider the focus to be the key to making their lighting design work. Many production lighting workers rate themselves by how good they are at focusing. Increasingly moving lights of all kinds are replacing the fixed lanterns that used do all the work. Even so, most lighting systems still contain a proportion of lanterns that require crew to get behind them to point and shape the beam. Getting the focus of the fixed rig right — first time and in time — is likely to remain an important skill for

---

[2] Trim height is the height that bars, trusses and other flown equipment will be at for the show. It is not always possible or advisable to set lighting bars at trim straight away, as they may be in the way or be vulnerable to damage. Whenever this is the case, the lighting crew needs to ensure that, before the focus is scheduled to happen, some time is allocated to setting all the suspended lighting positions (and the flown masking if it is to be used) to trim.

both lighting crew and lighting designers working in live performance.

In this section I will use the term LD interchangeably for lighting designer and lighting director. The latter is the person responsible for making the lighting happen but who has not necessarily designed that lighting. In this case that might be a chief electrician (Lx) or lighting manager in a repertory house, reproducing lighting for an absent lighting designer, or the lighting designer's associate or assistant, or a person appointed to look after the lighting design on a tour. The point is that it is not just lighting designers that run focus sessions.

Before the focus can begin, several things have to happen:

Pre-focus check list

- The rig should be thoroughly flashed out; each fixture proved to function correctly from the lighting console and have the correct colour and appropriate accessories.

- All suspended lighting positions need to be at trim, and all flown masking, including legs and borders, are in place.

- All ground masking should be in place, or at the very least, accurate markings to indicate where it will be.

- A dim safety lighting state should be established that will allow safe movement throughout the space but will not get in the way of the focus. In theatres this is often referred to as 'show blues'. It is especially important that any access steps, ramps, or unprotected edges and holes have some illumination to prevent accidents (which may result in injury and inevitably stop the focus).[3]

- A brighter state, ideally quickly accessible by the board operator, which can be brought up when access equipment needs to be moved, faults need to be fixed, breaks need to be taken, or in case of an emergency.

- All items of set that are required by the LD. (Prior to the focus the LD will have negotiated with the appropriate department heads exactly what is needed in terms of set and props, and what if anything, can be left off stage, or needs to be moved to provide clear access.)

- Appropriate access equipment available, which may be different for different positions. Clear, safe space from which to use access equipment.

- Focus crew ready and appropriately equipped to access, set and lock off the lanterns

- Stage crew to move the set into places if this is required in order to focus some lanterns, and fly crew to move flown set or lighting positions if this is required, or perhaps to adjust the trim of lighting bars if that proves necessary.

- A lighting board operator in communication with the LD.

If any of the above cannot be achieved, it may well be better to delay the focus session until they can be, but often this is not possible and so the LD and the chief have to come up with work-rounds. If some flown lighting positions are not able to be set to trim, or can't be accessed, or don't work, or their target is not ready to be put in place, they will have to be left until later, while the rest of the rig is focused. (If it is about lanterns not working, then any crew not involved in focusing the rest of the rig will be well employed fault finding.) If no stage-crew is available to move the set into place or out of the way, permission may be sought to allow the lighting crew to do this instead; local restrictions may prevent this happening so as LD, ask nicely, don't assume. The LD and the chief will need to be creative to overcome these problems — but

---

[3]Following accidents where technical staff have fallen from the edge of the stage, occasionally during a focus, some venues insist on placing a barrier along the front edge. Clearly this can be unhelpful to the lighting designer! I suggest trying to find other ways of reducing the risk of a fall, such as making the edge more obvious, e.g. with white tape or some safety lighting in the void, and removing anything such as music stands or construction debris that might increase injury should a fall occur.

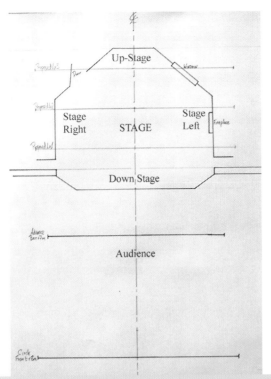

FIGURE 2. THE LD AND THE FOCUS CREW NEED TO AGREE A COMMON SET OF TERMS FOR DIRECTIONS. ON A PROSCENIUM STAGE WE USE THE CONVENTIONS OF **STAGE LEFT** AND **STAGE RIGHT** FROM THE PERFORMER'S POINT OF VIEW. OLDER PROSCENIUM STAGES WERE COMMONLY RAKED I.E. THERE WAS AN INCLINE SO THAT MOVING AWAY FROM THE AUDIENCE WAS GOING UP A SLIGHT SLOPE. THIS WAS TO ALLOW THOSE IN THE LOWER SECTION OF THE THEATRE A BETTER VIEW. FROM THIS WE GET **UP STAGE** AND **DOWN STAGE** AS SHOWN.

remember you can't focus the whole rig at once anyway, so if it makes others lives easier to focus a section at a time, why not offer that; it is what you would be doing anyway!

Focus from behind the lantern

Many top lighting designers for live performance have had some experience of being at the other end of the focusing process, behind the lantern as opposed to on stage. This experience is really useful; to be able to give good directions to the focus crew, to understand the potential problems faced by focus crew, and to understand the ways in which different lanterns work, which of course helps the designer to choose the right lantern for each job. Each different type of lantern presents its own challenges and has its own quirks. Anyone who takes focusing seriously should take time to discover the full range of controls on the lanterns they are working with. These will include:

- Suspension clamp, pan and tilt lock.
- Beam size adjustment e.g. lens movement on a profile, lamp tray and reflector on a Fresnel.
- Beam shape adjustment e.g. shutters on a profile, barn doors on a Fresnel.
- Field adjustment — usually screws or knobs at the back of a profile.

Not every lantern has all these controls, and some have more including gate rotation and shutter locking on some profiles, and power settings on some discharge lanterns. Before beginning a focus, the crew should ensure they have the necessary tools to operate all the controls, and especially to lock off each lantern. Few things in performance lighting are more frustrating than, having spent valuable time positioning a lantern exactly where it is required, to find that is has changed position because the crew member did not properly secure all the position lock offs.

Focusing a zoom profile

Zoom profiles generally have two adjustable lenses. This allows the beam angle to be varied as well as the edge quality to be adjusted. Although usually not as efficient in terms of light output compared to a fixed focus profile, the added flexibility has made them much more common in many markets. Zoom profiles come into their own in a repertory situation, where each unit may be asked to do a different job each time it is focused. For one show a lantern may be required to cover half of the stage, for the next the same lantern may be set as a special for a single performer on the far side of stage. In a busy rep, such as that found in many large opera houses, zoom lanterns become the natural choice. I am grateful to members of the lighting crew of English National Opera, where up to 200 lanterns are refocused most afternoons, for the following guide to focusing zoom profiles.

When you arrive at the lantern and before the circuit is brought up:

- Perform a visual check of the lantern, its cables, safety bond(s) and connector to make sure they are all undamaged.[4]

- Ensure the hanging clamp is securely fixed to the hanging position.

- Set the pan and tilt lock offs so that the unit can be pointed, but not so loose that it wobbles — this is usually between a ½ and ¼ turn from fully locked off.

- Referring to the current plan or paperwork, confirm that it has the correct colour in the frame, gobo if required, and that it is plugged to the correct outlet. Remove any diffusion material from the colour frame and reserve for later re-insertion.

- Move the lenses to the smallest beam size i.e. as far apart as they can travel. If you know the approximate direction that the unit is required to point, set it there.

When the circuit is brought up and the LD calls for the light:

- Unless directed otherwise, set the centre of the beam on the head of the LD.

- When the LD is happy with position lock off pan and tilt.

- By moving the lenses, set the beam size as directed by the LD — the front lens makes the biggest changes to size — try to keep the beam sharp at this point to help with seeing shutter cuts.

- Set shutters as directed by the LD.

- Adjust rear lens to gain required softness of edge, or replace diffusion material in colour frame, as directed by the LD.

- Check the LD is happy, and move on to next unit.

This is, of course, a generalised approach and assumes certain things of the LD and the schedule; that the LD will stand with their head in the centre of where they want the beam and that the centre once set will not change, that they are happy to set shutters with a hard-edged beam and then to make it soft, and that the schedule allows time for the pre-checks to be done. This last can be problematic, and in an ideal world all the checks performed before the unit is switched on (or brought up) would have been done before the focus began. In practice this is not always possible, but if time can be made for the checks it should be.

The very least that needs to happen before any focus is to check that each unit about to be focused is under the control of its assigned channel from the lighting console, or can quickly be turned on some other way.

In practice another way to allow time for checks is to have two crew focusing lanterns from different positions. Not only does this avoid losing time while a single crew member moves from one position to the next, it also means one person can be checking and preparing while the other one is focusing.

---

[4]As I have already mentioned, it is in the interest of anyone about to touch any piece of electrical equipment to check, as far as possible, that it is undamaged and not about to cause them injury. For anyone working in the UK, a pre-use check is also a legal requirement.

One aspect of focusing from behind the lantern that we have not mentioned yet is the need to get into position. In many theatres, the FoH lanterns are mounted in specially constructed positions with built-in access for focus and maintenance crew. In some larger venues, the over stage lanterns are hung from lighting bridges, which allow the crew convenient access from above the units. In most touring set-ups, especially those designed for one-night-stands, the lanterns over stage are hung from trusses. These can be accessed by specially-trained crew, again from above, protected from falls by wearing a harness attached by a shock-absorbing lanyard to suitable safety lines. Almost everywhere else (and sometimes even when the lanterns are suspended from trusses) access is by some kind of ladder or mechanical platform.

One thing the crew chief and the LD need to bear in mind is that dashing up and down ladders can be very draining and the last thing anyone wants is an exhausted person working above them! Rotating the crew who are doing the climbing during a focus session is generally good practice, and usually pays off by keeping everyone fresh.

A focus crew that has developed a good working relationship with the LD and have an understanding of the style in which they are working, can speed up the

Working at height in countries of the European Union

Recent legislation in the EU has placed some restrictions on what is and what is no longer possible when crew are working at height. Local rules vary but the guilding principle is that all equipment used to work at height must only be used as directed by the manufacturer.

This means, for example, if a large label on the access equipment says it must not be moved while someone is at the top of it, then to do so is breaking the law, and is probably also removing insurance cover from the person at the top, the people doing the moving, and the organisation they are working for and the owners of the venue. In other words, an accident could not only hurt those involved but could also make them very poor and result in bankrupting the organisation they are working for.

As a consequence of this legislation and for other reasons, there is increasing use of mechanical access platforms (single personnel lifts, cherry pickers, flying carpets, etc) in performance venues. These machines can be very useful, but they come with their own problems too. First among these is the need for trained and certificated operators, second is the need to re-enforce some stages and sets to take the additional weight of the machine and third is an annoying tendency for the machine to run out of charge half-way through the focus. (Most machines used inside are battery operated.)

Where mechanical access is not practical or not available for other reasons, the time spent going up and down ladders between each lantern or small group of lanterns can add considerably to the duration of the focus session. This can be used as an argument for more budget to hire or buy moving lights to replace some of the now hard to reach and focus fixed rig, but money is not available for such luxuries in many sectors.

Instead, the LD needs to think of other ways of making the best use of limited focus time; grouping lanterns together to make them accessible from a single point — making more use of gantry positions and bridges or accessible trusses, and perhaps more novel solutions such as bouncing light off a large suspended mirror over stage!

Unfortunately this is not a problem that is going to go away any time soon, and only the largest organisations have sufficient funding to buy into mechanical access or moving light solutions. It is up to resourceful LDs to come up with workable solutions for the rest of us!

focus considerably by having good anticipation of what is coming next. Very often, banks of lanterns are focused to work together in a wash. Once the first one has been set, the rest are likely to have the same beam size and edge. This helps to ensure that the light from each unit is similar enough to blend with its neighbour, and that they will all have a similar intensity when brought up to the same level. The focus crew can help out the LD by noting the settings on the first unit and transferring these directly to the rest of the units in that wash. Lanterns used in a wash generally have common 'cuts'. For example, lanterns from an FoH wash may all have an upstage cut in line with a particular feature of the set. The focus crew can help the LD by putting this cut in automatically. Many lighting rigs have symmetrical elements. If the focus crew remember where the stage right lanterns went, it can help the LD by offering the stage left into symmetrical positions. However, overdoing this kind of thing without consultation can annoy an LD, especially one not used to this kind of help.

There will be times when the person behind the lantern can see things the LD cannot see. For example, light from FoH lanterns spilling over the front edge of the stage. Different LDs will have a different approach to this. Most will welcome a call from the focuser to alert them to this. Some LDs will expect the focuser to deal with such things with out being asked, but occasionally an LD will get irritated by this kind of initiative. A good focus crew will support the way the LD is working, and a good LD will make full use of the talent available within the focus crew. As so often in lighting, making good relationships makes the work easier and usually leads to better results.

Beam edge, diffusion and gobos

The range of diffusion material now available, from heavy frost to almost clear, has begun to change the way many LDs focus profile lanterns. Rather than softening the edge of the beam by adjusting a lens, it is becoming common to focus the profiles with a sharply-defined edge, and then create the softness that will help beams to merge together by using diffusion in the colour frame. This has the advantage that each

lantern's beam will look more like its neighbours, producing a more uniform wash of light from several lanterns. It is much easier to achieve a consistent hard edge and then diffuse it than to produce a consistent soft edge by moving a lens with a consistent accuracy whilst also working at height. The choice of diffuser is critical, especially when the lanterns are in the auditorium. Too much diffusion and there is a tendency for a significant proportion of the light to scatter away from the main beam and light up the surrounding walls and other features. Generally speaking, we don't want this because it draws the attention of the audience away from the stage. Too little diffusion and we still have the sharp edges — the rapid change in intensity — that the human eye and the camera pick up on, again causing distraction. In an unfamiliar venue, it is as well to have several different qualities of diffusion available.

One place were we cannot usually use diffusion is in front of lanterns with a gobo. Clearly, if the pattern is meant to be crisp, for example if it imitates the words of neon signs, or the outline of a window, we will not want any diffusion or softness. Very often, however, gobos are used to add more or less subtle texture to the stage picture. Rather than use diffusion to control the edge, most LDs will resort to softening the beam by using lens adjustments. As the lenses of a profile lantern with a break-up gobo are focused away from sharp, two different effects are observed. In one direction blue fringing appears and in the other brown fringing appears.

It is usually easier to merge the beams of brown focused lanterns than those of blue focused ones. Also the brown edge is usually considered more pleasing. Whatever the designer's choice, if a set of lanterns with gobos are to be focused to create a soft edged and more or less even cover, the focus crew and the designer should all be clear about which soft focus they are going to use, blue or brown. Once the edge has been agreed on, it will need to be replicated as closely as possible in the other units of the cover. Many lanterns have graduations or other marking along side the lens adjustment controls. It is a good idea to make a note of the settings here, though unfortunately, for many makes of lanterns, reproducing these settings on adjacent lanterns is no guarantee that the edge will be the same

Focusing a gobo cover can be time consuming and difficult, especially if the position of each unit has not been fully thought through. It can be very useful to the LD and speed up the process if the focus crew has a good memory of where they have already set lanterns, and what the beam looked like. Alternatively it is often necessary to bring up the group, i.e. all the units that form part of the gobo cover, each time a new lantern is to be focused. For this reason, it is sometimes useful to point lanterns to be used in a gobo cover away from stage when they are hung, so that un-set lanterns will not confuse the focuser or the LD.

Calling a focus from the stage

Leading the focus of a lighting rig, often referred to as calling the focus, is a demanding task. To do it you will have to walk across the stage many times, stand in the only pool of light on stage, and call out to crew in distant parts of the venue, either to direct their actions behind a lantern or to ask for channels, or perhaps for quiet. You will do a lot of walking so wear comfortable shoes.[5] You will do a lot of talking, often in a voice much louder than your everyday voice (have water available[6]), and perhaps boiled sweets or mints to suck on.[7] You can take a tip from the performers and warm up your voice (and the rest of your body) before a focus session.

You will be working in conditions of high contrast, moving about a potentially difficult space often in the dark (remember the unprotected drop at the front of most stages, the one into the orchestra pit or the front row of the stalls). You will be trying to read your notes, and perhaps the lighting plan too so have a reliable torch. You will often get stressed out so develop ways of calming yourself down, such as breathing or stretching exercises, which you can do while the crew sort out a problem or simply as you move from one position to the next.

You will be exposed, standing on a stage, often literally in the spotlight, making strange signals and shouting up to unseen technical personnel. You will be visible to everybody in the venue, most of whom will be invisible to you. This is a little of what a performer feels; if you are not a natural improviser, it is a good idea to have a script, a set of words you have thought out and are comfortable with to ask for channels and to direct focus. Most importantly, you will need to command the space. You are doing an important job. It needs to be done quickly and well, and to do that you will need the co-operation of most if not all of the other people working in the space. You will need to be polite but firm, and well very organised.

Ideally, the LD would have plenty of time, a quiet blacked-out space to work in, and quick easy access to every lighting position for the skilled focus crew. In this ideal world, every necessary item of set would be in place as it is required, and out of the way when it is not, the masking would have been finally adjusted, and the blocking of the performers would also be complete.

---

[5]Stages, especially during a fit-up, can present numerous hazards to unprotected feet. Everything from sharp unfinished edges to carelessly placed tools and equipment, to gaps in the surface required for the tracks of stage trucks. Many venues insist that all personnel working on the stage during the fit-up wear safety footwear. This does not usually mean heavy boots (though it can) but it does mean that flip-flops and light-weight tennis shoes will be frowned on, if not banned. It is a good idea to get buy yourself some comfortable safety shoes, both to satisfy rules and regulations, and for your own protection.

[6]It is not a good idea to have open containers of liquid on a stage. Indeed most venues will specifically prohibit this. The reason being it is too easy for the liquid to spill and cause damage, either to the paint work or drapes of a set, or to electrical systems. Also spilt liquid makes floors slippery, increasing the chances of slips, trips and falls. Most venues are happy if you use bottled water carefully, leaving it in an agreed safe place at the side of stage, with the top securely in place.

[7]It is often possible to use radios to communicate during a focus session, or even a radio microphone on the LD. If you do, remember that the crew member may not be able to respond using the radio, especially if they are using both hands to perform the task you have asked for!

Ideal worlds don't happen very often and it is a fact of life for most lighting designers working on live performance that many focus sessions have to be shared with set builders, painters and others. They will be making noise and will need working light. Someone on the lighting team will need good negotiating skills to try to persuade those who need light to work that there may be other jobs they can do during the time allocated to focusing the lighting — sometimes this will not be possible or useful. We will come back to this later.

For the moment, let us assume we do have a reasonable quiet and dark space in which to call the focus. Based on a considered design and good planning, the LD will have a set of focus notes (the script), which should define where each of the lanterns in the rig will point, what each will light and what each will not light, and which ones will work together in washes, and which alone as specials. Get the focus notes arranged into the order that you will focus the lights. An experienced LD will usually aim to work quickly to set each lantern as the crew arrive at it, working along a bar or truss, regardless of the function of the lantern. This is the ideal and even top LDs sometimes need to go back and forth between positions or along a bar, especially when working on a design for the first time. If you are calling a focus, try to think through what you want from every lantern before you begin. Wherever there is some doubt about whether a particular unit can achieve what you want or need, have a back up plan. But if all this fails, try to make time to go back and fix mistakes within the focus session, because otherwise they will become part of the cues you will soon be making, and then it may be too late to fix them. It is often a good idea to leave easily accessible units till last since it is usually possible to set these in between other activity later, say a tea or coffee break during rehearsals.

There are several different and equally valid ways to call a focus. There are also different techniques required when focusing units that will light performers or three dimensional objects, and units that will light the walls, floors or other basically flat features of a set, and for lanterns whose beams need to blend and those that will work alone. No one is born being able to call a focus — as with most things practice makes us better. When starting out, it is a good idea to watch others, picking up their good practice to inform your own. Experienced LDs will be able to carry focus notes for generic washes more or less in their heads. They may focus with just the lighting plan as their script or perhaps completely from memory. This ability comes from years of having done it and is an ability that should not be under estimated. If you are new to calling a focus, there is no substitute for planning. Plan as much as possible: visualisation programs allow today's lighting designer to try out a focus on a computer before calling it in public. This can be very useful for planning how to focus a wash. It takes time, but it is time spent outside the venue to save time on stage, and this is one of our key aims.

If the crew who are focusing are working along similar lines to the way the ENO[8] crew work, the LD works as follows:

- Stand with your head in the centre of where you want the beam, with your back to the lantern.

- Call up the channel. Ask the console operator to bring up the channel — by radio if possible to save your voice. Sometimes it works well to bring the channel up to check, i.e. a level less than full, so the crew member can see where it is and it does not get too hot whilst they are getting to it.

- Direct the crew member to set the beam where you want it. Use bold gestures with your hands well away from your body for maximum visibility. When you are happy, make an agreed signal, such as thumbs up or shout 'Lock off there, please'.

- When you are told the lantern is locked off, set the beam size, again using bold gestures agreed between you and the focus crew. When you are

---

[8]English National Opera, based at the Coliseum Theatre in London. The ENO lighting crew on an average day focus between 150 and 200 lanterns between them to facilitate the repertory system common in most large opera houses.

happy, thumbs up or some agreed command, such as 'That's good!'

- Using bold gestures, indicate where each of the shutters or barn doors should go to shape the beam. For any shape out of the ordinary try to indicate your whole intention first, then each individual cut. Remember that some profiles have a rotating gate and barn doors should rotate too. This may be helpful but only if the person focusing knows what they are trying to do with all four shutters. Most barn door sets have two long doors and two short ones. Be clear about where you want the long doors (which will usually be to do the most substantial cut.) Not everything is possible — be prepared to re-think and to take advice from the person behind the lantern.

- Set the edge of profiles, either by asking for lens movement or diffusion. Remember to be clear about when you are happy with the edge.

- Check there is no unintentional light, for example spill onto masking or the front edge of stage, or from between barn doors.

- Once you are happy, make sure everyone concerned knows they can move on — either call for the next channel or for work-light to allow the movement to the next channel. **Tick off the set lantern on your focus plot,** and move into position for the next channel.

So, before any the focus crew sets any lanterns, the LD needs to agree signals and directions. As we have said, on a proscenium stage we usually use stage left, stage right, up stage and down stage. In any other situation there is unlikely to be a natural set of directions, unless everyone has worked in that venue for before.

One of the more important signals to agree is the 'OK!' indicating the LD is happy with the current action and is ready to move on to the next, or that the focuser is locked off and ready to move on. Once you have this signal sorted out, the LD can give it, and move out of the beam to look at its effect without the beam following them like a follow spot. Also LDs will not find them-selves waiting unnecessarily, thinking they are waiting for a crew member, while the crew member thinks that they are waiting for the LD. Once an understanding of signals exists between LD and focus crew, the focus can happen quickly, with a good deal less shouting, which usually reduces everybody's stress levels.

It is very tempting at times to look into the lanterns rather than to stand with your back to them. This is not a good idea, and can lead to permanent eye damage — not a good idea for anyone beginning a career in lighting! Get used to judging the position of the lantern by observing your shadow on the stage. Standing with your back to the lantern makes it even harder for the focus crew to hear you so your signals become even more important.

Making a wash work

The above method will work well for individual lanterns, but most often we need units to work together, and blend into a wash, or a gobo cover. We have already looked at a gobo cover and compared it to a wash, that is easy! A gobo cover generally only has to blend in two dimensions, across the stage floor, or perhaps a cloth or a wall. A wash is normally required to light performers as they move their three dimensional bodies through three dimensional space. It is important to begin with a clear idea of the volume that needs to be covered by the whole wash, and by each individual lantern. In Chapter 6 we looked at the need to think in terms of cubes of useful light within the conical beam of each lantern. In the focus, the LD needs to match these cubes together. At first, try not to worry too much about what happens to the spare light that illuminates the floor or walls beyond the area that is usefully lit for your performers. With design experience comes the ability to plan for this and make best use of it.

Before anybody has to focus a wash of lanterns under the pressure of a production deadline, they should practice. Getting it right is as much about an instinctive grasp of three dimensional geometry as any-thing else. Trying to work this out on the page needs some sophisticated maths beyond the scope of this book. Working it out practically with real lights in a real venue is easier for most of us.

I strongly recommend that any aspiring LD tries the following exercise — make a wash with three lanterns

175

from the same angle. You will require a colleague to be behind the lanterns, which need to be at least 5 to 6m from the stage. Have a clear picture in your mind of the outline of the cubes that make up the wash on stage. If you like, mark out the squares that make up the bottom face of the cubes. Start with the lantern that will illuminate the central cube — it makes it much easier.

1 Begin as before, standing in the centre of the middle cube.

2 Once the lantern is locked off, move to the corner or side of the cube that is furthest from the lanterns. Unless you are well above average height, hold a hand above your head and signal for the beam to be spread until it illuminates your hand. Move along the edges of your cube and check you are illuminated everywhere, from your feet to the top of your raised hand. It is not uncommon to have to make small adjustments to the pan and tilt of the lantern at this point — again, with experience, this happens less and less. Ask the crew to note the setting of the lenses for future reference.

3 Once you are happy with the overall size, you can call the cuts. I usually start with the cross stage cuts — the top of my cube. Standing on the furthest side of the cube again, I call for the cut to include my fist, but not the tips of my fingers (I am about 1.7m high and this usually works; you will have to adjust to your own size, and perhaps the sizes of your performers.) Make sure the cut is parallel to the imaginary side of your cube.

4 At the sides, follow the same procedure, ensuring once more that the cut is in line with your imagined cube. Check by walking along the line of your cube with your hand up, to see where the edge of beam lies. You can look at your shadow on the stage floor, or the light on your hand. It can be very difficult for the crew to get side cuts precisely in line — experience will inform the LD's decision about where the compromises need to be made.

5 On the side of the cube nearest the lanterns, the cut lies at stage level.

6 Once the cuts have been set, you can set the edge.

Again this takes experience to get right every time. A good crew who know their venue and equipment will often be able to help. Be aware that the size of the beam will change when you soften it with lens movement (another reason to use diffusion material). Even using the subtlest diffusion increases the size of the beam a little though.

In a production situation, try to focus the centre unit first. It is likely to be the most important — as we have already noted, directors and performers both tend to favour centre stage, and it is often the centre of the audience's field of vision. It is worth taking time to get this one right; the others will often be quicker to set if you are confident of having got the first one right. Subsequent cuts will very often lie along the similar lines to first ones and once one edge is agreed upon, the rest can be copied.

7 Move onto the next lantern, with a clear mental picture of where you put the cuts for the first one. Many LDs find it easier to work on the next lantern with the first one still on at check, just as a reminder. Again stand in the centre of your next cube (having made any adjustments to where centre is based on the experience of focusing the first unit).

8 Once the unit's pan and tilt are set, zoom it to the same settings as the first unit. This will help to give you a similar intensity on stage from each of the lanterns in your wash at each percentage setting on the lighting console. Hopefully the size will be big enough. If it is too big, don't worry as cuts will deal with this. (If it is much too small, you may have made a mistake in specifying the lanterns, and you may have to go back to the first unit and make it bigger, or reduce the size of your imaginary cube for this second unit.)

9 Make the cross stage cuts, matching as closely as possible the line of the previous lantern on stage. Make the side cuts as before. Do not try to match up the side cut adjacent to your first lantern on the stage floor. Remember you are not lighting the floor with these units — you are lighting performers, and usually their faces are more important than their feet. You need to blend the beams at

about face level, so trust your cube and make the cut to that.

10 Set the edge, then have both lanterns on at full. Face away from the lanterns and place your hand about 0.5m in front of your face. Move across stage through the two beams looking at how your hand is illuminated. If you can see a sharp line, the edge of one or both lanterns will need to be softened. If there is a bright patch or a dark patch between the two beams, you will need to make adjustments to get rid of this as much as possible. Merging beams in three dimensions is about compromise; this will not be perfect, but making it work gets easier with experience.

Why it might not be working

Successfully merging the beams of two lanterns relies on several things. One of the most important is matching the fall off in intensity towards the edge of each beam with the amount the beams are overlapping. What we want to achieve is the same intensity where the two beams intersect as that in the middle of a single beam (i.e. the peak intensity). This works if we merge the beams where the intensity is half the peak intensity. In one dimension i.e. along a line, this is relatively easy.

Even in two dimensions there are problems. The intensity of a lantern's beam generally falls off as a circle. These two beams will only match intensity along the line joining them together.

If we don't cut too far into the beams, and soften the edges a lot, we can make a good approximation to an even intensity across a larger area than before by merging them at about the half intensity point of each beam.

Go back to the exercise, and take out all the cuts. Make sure the beams are only just big enough to illuminate each cube. Put the cross stage or top and bottom cuts in and diffuse or soften the edges. Leave the side cuts out. Now walk across the beams — the chances are that they are much more even across the stage without side cuts. This is because by making the beams only just big enough for the cubes, you are now making use of the natural fall off in intensity of the lanterns and you

FIGURE 3. LIGHTING DESIGN STUDENTS LINE UP ACROSS THE STAGE TO SEE HOW EVEN THE WASH THEY HAVE JUST FOCUSED IS.

are not introducing any potentially sharp edges across stage. In a real life lighting design, if you can adjust your cubes to fit the particular beam angle of the fixed beam profiles available, you will not only stand a good chance of getting your wash to work first time, but you will also potentially get more light on stage (remember fixed beam profiles are usually more efficient that zoom ones).

Focusing moving lights

Since moving lights can be moved into position from the lighting console, during a lighting session or during rehearsals, why do we need to focus them before we have to use them during the lighting session or the rehearsals on stage? Here are four reasons.

1 Moving lights are an expensive choice to add to your rig — you should know what you want to do with them before the lighting session and stage rehearsals. You will be able to concentrate on doing this well if they can go quickly to the positions you have planned each time you want to use them.

2 It can be hard to set a moving light in exactly the right place from the sometimes distant lighting console — harder still to set several into the same area, or adjoining areas, especially with the distraction of the rest of the lighting rig on.

3 Moving heads have two ways to point at any given position. If we want them to move live, say across the stage, each position on stage needs to be planned with care so that they do indeed move across stage, instead of moving their beams out into the auditorium and then back again.

4 Just as it is a challenge to focus an even wash with fixed lanterns, so it is with moving lights, whether they have shutters or not. To do it well needs some time, and usually two people, one on stage and one at the console.

So it is a good idea to record at least some focus positions for your moving lights before any lighting session or stage rehearsal with light.

It is possible to use the same outline procedure to focus movers as we used to focus the fixed rig. If the preset focus is for a look that illuminates the set or the

floor, make sure the programmer or operator can see that. If it is for illuminating people, make sure that is what it is doing, either by getting someone to stand for the programmer as a target, or by directing the programmer yourself as LD, from the stage.

If you are making a moving light wash, set lights individually. Set each of the attributes you want to use which will often only be pan and tilt, but may at times include beam size and edge, and try them together to see how well they merge into an even wash. If beam attributes are used, make sure they are stored, and recalled whenever you want to use the wash.

Once each preset focus position is stored, it should be named. Getting the right name is important, as we will see below, and it is quite usual to start with a position down stage centre. By starting with this one in first, and then building all the other stage positions from it, you can be fairly sure that the lights will move predictably from any place on stage to any other without going up the side walls or out into the auditorium — unless you want them to!

One other tip for moving light positioning: always move the tilt first, and always in the same direction first too. This will help to control 'flipping' which is where the moving light head thinks it should turn up-side down to get from one position to another. If you always have the movers the same way up over stage, the gobos will always be the same way up and the shutters will always be (more or less) where you expect them to be.

There is another perhaps more technical, but even more important reason. Storing a position on a moving light console does more than simply give the programmer the ability to recall that position at the press of a single button. Every cue that is made with units in a recorded position can be updated simply by changing the recorded position.

Supposing we have a solo spot for a song or some other action down stage centre: there are several cues for the solo, building — changing mood — and then fading down at the end. Half way through rehearsals the director decides that solo should be from the platform centre stage. By changing the pan and tilt of the movers to point at the new location for the solo spot, and updating the recorded focus position, every cue that used that position is automatically updated. So if we had a focus position solo spot, we would re-focus the light, re-record the focus position, and the lights would be in the new position for all the solo spot cues.

But what happens if instead of a recorded focus position called solo spot in the original cues we had used down stage centre. If we updated that focus position, every cue in the show that had had units pointing down stage centre would now have those lights pointing to the centre stage platform. This is just one example of why it is necessary to be thoughtful about naming and using recorded focus positions.

Recording and naming palettes/ presets/focus groups[9]

Ideally, the lighting programmer should have rapid access to every gobo, fixed colour, and mixable colour likely to be used in making the lighting for the show. This requires each attribute setting to be recorded as a pallet or preset or focus group, so that it can be accessed through a single button press. Many modern lighting consoles will do this automatically, but many lighting programmers will want to customise aspects of the process.

Just as we called the focus positions by names in the last section, it is extremely useful to have names that mean something for all the other attributes of the moving lights. Firstly because it usually makes it easier for the programmer to take the movers to that particular setting if they are looking for a button with a recognisable name on it rather than a more or less random number. Secondly because when you look at the console's display, it is much easier to see what each unit is doing if the attributes are labelled with a meaningful name rather than containing a percentage or dmx 512 value. Just as calling focus positions for movers by common names makes sense, so too does having the colour and beam selection by name rather than by a

number. The lighting designer and the programmer just have to agree on what that name will be. Generally, since it is the lighting designer's show not the programmer's they should be allowed to choose the names — hopefully with some consideration for the way the programmer and the lighting console work. For colours, it could be the nearest match in a favoured swatch book (L200), the colour names from one or more swatch books (Double CTB), or a name that means something within the show (Mick's Back Light Blue). For gobos, the same applies, catalogue number (DHA 407) or name (Dapple) or function in the show (Woodland Act II).

It is useful to think about how names will be displayed when you are choosing them. There is usually a limit to how many characters will be displayed on the screen or on the button, and it will usually be the beginning of the name that is displayed. Suppose we have three different blues:

Blue Act I
Blue Act II
Blue Act III

On a seven character display they will all be displayed as Blue Ac. Even if the whole name is displayed, it will not be easy to distinguish between fixtures with Blue Act III and Blue Act II on a very full display. Perhaps better names might be:

A1 Blue
A2 Blue
A3 Blue

Each pallet is now recognisably unique on the screen display and still meaningful. There are lots of other considerations that are specific to particular lighting consoles or programmers' working methods. It is in the lighting designer's interest for the programmer to be able to work as quickly and efficiently as possible, so as elsewhere in the process, some consultation between the two on naming palettes is a good idea.

---

[9]Palette, preset, focus group all mean much the same thing on different consoles. As I have said before some manufacturers of lighting equipment have patented or copyrighted the use of these words, which makes it difficult for the rest of us to decide which one to use when we don't want to be specific about one particular console, and I wish they had not.

As well as gobos and colour palettes, it is usual to store what might be called beam quality palettes; sharp for each gobo wheel, a particularly useful soft, and different sizes of beam, for example. Some shows may require special effects such as strobe[10] and stop strobe or rotating colour wheels, and these too can be stored under a single button.

Just as with the stored positions, updating the contents of colour and beam palettes/presets/focus groups changes the contents of all the cues that refer to those palettes/presets/focus groups. Usually this is just what is required, but it is as well to be aware that it can occasionally lead to surprises.

Now the rig is in place and focused, and the moving lights (if you have any) have at least some of their required palettes/presets/focus groups, it is nearly time to start making some lighting cues. Before that though, there are any number of things still to do or at least to check. These might include:

■ Smoke and haze (if used) ready, and not about to trigger the fire alarms.

■ Scrollers all lined up so they all produce the right colour for each instruction.

■ Gobo rotators, effects projectors and other equipment requiring additional power working as required.

■ Communications — between lighting designer and operator(s) and programmer(s); between lighting designer and stage manager or show caller; and importantly between lighting designer and the director, choreographer and other designers.

■ Stray light — making sure there is no stray light from off-stage workers or exit boxes.

■ House lights — under control and working as they will when the audience is in the venue (including emergency lighting which may have to stay on when the audience is in).

■ Follow-spots — working and gelled up, with operators in communication with the lighting designer and ready to begin.

Ready now?

---

[10]Strobe light — rapidly flashing light — can work very well in the right circumstances, but can also trigger epileptic seizures in a proportion of the population. In performance it is usual to warn the audience by a notice on the auditorium doors or in the programme. In rehearsal, it is worth checking that none of the crew or performers are photosensitive before using significant amounts of strobe lighting.

working in the performance space — II

Making states and cues

This chapter concentrates on creating lighting states on the performance stage. Anyone who does not appreciate what goes into the creation of good performance lighting might think that taking eight chapters to get to the heart of what a lighting designer does is rather a lot! I hope that by now the reader will have gathered that creating good performance lighting actually involves a lot of preparation, knowledge, thought and skill. To begin plotting lighting states and cues there needs to be a fully working, accurately focused rig in place,[1] and we are now aware of many of the decisions that have gone into making that happen.

In this phase of the production the lighting designer is likely to find themself under considerable pressure. Time is usually tight and even in the best planned productions there are always limits to the resources available. The lighting designer will need a good technical understanding of what can be achieved with the lighting rig,[2] a good eye for how light is shaping the visual world to be presented to the audience, and very

good people skills. There is always a danger of becoming isolated as a lighting designer, especially in this phase of the production process. If they become absorbed in technical detail and forget to keep talking to the director and the other designers, the rest of the creative team will almost certainly stop talking to the lighting designer until they feel things have gone completely wrong, at which point it becomes very difficult to get the lighting design back to something that everyone can live with. By neglecting proper communication with the rest of the lighting department, the lighting designer almost certainly limits what will be achieved by these people to enhance the lighting design. Sometimes people skills boil down to never be too busy to say 'Hello, and how are you?' — keep the communication channels open.

Lighting states, lighting cues and the prompt copy

A lighting state is a selection of channels recorded at particular output values, for a particular purpose, scene, or part of a scene. It can be static; that is all the

---

[1] For all kinds of reasons, many lighting designers have to, or choose to, sit down to create lighting without the rig in anything even close to a finished state. We will discuss this further in Chapter 10, but for now let us assume that we are in a perhaps idealised position of having had enough time, money and people to have our perfect lighting rig in place, fully functioning, and fully focused.

[2] Many lighting designers have a wide interest in all aspects of technical presentation, from the technology involved in moving scenic elements to the ways in which particular departments run, the more we know the more we understand and the more can be achieved.

lanterns maintaining a constant intensity, moving lights stationary and the effect on stage the same from moment to moment. Alternatively a lighting state can be dynamic, including within it changes in intensity (a chase in a fairground festoon or the simulation of flickering fire light) or movement of moving lights or their attributes (search-lights sweeping a night sky, or a colours rapidly changing to simulate firelight).

Strictly speaking, a lighting cue is the point in the show when the lighting changes. There will be a time over which the change occurs, and this is called the cue time: more on this later. However, we often refer to lighting states as cues and the stack of lighting states as the cue stack. When a recorded lighting state is played back we say the cue is live on stage. In the time before it reaches the final recorded state — for a static cue this means when the levels are still changing — we say the cue is running in. Just to make matters potentially more confusing, the total lighting state on stage may be the result of several live lighting cues at the same time including some running in and some running out.

The most common method of creating lighting states is for the lighting designer to call up channels or groups of channels, and for a lighting programmer or operator to press buttons or push faders to implement these requests. When the lighting designer is happy with what they see on stage (or wherever) the state is recorded by the programmer or operator, given a number or name, and usually a time or times, and a place in the running order of the piece is defined as the point where this state will be triggered. If the show has a script or a written score, a particular line, or word in a line, or bar of music may be defined as the cue point. If the show is called, that is following the British and North American theatre tradition, there is a show caller responsible for cueing the show, each cue position will have a number. At every performance, when that point in the show is reached the show caller will say 'Lx NN GO' (where NN is the cue number and Lx is an abbreviation for electrics). On the command 'Go' the lighting operator will perform the necessary actions to begin the process of making lighting state NN appear on stage in the recorded cue time(s), usually pressing a single button on the lighting console.

The position of each cue is recorded in the prompt copy, also sometimes referred to as the book. This marked up copy of the script or score will be used by the show caller each night. As well as the position of all the called lighting cues, it will have all the other called cues (e.g. for flies, sound, set, etc) all the warnings for these cues (e.g. 'stand by Lx NN') and the calls for the performers (announcements to be made to the dressing rooms to warn each performer to be ready for an entrance) and any other information needed to call the show. In this system, it is the show caller's responsibility to make sure the show runs smoothly and safely, and when the show caller says 'Go', the only legitimate reason for the operator not to make the cue happen is if it would be dangerous to do so. As a lighting designer working with a show caller, it clearly just as important to make sure that your cue positions are correctly recorded in the prompt copy as it is to make sure the contents and timing of your cue states are correctly recorded in the lighting console.[3]

Traditionally, for ease of working, lighting states have numbers. When they are recorded electronically they have a memory number. On older theatre lighting consoles there is only one set or stack of these numbers, that is there is only ever one state 101. Many current lighting consoles have more than one stack of states, which can lead to some confusion. However, these consoles allow the user to give each state a name as well as a number, which is some compensation. To significantly reduce the possibility for confusion it is standard prac-

[3]Not that long ago, computer power and memory was much more expensive, and lighting cue states were universally recorded on paper. Many shows still keep a paper record of the level of each channel in each lighting cue state. For simple lighting systems there is nothing wrong with recording the contents of the cue state on paper, indeed many small and medium scale tours still do this to avoid the problems of incompatibility between different makes and models of memory lighting console.

tice to use the same number for the cue number recorded in the show caller's book, the state number in the lighting designer's cue synopsis, and the memory number used to recall, replay or modify the recorded lighting state in the lighting console.[4] This goes some way to account for the interchangeability of the words state and cue. As we have seen with other potentially confusing double meanings, context will usually tell us what is meant at the time.

Other ways in which the cue might happen for each performance include automatic triggering from a sound track, perhaps using midi or time-code,[5] remote devices sending a signal to the lighting console, perhaps triggered by the performer rather than an technical operator, or the operator might learn the show by heart and cue themself. This is what usually happens in live music concert lighting and perhaps brings the operator closest to the performance. As lighting designer you will need to be aware of whatever system is used to initiate changes in the lighting, and make sure that the correct information is recorded — digitally or otherwise — to enable your vision of the lighting to happen for each performance.

The lighting plan, magic sheets and groups

In previous chapters we have mentioned the importance of making the lighting plan intelligible for the different users that need it. One of these was the lighting designer making cues in the performance space. For this use we said we needed the channel numbers to be most prominent so that the lighting designer can call up lanterns and groups of lanterns using these numbers. On any lighting system with a soft patch the channel numbers do not have to be the same as the dimmer numbers. As lighting designer, whenever there is an opportunity to decide what the channel numbers should be, you should take it. Make the numbers mean something to you. The simple rig for *Bullie's House* in the last chapter took this approach. Channels that were likely to be used together were numbered consecutively and consistently. For example, the front light channels are numbered 1 through 4 with 2 and 4 as centres; the red top/back light channels are numbered 7 through 10 and again even numbers 8 and 10 in the centre. Even here on this small rig, however, there are inconsistencies. For example, the three overhead specials are numbered in the order that it became apparent they were needed. Originally there were two more, channels 16 and 17, hence the cyc floods start at 18. However, the furthest off-stage floods were added later in the process and had to use whatever number was still un-used at that point, in this case 30. Even on this small lighting system, numbers did not remain logical for long.

On a larger rig, the lighting plan has to be bigger in order to remain intelligible. It will be a larger piece of paper with more lanterns, more channels and more numbers — harder to make sense of in a hurry, taking up too much space — difficult for the lighting designer to use when making cues. By this stage in the process they will have focused the lighting rig so it is reasonable to assume that they know where all their units are located around the building. What is more important now is the area on stage that they light up, which direction their light comes from and what colour that light is. And this is where the magic sheet really comes into its own.

The magic sheet is usually a map of the stage with notation to indicate which channel will provide what

---

[4] Sometimes this is not possible, but the potential confusion arising from almost any other system is rarely worth going through.

[5] Midi is a set of codes developed to allow digital musical instruments and other devices to communicate with each other. Many lighting consoles have midi input and output. Time-code was developed to allow film editors to synchronise images and sound recorded on different machines at the same time. Uses for time-code have developed way beyond this and it can now be found synchronising the output of all manner of devices in situations from amusement parks to professional theatres and large events. Both midi and time-code provide opportunities for synchronisation and automation of lighting and other performance media well beyond the scope of this book. For more information on this complex but fascinating subject, start by looking up show control.

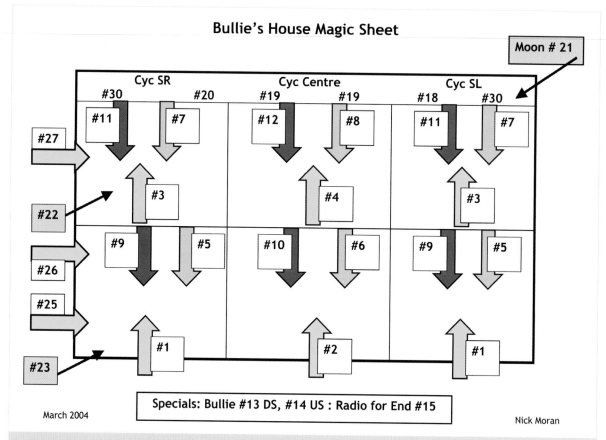

FIGURE 1. *BUDDLIE'S HOUSE* MAGIC SHEET.
THE LARGE RECTANGLE REPRESENTS THE STAGE, SPLIT INTO SIX AREAS, WITH THE CYC AS THE SECTION AT THE TOP. THE COLOURED ARROWS REPRESENT THE ELEMENTS OF THE MAIN WASHES, WITH THE CHANNEL NUMBER APPROPRIATE TO THAT AREA IN A BOX BESIDE THE ARROW. THE COLOUR OF THE ARROWS IS A CRUDE REPRESENTATION OF THE COLOUR OF THAT WASH. THE SOLID ARROWS ARE DISCRETE CHANNELS THAT GENERALLY WORK ALONE. I HAVE INCLUDED SL AND SR ON THE SHEET BECAUSE I SOMETIMES MIX THEM UP AND THIS PROVIDES A USEFUL REMINDER.

kind of light for each area. Most working lighting designers who use this approach develop their own layout, what is important is that it is clear to the user. As lighting designers we generally make these documents for our own exclusive use so the only person it has to be right for is ourselves. Here is a very simple magic sheet for the very simple rig for a show I lit called *Bullie's House*. The production toured studio theatres without a dedicated lighting crew, and with very little time to build or tech in each venue, so the documentation had to be easy to work from.

Most lighting rigs will need more than one magic sheet to keep things clear enough to be useful. Usually when a lighting designer is balancing levels we are dealing with one or two systems at a time, for example

back light and front light over a particular section of stage. The systems which are likely to work together are usually most usefully kept on one sheet. Later on there is another example of a magic sheet for a different type of rig.

Lighting design is not, however, about numbers, it is about light. Some people are very happy expressing their ideas in numbers, but most are not. Why talk about the back light as 'channels five through eight' or 'nine through twelve' when what we mean is 'cool back light' or 'red back light'? Many professional lighting consoles now allow us to do just that. By recording a selection of channels as a group, giving that group a name, and allocating a button on the lighting console to that group, the lighting designer and the lighting operator/programmer can select a system of light without any numbers being spoken.

We will probably want to balance the output of the channels within the group. If a particular balance of intensities is going to be useful more than once there are ways to record the group with that balance built into the selection on almost every professional lighting console.[6] For now at least we may have to return to channel numbers to do this, but if the individual channels within the group have been numbered in a logical way, this will be easier. Most lighting designers prefer working with groups with names than working with just numbers. It is common practice to record the groups before creating cue states, often before the focus too, since bringing up the group can be a good check that the focus will work. To the right is a group sheet for *Bullie's House*, with the contents of each group in the second column. The order of the numbers written in the second column mirrors their effect across the stage looking from the production desk, which should help us if we need to balance the levels within a group.

Some lighting consoles, whilst allowing groups to have names, have no facility to label the button associated with the group, or do not have sufficient buttons to give each group its own. This means the operator still has to use numbers to access a group, even though it has a useable name. Where this is the case it can be very helpful if the lighting designer knows the group numbers, to speed up the process of accessing channels.

The purpose of these documents — lighting plan, magic sheets and group list — is to help the lighting designer do the job of making lighting cues. It is worth spending some time preparing the type that suits you best, and this might change from rig to rig. The important thing is to make sure they are tools that help to get the show lit, and not burdens that drain creative energy or limit what can be achieved with the rig.

Gp no.	Group name	Contents
1	Front light	3 ; 4 ; 3 1 ; 2 ; 1
2	202 back light	7 ; 8 ; 7 5 ; 6 ; 5
3	Red back / top	11 ; 12 ; 11 9 ; 10 ; 9
4	DS high cross	26 25
5	US high cross / ¾ back light	27
6	Cyc	30;20;19; 18;30
7	Moonlight key	21
8	Moonlight fill	22 23
9	Death specials	14 13
10	Radio special	15
	House lights	? ?

FIGURE 2. *Bullie's House* Group List

The production desk

The lighting designer will need a place to work from, and this is usually the production desk, often in a central position in the auditorium. This position needs to be a centre of operations for the lighting designer. It needs to have a good view of the whole performance space and it needs to have good communication links to all the people that will be working to make the lighting the best it can be. The production desk is the lighting designer's

---

[6]Usually the word 'proportional' comes into the description of this function, e.g. proportional patch, proportional group, etc.

FIGURE 3. LIGHTING DESIGNER PAUL PYANT AND ASSOCIATE DAVID HOWE AT WORK BEHIND THEIR PRODUCTION DESK FOR *LORD OF THE RINGS.*

work space during much of the build and technical period, and often up to the first public show and it needs to be treated as such by everyone.

The production desk is where the lighting designer will keep the show paperwork.[7] As well as the lighting plan, magic sheets and group list, there will be a cue synopsis outlining the provisional composition of each proposed lighting state and the position of each proposed lighting cue — all ready to be referred to and updated as the lighting states are made and recorded. Most lighting designers will want remote monitors from the console displaying the contents of cues and the details of the cue sheet. While the lighting designer will be concentrating on the stage most of the time, and should know the rig well enough to be roughly aware of the effect of each channel on the stage, it can be very useful to be able to see exactly which channels are at what level. Many questions can be answered by a quick look at a well laid out console screen; for example, the dull glow at the top of a flat are channels we forgot to take out from the last

[7]Of course this 'paperwork' could be digital, stored and accessed by computer. If it is be sure you have back-up copies, on a memory stick you take everywhere with you or perhaps remotely stored on your own private website, accessed over the internet and protected by password. You cannot work without this information so you need to protect it.

scene, the lanterns with scrollers look too yellow because they have the wrong colour rather than because they are dimmed down or the cue we are just about to modify is not the one we should be working on! However, the lighting designer needs focus on the stage more than numbers on screens, and we will need to make sure that monitors do not interfere with our view of the stage.

The production desk will be home for some hours — perhaps some days or weeks — so it is worth making sure it is reasonably comfortable.[8] However, I would strongly advise all lighting designers to make sure they regularly get out from behind the production desk, to look at the performance area from other perspectives and talk to the director and others face to face, away from the technical paraphernalia that can easily inhibit creative discussions.

Do not under-estimate the potential for stress at the production desk, or the often destructive consequences of not dealing well with that stress. At the end of the last chapter is a short check-list. It is worth adding some things to that list that the lighting designer can think about providing for themselves. We usually feel better when we have elements of our immediate environment under our own control. Each person will have their own tools and favourite things that can provide comfort or relieve stress. These will probably include supplies of favourite mess-free foods or sweets and bottled water. (All of this generates rubbish so make sure you have something for that too.)

For many the comfort of your own laptop computer (with or without peripherals such as printers, speakers, web cam, media drive etc) is essential, whether or not the machine is used for making lighting or documenting the show. You may have a charger for your mobile phone or PDA. You might have a personal work-light, or a mascot, or a stress ball. You will need a note pad and something to write with — don't rely totally on the computer unless it really does go everywhere with you. Even then, you will often want to give written information —

lists of missing items, a request for colour or gobos, or just the lunch order — to an assistant or other helper.

Try to avoid liquids and messy food at the production desk, even though it is often easier to stay there for your break. In the dark it is all too easy to knock over a cup or container and spoil a plan, make important notes un-readable, or wreck a computer. Best to stick to dry snacks and to take regular breaks for coffee, tea or whatever away from the production desk.

At the top of the check-list was communication. It is worth reminding ourselves once again that an lighting designer rarely works alone. They will need to be in communication with:

■ Members of the technical team, for example the pro-grammer or lighting console operator, the chief or production electrician, and perhaps the follow spot team.

■ The team running things on stage, for example the DSM or show caller and the stage manager, and . . .

■ The rest of creative team.

Each of these three teams requires a different kind of communication. With the technical team, the lighting designer will often need to communicate specialist information using technical language specific to per-formance lighting; for example, talking about moving light attributes, colours referenced to swatch book numbers or console procedures, and almost inevitably, lots of numbers. With the stage management team the communication will focus on the correct timing and placement of lighting cues in the script, and other matters concerning the mechanics of how things will run on stage. There will be lots of numbers here too; page numbers, cue numbers, even bar numbers (both musical bars and flying bars), numbers of seconds and minutes, numbers of people on stage and lots more. Communication with the creative team should be much less about numbers, much more about ideas — it should be creative! At times the lighting designer

---

[8]That includes knowing the route to the nearest comfort zones — the best way to a place with some fresh air, perhaps a coffee shop or tea room, and of course the nearest rest rooms or lavatories.

becomes the conduit between director and stage manager, translating creative ideas into the technical language required for their realisation, and a good lighting designer will need to handle this alongside all the other stuff. It can be hard jumping between these different modes of communication and remaining polite, but that is almost always part of the job. It many not be in the job description of the lighting designer to ensure that all the equipment for this essential communication is in place and working, but a wise one will check. Well in advance of the time allocated in the schedule for stage rehearsals with lighting, the lighting designer needs to make sure they will be able to communicate effectively with these three groups.

There is more to communication that having the physical channel set up (that is the head-sets and talk-back systems, or just being close enough to talk face to face.) It is a good idea to know not only everyone's name, but the form of their name they would prefer you to use; for example, Sir, Mr Smith, Philip, Phil or darling. Often the lighting designer will hear a voice at the other end of the talk-back system, and may need to talk to that person for hours without ever seeing them. This can take some getting used to. It is a good idea to adopt an etiquette on talk-back that acknowledges the missing elements of communication between people — you can't see each other. This may mean people need to limit their use of irony and sarcasm as these can easily be mis-read over talk-back. Also assume that you are being listened to by the person you are talking about, or a close friend of theirs — because you just never know . . .[9]

Catching up with creative collaborators

If you have been busy with all the business of overseeing the preparation of your rig while the director and others have been in a rehearsal room with the performers, you may need to re-establish good relations with the creative team. As lighting designer you will need to find out if anything significant has changed since you were last in the rehearsal room. You will need to make your creative collaborators aware of anything you have discovered which might impact on your work together in the coming hours, days or weeks. (However, there is little point in raising levels of stress and tension by telling them tales of woe at this point — it won't make your life any easier.) Along side the work stuff, you will want to know what sort of mood everyone is in since this should affect how you communicate with them. You are likely to be working long hours with these people and it will usually be easier if everyone can be as relaxed and open as possible with each other.

The director is not the only person who can fill you in with information on changes and moods. Indeed unless the director has a strong technical focus they may not even be the best person to do this. The stage manager or the production manager should know if there have been changes that impact on the technical realisation of the show — anything from changes in the location of a scene on stage to a major re-ordering of scenes has been known to happen in the final days in the rehearsal room. The DSM or show-caller will the best person to let you know about any more subtle changes such as small changes in the script or blocking changes.

All the lighting designers I talked to say that if at all possible, find time to sit down with the director to agree a way of working before making your first lighting states. It is important at the beginning of this process to establish trust — the lighting designer needs to ensure the director maintains a belief that they can successfully light their show. This is especially important if the lighting designer and director have not worked together before. For example, the lighting designer needs to be

---

[9]The same applies on stage — most theatre spaces have a microphone over the stage to relay the performance into the dressing rooms and back stage areas. The idea is that during a show, the performers and crew can hear what is happening without everyone having to wait at the side of stage all the time. It is always best to assume this stage relay system is on and that people you can't see are listening to you whenever you are on a stage.

---

clear if they are presenting states as a work in progress or as more or less finished. Many lighting designers like to sketch in ideas to begin with, holding back on adding too much detail too early and waiting for a 'language'[10] to develop. This way of working allows the team to write a lot of lighting states relatively quickly and define an approach that has a consistency — that language we were just talking about. Fine adjustment such as balancing levels to more subtly focus audience attention or remove distracting shadows can come later, perhaps when the blocking is more settled. If the lighting designer is not clear about this way of working, the director may be horrified by the sketchy states presented as finished work and lose confidence in the their ability.

Trying to create the right lighting state for some scenes can become time-consuming, slowing down the creative process and leading to frustration.

Many lighting designers use the idea of a placeholder cue — a cue which we know we will have to come back to, but which allows us to move on — in these situations. This has proved to be an especially valuable way of working for many less experienced designers. It gets the creative process moving again without undermining the lighting designer's position in the creative team, and can allow difficult lighting problems to be solved later when there is less pressure, say during a break when the whole cast and crew are no longer hanging around while lighting sort themselves out! Think of this idea as a kind of get out of jail free card though, and don't try using it too often or it will stop working. A conversation with the director before the session begins will often give clues as to their mood and degree of nervousness. (Don't think that the lighting designer is the only one with nerves at the beginning of rehearsals on stage. Many directors find technical rehearsals very difficult, often because it is a part of the process they feel they cannot properly control.)

As well as letting the director know how you intend to work — or rather agreeing a way of working to create the light for the performance with the director — as lighting designer you need to know how the director will be working with the performers on the stage. How close to a finished product is what will be presented at these first stage rehearsals? How much work will the director still be doing with the performers on stage and how much time will they have to attend to other matters, including the lighting?

One of the key things the lighting designer needs to establish is how much the blocking[11] of the performers might change. For example, how close will the positions to be taken by performers on stage in the coming rehearsals be to final positions taken when the piece has an audience? If there is to be a period when the director is trying blocking ideas out, can they give you some idea about when positions will become final? There will be aspects of the performance that are affected by the change in space from the rehearsal room to the stage, and it will usually be the director's primary concern to work on these things first. As lighting designer you may well need to explain why confirmed blocking is important for the realisation of the lighting design (if it is), and if it is important for particular sections of the piece only.

---

[10]We are borrowing here from modern linguistics and semiotics. The idea is that, as with other signifiers on the stage, lighting can work best if its signifiers are allowed to work as a 'natural language'. By analogy with the generally consistent meaning of words in language, if light of a particular quality signifies a particular place or time of day once, when that place or time of day needs to be signified again, the same quality of light is used. Each different quality of light used relates to the others — in intensity, direction, colour, etc, in the same way the words in a sentence relate to each other and help us understand the whole sentence. If we don't push this analogy too far it can be very useful.

[11]Blocking refers to the moves and positions of the performers. Sometimes a director will be very definite about where each performer is at every moment of the piece — in a dance piece, for example, this is normal. Other genres are more relaxed about where the performers are on stage at any particular moment. There is little point in making tightly-defined areas of light for a particular scene if the performers have not yet become comfortable with the space of the stage, and therefore do not have tightly-defined places to be for that moment.

If possible the lighting designer should find out if there are particular parts of the piece that the director is nervous about; maybe a section is not working in the rehearsal room, or there is uncertainty about how to play a particular scene. Ask if the director needs help from the lighting designer or perhaps wants this section left in something like work-light until a way forward becomes clear. Perhaps there is a particular section that everyone has said will be solved by lighting and now the director wants to be sure that it can be. Decide if you both want to solve this problem first or leave some time later — once the language for the lighting is clearer to you both.

Most important, decide if it will be possible for the lighting designer to try things out during rehearsals. Clearly the lighting designer and the lighting team will need to assure the rest of the company that they will not be plunging the stage into darkness at inappropriate moments during rehearsals, but that said, try to establish that it will be alright to add or subtract light, change its colour or shape, and generally work on a lighting state while the scene is being rehearsed. Sometimes directors find this too distracting from their main focus, which may still be getting a good performance from the actors. However, if the lighting designer can make use of the populated stage to work on lighting states it is generally better for all concerned. Sometimes it is possible to work on lighting states for a scene other than the one being rehearsed. It is often enough to just make the director (and set designer) aware that this is what is happening (and to ensure there is enough light on stage for everyone to see what they need to see). For example, during the rehearsal of a long daytime scene with few cues, the base states for a sunset in the following scene might be tried out and recorded. So long as everyone knows what is going on this is not usually a problem, and it reduces the time needed to plot these states when the rehearsal moves on to the next scene.

Making cues

Let's take a moment to check we have everything in place to begin lighting the show:

- The lighting rig is fully focused and fully working.

- The lighting console is fully working and the operator/programmer is ready to work.

- All other necessary operators are standing by to do their jobs.

- Communication systems are in place, tested and working for all the people that need them.

- The house lights are under control, and the emergency lighting is as it will be during a performance.

- The lighting designer is comfortable at the production desk, snacks and liquid refreshment on hand.

- The production desk has at least one functioning work-light that the lighting designer can turn on and off.

- The paperwork (plans, magic sheets, group lists, cue synopsis) is accurate and up-to-date and available to the lighting designer at the production desk.

- The lighting designer's script/score/running order is accurate and up-to-date and available at the production desk.

- If we are plotting a called show, the show caller is standing by with the book ready to enter cue points and call cues.

- The lighting operator/programmer has a suitable emergency state that will put light on stage no matter what else is happening — just in case!

- The director is in a good mood and ready to collaborate in the creation of the lighting for the show.

- All parties concerned have agreed where in the piece they are going to start work. Very often this is not the beginning or the show, and if that is the case, everyone needs to be aware and ready.

Lighting over rehearsals vs. lighting sessions

It would be an extraordinarily confident lighting designer who, after finishing the focus, could walk away from the performance space without wanting to see how their cue ideas were going to work in reality. Most of us want to try a few things out and examine how the pictures in our heads (or on a computer monitor) compare to combinations of light from real instruments in the real performance space. After standing in the beam of the lanterns for the focus, we want to see their effect from the auditorium. Trying a few things out before the first lit rehearsal, however, is not what most people mean by a lighting session.

In the past the lighting session was an important part of almost every production period in theatre, opera and elsewhere. The idea is that a block of time is given over to the lighting designer, and (usually) the director and set designer, to work on lighting states and transitions without the cast. The expectation was often that every lighting cue would be built and recorded during the lighting session, and then just played back over the dress rehearsal. Often this block of time would be late at night.

One problem with this approach is that what most lighting designers want to focus their attention on is the light on the performers, and with no performers on the stage this is difficult. Sometimes the junior members of the stage management department are available to stand in for key performers and walk the stage, but this is rarely a satisfactory substitute. All too often so much adjusting of the lighting of the performers has to be done once they start rehearsing under the lights that all concerned begin to feel that the hours spent in the lighting session could have been better spent else-where — in bed asleep perhaps.

This is definitely not to say that a more satisfactory solution is for the lighting designer to begin the first lit rehearsals with nothing in the desk — no lighting states ready to try out. Experience and local practice will help the lighting designer decide how much useful time should be spent plotting lighting states and transitions without the performers in place. Clearly, complex transitions or scene changes where the primary focus is not on the performers will benefit from some preparation. No one will thank the lighting designer for working on a multi-part sunset on the cyclorama while performers and others sit around waiting. Indeed, in the professional world where each person's time is money, the production manager or producer will quickly point out how much each hour with performers and full crew on stage is costing. At the same time, lighting that is sensitive to the moves and moods of the performers is all but impossible to create without those performers present. How can we judge the quantity and quality of light that best supports a performer at key moments in the piece without being able to see that light on the performer?

So what use should the lighting designer make of lighting sessions? If we can no longer expect the lighting session to produce a finished product, it can still be useful in a number of ways. This may be the last chance to check the focus of all the units in a group to make sure they work together. Lighting sessions are a time when the lighting designer can try out the elements of the rig and to see for the first time if they will work as planned. If they are working with a cue synopsis that includes the groups and specials planned for each state, these can be looked at working on stage together and evaluated. Even a relatively inexperienced lighting designer should be able to tell most of the time if the general idea is going to work or not, without the performers being there. There will always be surprises, usually some good and some not so good: a particular wash that works surprisingly well to do two different things at different intensities; a cross-light special that beautifully sculpts a scenic element it was never meant for; or a particular combination of scenic colour and light colour that is just not going to work! A lighting session can be very useful for discovering these things too.

Another use for the lighting session is to reinforce the relationships between the lighting designer and the rest of the creative team. Often the lighting designer will be seen operating primarily in a technical role during the process of rigging and focusing. The lighting session can be a time to demonstrate once more their artistic side. As we have already commented, it is necessary for the director to trust the ability of the lighting designer to work in a style that complements their own. If the two have not worked together before it is especially important to establish that trust quickly, and a good way to do this is to sit together and discuss light on the stage without too many distractions. In the early chapters we commented on how hard it can be to talk about light in performance, especially with non-specialists. It so much easier to show your collaborators the quality of light you wish to use to evoke a particular time, place or emotion, than to describe it.

However, in British theatre and elsewhere the dedicated lighting session is disappearing. Prohibitions on overnight working and a general wish to control overtime costs of staff are both factors in its decline and this is not entirely a bad thing. After all, how fresh is the creative team on the morning of the first stage rehearsal, if the night before they were looking at lighting states till 5am? It is usually worth stealing some stage time to look at lighting states — preferably with the scenery in position — before lighting the performers for the first time and if this can be done with the director and set designer, all the better. If there is no scheduled time of a lighting session, many lighting designers will attempt to build a session into the end of the focus time, or by agreement work over a scene change rehearsal, being careful to ensure that this does not make things more dangerous in any way.[12]

By whatever means are available the lighting designer needs to be sure that, before the first lit rehearsal with the performers, there are lighting states recorded and ready to be played back on stage. If the opportunities for a dedicated lighting session are limited, many lighting designers will now opt for pre-plotting using visualisation software such as WYSIWYG or LD Capture. These can be very useful if the lighting rig has a large amount of technology or is required to work in a particularly intricate way. However, at present these systems have major shortcomings including poor rendering of the effect of light on the moving human body.

Whatever means have been used to get the basic states recorded, once the performers are on stage, there will inevitably be a need to modify those states. This is referred to as lighting over the rehearsal, and it requires quick thought and consideration for others if it is going to be productive. Even with the basis of each cue recorded in the lighting console, as the performance evolves of stage, the lighting needs to evolve with it. Perhaps some action on stage is reblocked to a new area; the focus of the lighting will need to move to this new area too, meanwhile restoring the old area of focus to a less prominent condition. But this is a relatively major change and there is every chance that the rehearsal itself will stop while the new blocking is worked out in detail. This will usually give the lighting designer and their team plenty of time to modify the states before the rehearsal continues.

More difficult to catch and repair are states that almost work but still have some flaws. If the agreement between director and lighting designer is that the rehearsal will only stop for lighting as a last resort — and this is often the case — catching and fixing these flaws requires everyone in the lighting team to be working quickly and efficiently. Perhaps a costume catches too much light and takes focus from where we want it; a channel within a group will need to be reduced in intensity or otherwise dealt with in order to restore the state to something that works with the other elements of performance. Perhaps the balance of key and fill is not quite right in one area of the lit stage. Again, the offending channels will need to be located and levels adjusted accordingly, but at the same time as the rehearsal continues and cues are being called and executed. The flaws in a particular state may only reveal themselves for a short time as rehearsals continue — long enough to distract audience attention, but not long enough to diagnose the problem and fix it — unless:

- The lighting designer is very aware of what each lantern in the state is doing.
- The lighting designer can decide quickly on a remedy.
- The operator of the lighting system can make the adjustment, and record the change, hopefully while whatever revealed the flaw is still present and before the next lighting state is required on stage.

A speedy and focused response to any flaws is important. When things can't be fixed in time the lighting designer needs to make a note of the problem, and hopefully come back and fix it later.

---

[12]Remember in the preparations for making lighting states we mentioned having a fader on the console that brings up light on stage in an emergency.

As the creative team begin to define and build the visual languages, including the language of the performance lighting, the lighting designer may find themself moving away from the original ideas that were discussed before the piece took life on stage. Whole scenes may finish up looking very different from the way they were originally envisaged, as the director, the performers and the lighting designer discover what works well and what does not. This can be an exciting time — often fuelled by adrenalin and coffee. Everyone on the lighting team will need to be able to work quickly when required, especially the lighting designer and the person entering information into the lighting console.

Enter the programmer!

Over recent years a new role has emerged in the lighting department, the role of programmer. We have already mentioned this, and talked about the need to establish good working relationships to be able to work quickly together. So what is the difference between an operator and a programmer?

In North American practice, it has been common for the lighting designer to instruct the console operator key stroke by key stoke how to enter and record the information into the console. This practice remains common in other areas too. However, with the increasing use of moving light technology, and the increasing numbers of cues now employed per show, a new discipline was required to master the control of this complex lighting. The consoles and lights can do more so more is expected. The lighting programmer — a lighting person with an expert level knowledge of the lighting console and the lights it controls — became an essential member of the team on larger shows.

If the system is largely conventional lanterns, it is perfectly possible to make groups and put the intensity of those groups on faders. The lighting designer may then wish to push these faders up and down themselves, as appropriate, balancing washes and specials on stage by hand. As things get more complex — moving lights and colour changers, for example, need to be in the right position before they come on — a more sophisticated approach becomes necessary. The lighting designer is paid for their eyes and how they see

the stage. With the lighting under the control of faders, these can be moved up and down whilst still looking at the stage. With more sophisticated lighting systems comes the need to program the lighting rather than just plot it. Many key strokes and other adjustments are needed to get the moving lights into the right place at the right time. The eyes of the programmer will at times inevitably be focused on screens and keypads rather than the stage. The programmer's brain will be focused on the best technical way to enable the latest lighting state on stage rather than on the dramaturgical reason for that lighting state. Very few people can successfully accomplish the two roles of organising and entering data, and designing lighting states simultaneously — the novice should not attempt it.

Cut and paste

Very often, we want to use the same basic look more than once. It may be a whole scene. For example, we might have several scenes set in the same location at the same time of day (or a location where time of day does not affect the light). Or we might only want to use selected channels from a scene, say the channels dressing a particular scenic element or perhaps a particular cyclorama look. It is common practice to copy the channel levels (and attributes of an automated lighting) and paste them into the other cue or cues, either as a basis to build on or as a finished cue. It is important that the programmer understands exactly what the lighting designer wants to do in these cases as there are usually several different ways of working on modern lighting consoles, each may have slightly different results. Approaches include:

■ Copying a whole cue and pasting it into the new cue, either with or without the associated timing information. This can result in unwanted information in the new cue, such as positions of moving lights that are not actually used, and is usually the least satisfactory way of working.

■ Copying only the active components of the cue — intensity channels above zero and the status of any associated automated lighting attributes. This is usually the most flexible way of working, but may not be the easiest for the programmer on some consoles.

■ Storing frequently used cues as a preset focus or set of preset focus groups (or equivalent). This means that any change to the preset focus will automatically update all the cues that have used it as a basis but probably means the fewest number of buttons need to be pressed by the programmer to get the state on stage.

Since copying cues and pasting the contents into new cues can be extremely efficient way of working, it is something every aspiring lighting designer should investigate the particulars of on the consoles they will be using.

Tracking

While we are discussing lighting programmers again we should talk through the pros and cons of the two most common ways of recording cues in memory consoles — tracking and cue only. In essence the difference is clear:

■ In cue only the console records the output of every channel in each cue.

■ In tracking the console records only the changes from the previous cue.

Why the difference? Well, the first computer consoles had very little memory, so many manufacturers made a virtue of necessity and maximised the usefulness of that memory by storing changes rather than whole cues. After all, the guys (and they were mostly guys) who recorded by hand the cue information for the manual boards of old were only interested in what they had to change, so that is all they recorded on paper. When memory became cheaper, some manufacturers allowed their consoles to record everything with every cue, and for a while many of us thought this was no bad thing. Admittedly it did bring a few problems: imagine a show has a big sky cloth and we run a long cue simulating a sunset using cyc floods. Then a performer pretends to operate a light switch and we have a second cue that quickly brings up some channels to simulate a desk lamp

going on. So long as the sunset cue has finished there is no problem. But if the performer is early and operates the light switch *before* the sunset cue has finished, the cyc channels would jump to their final state with the go of the desk lamp cue. This is because when the desk lamp cue was recorded the console took the level of all the channels including the cyc ones, and stored them, so the cyc channels were recorded in their final state. When the desk lamp cue was played back, the console told all the channels, including the cyc ones, to go to the values they were at when the desk lamp cue was recorded.

If the same cues are recorded in tracking mode, only the changes in the channels associated with the desk lamp are recorded in the second cue. The sunset cue will continue to its conclusion in its recorded time, no matter when the desk lamp cue is taken. Some lighting consoles that record all channels in every normal cue have work rounds such as the move fade, but when we start to use moving lights and scrollers on these lighting consoles things can get difficult. With tracking it is possible to record the position and other attributes of a moving light at the beginning of a scene in which it is used and then focus only on the attributes that change during the scene. If the intensity changes from cue to cue that is all that will be recorded in these subsequent cues. If later we decide that the beam was too small for the scene, we only need to change it in the first cue and it will be correct for all the rest. This may seem like a small thing when you only have a few moving lights and you are using them individually. Once a lighting system becomes dependant on moving lights, the increased speed and other advantages of tracking make it the only logical choice for most lighting designers.

What tracking allows us to do, as well as running several cues at the same time without them affecting each other, is to simplify the business of using moving lights in a theatre style play-back or stack of cues. The detailed implications of working in tracking mode are primarily the concern of the lighting programmer[13] and

---

[13]Good books on this subject include the *Automated Lighting Programmers Handbook* by Brad Schiller and the comprehensive *Automated Lighting* by Richard Cadena.

in any case will change from console to console. However, here are a few things the lighting designer needs to consider when working in tracking:

- Two or more cues controlling separate selections of channels can run simultaneously without affecting each other — the sunset will carry on to its programmed conclusion in its programmed time no matter when the desk lamp cues GO.

- The channels that don't change throughout a scene, for example channels involved in lighting the setting, only get recorded once in the first cue of the scene — if half way through the rehearsal of that scene we want to change the look for the whole scene, we only need to update the first cue and all the rest of the cues will look right too.

- It should be simpler to see on the console display what each cue is actually doing, since only the channels that change will be in the contents of the cue.

- It should make cutting and pasting lighting cues and parts of lighting cues a lot simpler. Moving light and scroller positions associated with intensity channels at zero will not be in cues we copy from, and so we won't end up with unnecessary noisy and distracting moves in the pasted cue.

However, tracking can catch out the unwary, especially if there is a need to record cues out of sequence. For this reason we frequently use blocking cues. A blocking cue includes every channel, including every attribute of every moving light. It means that any changes made to cues before the blocking cue in the cue stack will have no effect on those after the blocking cue. In multi-act drama or opera for example, it is a good idea to record the first cue of each act as a blocking cue.

As with the details of the options available to cut and paste, getting to grips with tracking as implemented on the consoles you use regularly is something every aspiring lighting designer should do.

Timing cues — transitions

As well as consideration of the finished lighting state, we also need to think about how we get into that state and how we get out of it — hence transitions. Let's begin this discussion with some definitions of cue types:[14]

- Snap cue:

A jump from one lighting state to the next in the fastest possible time.

- Normal cross-fade:

A transition from one state to the next where the intensity of some channels fades out at the same rate and starting at the same time as the other channels increase in intensity.

- Split time cross-fade:

A transition from one state to the next where the channels associated with the new cue state move at a different rate to the ones fading down from the old cue. Usually represented as UU/DD where UU is the time taken to build the new state (up time), and DD the time for the old state to fade out (down time).

- Delay time*:

Used when the fade in and fade out *start* at different times. The delay time is the gap between the action of pressing GO and the delayed fade in or fade out beginning.

- Follow-on cue:

Is a further cue that happens at some point after the first transition has begun. It will

----

[14]See also the boxed section on p. 99.

----

often start when the first cue is completed, and may be triggered automatically (auto-follow).

■ Wait time*: Is the time between pressing GO and the cue with that wait time beginning — most often used with follow-on cues. Some consoles take the wait from the end of the first cue rather than the GO of the first cue!

■ Link cue*: A cue that changes the standard numeric order or cues in a stack. It may link around cues that are not required, but that you don't as yet want to delete, or may be used to create a loop of cue states to form a chase. Does not usually have any channel information.

■ Part cue*: A single cue in which different channels or groups of channels move with different rates and/or have different delay or wait times.

* Warning: some console manufacturers use these words in different ways, and some use different words — always check if you are at all unsure.

Complex rigs of moving lights can require cues with multiple timings. For example, imagine a cue where some moving lights required for the next cue, pan tilt and change colour ready for that cue — but very slowly in order not to cause a distraction — at the same time as other channels snap on to mimic the effect of a light switch being turned on; or the fade up of some units

The mark cue

Mark cues are particular to moving light consoles and again the name comes with a warning. Different console manufacturers call it by different names, and implement it in slightly different ways, Generally the mark cue is a special cue that the console itself calculates the contents of. A mark cue is an automatic follow-on, once the cue before it has completed, the console will automatically trigger the mark, which should have no effect on the lighting state on stage. Once a mark has been placed in a cue stack, the console will look ahead to the very next cue. All the moving lights or lanterns with scrollers that are at zero intensity in the current cue and are on in the next cue, i.e. are at a non-zero intensity, are moved into position ready for that next cue — correct colour, beam, focus position, etc. If any change is made to the 'next cue' these changes are automatically reflected in the mark cue. This function is very powerful when it is properly implemented in the software of the console and understood by the programmer. On good moving light consoles, the mark cue or equivalent can be given its own time, so if things need to be in place quickly they can, but if on another occasion they need to be moved slowly to reduce noise or distraction, they can do that too.

Some consoles have a global function that puts moving lights and scrollers into position automatically with a global time. This can be useful during technical rehearsals because it will (usually) avoid unwanted sweeps of movers or scroll changes while the lantern is on — called live moves. However, the feature is rarely flexible enough to deal with every preparation cue discretely and a good programmer will strive for the added control afforded by an approach tailored to the individual cue state and taking account of the context of the show, e.g. is this a noisy or quiet part of the performance?

with scrollers being delayed for a few seconds while the scrollers change to the correct colour. For a dance number (or for other reasons) we might want each of say six moving profiles to sweep from up stage to down stage. Instead of them all moving together, we might want the first to set off, and as its beam gets to mid stage for the next one to set off, and so on. And then we might want the later ones to move more quickly than the first few — to catch them up so to speak. If we also decided that these lights would change colour in sequence as they moved down stage, and perhaps intensity too, we might be looking at up to 36 different values of fade time and delay time for just these six lanterns in just one cue! If we were using part cues, this could be a 36 part cue. Most contemporary moving light consoles, however, allow the programmer to do this ways that are much easier to see and to edit.

Snaps

A transition between two lighting states that has cue time of zero — a snap cue — will clearly have a very different effect than the same transition with a longer time. The shock effect of a sudden change in intensity (or colour or beam for that matter) draws attention to the lighting. If there is an obvious cause for the change — a performer switching a light switch or the sound effect of thunder — then the motivation for the change is clear, and the shock effect is diluted. (After all, our audience is used to sudden changes in intensity resulting from operating a light switch.) A snap cue that does not have such a immediate physical motivation[15] is a powerful signifier — usually provoking an audience response along the lines of 'What was that?' as the audience searches for the cause. It can be like a metaphorical slap for the audience, and so snap cues need to be handled with care. Making sure they happen in exactly the right place in the show every night is worth spending some time over.

One specialised use for the snap cue is at the end of musical numbers, where it is called a bump. A well-executed bump signals applause to an audience used to American and British musical theatre. It is part of the language of that genre. There are many ways of executing the bump cue. For anyone wanting to light musicals, this is just a small part of the language to be learned from observing the work of acknowledged experts. It is said that a well-executed bump can wring applause out of the audience — even if the musical number itself is indifferent.

Cross fades

A cross fade that, for example shifts focus from one stage area to another, will have a different impact depending on the timing of the transition. It is important to be clear about what the performance is trying to achieve at that point if the lighting is to support it. For example, in a two room stage set, if our intention is to transfer attention from one room to another in a clear and obvious way, a simple relatively rapid cross fade will probably be appropriate. On a more open stage we may want to make the audience slowly aware of some developing action away from the current area of focus, and then once that new area has been established, reduce the focus on the original area. We can do something more ambitious with timing the transition here; perhaps a slow build on the new area over say 20 seconds, and as this is establishing a slightly quicker fade on the original area. This might be represented in a cue synopsis as 20/10 Delay 15, meaning a build over 20 seconds, followed 15 seconds into that fade up by a 10 second fade down of the original area. On a simple time-line it looks like this:

Seconds	0	5	10	15	20	25
New area	Build starts				Complete	
Original area				Fade starts		Complete

[15] Remember our maxim from Chapter 5 about lighting cues being like method actors and needing a motivation.

If we wanted more subtlety, we might establish the new area in parts — first bringing in the back-light to reveal a silhouette, then a key from the side to reveal a more three dimensional form, and finally something to reveal faces. If we did this with a part cue, the timing and notes might be written down like this:

Part no	Time in/out	Delay time	Notes
1	20/20	0	Back light & cyc in new area
2	15/15	5	Add side key
3	10	15	Add face light
4	20/20	20	Lose much of original area

Let's look at this on a time line:

Time in seconds	0	5	10	15	20	25	30	35	40
Back light	Build starts				Build complete				
Side key		Build starts			Build complete				
Face light				Build starts		Build complete			
Original area					Fade starts				Fade ends

Recording this kind of transition as a part cue is not the only solution. If the lighting console is working in tracking mode where changes associated with each cue can be more or less unaffected by other cues running at the same time, each build or fade can be a separate cue state. We can set up the console to make the first cue — the back light build — trigger the others automatically after the programmed wait time, or we might have each cue triggered by separate hits on the GO button, allowing the operator or show caller to judge the best moment to begin each stage of this reveal according to the small differences in the performance from show to show.

Very often in performance we are manipulating time — the time of the piece may or may not run at the same pace as the time of audience — hours may pass in stage time in the seconds of a transition. There are ways the timing of our lighting cues can either support or undermine effects like this. For example, we have mentioned already that simulation of the changing position of the sun in the sky can be a way for lighting to indicate passing of time, and how this may often go unseen by an urban audience no longer used to judging time by the position of the sun. However, if we allow the key source or sources to lag in the fade out and lead the build into a new lighting state, the strong shadows will be more present for a while, and more available to signify time of day. Another example might be a transition into a dark night-time state. This might begin with little light and the audience struggling to see, and then follow on with a very slow build that brings just enough light to make the key performers visible by the time they are saying or doing important things.

Time on stage may or may not be linear — the piece may include flash-backs or scenes from other specific or non-specific time periods. Usually lighting will play a big part in signalling of slips in time to the audience. Unusual key light angle or colour may be used to signify unnatural time or place, but so can fractured transitions accomplished using part cues. We are in the territory where performance lighting draws attention to itself as conscious signifier, which means we need to be especially rigorous in our approach. Once a language has been established that works within the genre and is coherent with other signifiers on the stage, representation of nature can become less necessary, so long as the lighting is still supporting the production.

Constraints of genre will need to be considered. If the piece is a conventionally presented play in a naturalistic box set[16] it is unlikely that the audience will read a fractured transition as anything other than a technical mistake. If we are making a musical in the West End/Broadway tradition, the audience will expect there to be enough light to see all the faces (almost) all the time, but will probably be accepting of quite a lot of unnatural coloured light. If the genre is large-scale opera, very often light can be a conscious and overt signifier, while in the world of classical ballet functional revelation of the dancer's form must be the prime consideration.

There is also an argument that in general, the shorter the transition the more critical is the cue placement. Some instruments respond much more slowly than other — generally high wattage units are slower than low wattage ones, but PAR 64s are often quicker to respond the 1kW Fresnels (same wattage) or birdies (much smaller wattage).

Making use of rehearsal video recordings

Sometimes there is just no possibility of working fast enough to program all the required cues in a particular section of a piece. Maybe an intricate dance number where the design idea is to both follow the rapidly moving centre of action of the piece and change the mood of the light to follow the mood of the music. Sometimes the lighting designer is simply told that it is too dangerous to light over a particular rehearsal, and it will happen first in bright work light. Maybe a complex scene change involving a number of flown and trucked elements breaking apart and reforming. The first stage rehearsal of this kind of activity is unlikely to be the right time to try out lighting states and cue transitions. All concerned are likely to want to perform difficult or dangerous transitions in an evenly lit space without having to worry about performance lighting, perhaps blinding, perhaps plunging into unexpected blackout.

One response to this is to take a break and come back when the others are sufficiently prepared for lighting to continue. Another response is to take a video recording — preferably including the show caller's cues on one of the sound tracks for reference.[17] The lighting team can then record lighting states and transitions with the video and the show caller's cues as a reference. This technique can work really well for dance numbers requiring a lot of specials — especially if the video images enable the lighting team to see where on stage each special needs to be focused. Generally speaking, dancers are good at hitting the same spot of stage every night, so specials can be tight and if you discuss ideas with the choreographer this can be very effective.

When it comes to making best use of a lighting session, having a video reference for scenes goes a long way to compensating for not having the performers on

---

[16] Box set: a naturalistic representation of a room on stage with the fourth wall missing to enable the audience to see and hear what is going on — like our melodrama of previous chapters.

[17] You will need to check that everyone is happy with you taking a video, as people can get quite touchy about unauthorised recording. Be clear why you want to make the recording, what you will use it for, and be prepared to hand over the tape when you have finished working with it!

stage. At least you know where they were in the rehearsal, and at what moment.

These days it is possible to use a web cam and record a rehearsal directly to the hard drive of your lap-top on the production desk. This can be very useful for fixing cues — refocusing the moving light to where the per-former actually stands, or moving the position of a cue a few lines to go with a particular move. The quality will not be great and the colour will be nothing like real, but think of this as a video note-book, one of a set of tools that will help the lighting designer make the lighting the best it can be by opening night.

10

through to opening night and beyond

Watching a run-through

The first stage rehearsals of most productions proceed in a stop-start way, as everyone works out how the piece fits into this new space. The lighting designer can make use of these stops to do work on cues, and not only the cues relating to that particular section of the piece either. Soon though there will be an attempt to run the piece, or sections of it, without stopping. During these runs it becomes more difficult to do much more than tweak the occasional level or time, especially if there are sections with many cues. The lighting designer will need to take notes of flaws and errors, ready to fix them later. In heavily-cued sections of a piece, for example a dance number or complex scene change, it is usually more important to make sure the cues are in the right place in the script rather than that the state is perfect. The state can be fixed later when the dancers or scene-change crew are on a break and there is less pressure — hopefully with the help of someone who knows the sequence well or using a video recording of the rehearsal.

For a lighting designer, watching a run can be frustrating, even at the best of times. They will often think that if the proceedings could just be stopped for two minutes a lighting state or transition could be fixed but that can't always happen. Instead they need to make a note of the cue states that need attention, and then arrange a time to work on those states.

Visual dramaturgy

During a run, the lighting designer needs to keep concentrating on the whole picture on stage, trying to see it from the point of view of someone who has not seen this piece before. Is what should be visible sufficiently visible and what should be hidden suitably hidden? Is form revealed appropriately through combinations of shadow and highlight, colours and textures? Is the attention of the audience suitably guided to the most appropriate place for the production at each moment of the production and left to find its own centre of attention where that is appropriate? Are states that support a particular location, time or mood doing that? Are the transitions working, and do the states work in sequence? This may be the first time anyone has seen all the states next to each other. It may be the occasion when something that looked great when plotted in isolation looks wrong in the context of the cue states before or after it.

This is the part of the production process where the lighting designer's role as visual dramaturge becomes most important. In the northern European theatre tradition the dramaturge is the literary manager of a theatre company. Their role in the rehearsal room and the performance space is to ensure the company's necessary attention to details during rehearsal does not stop the piece working as an integrated whole, and to maintain the integrity of the overall artistic vision of the company. This may sound like rather a grand role for a lighting designer, but consider this: who else is responsible for all the things we have just talked about and why are those things important? Just as the literary dramaturge is most often not the original creator of the text of the play, the lighting designer is most often not the original creator of the visual side of the performance, but both take a responsibility for ensuring the way the piece is presented to the audience works.

We have already said that the lighting designer needs to develop and maintain the visual logic of the piece, working with and enhancing the visual languages of the production. Of course each member of the design team will also take some responsibility for these things too, and the lighting designer cannot do anything alone. But the fact that the work of the lighting designer is to make visible that which is seen, determine the way in which it will be seen, and to hide that which is not seen, puts an overall responsibility heavily on their shoulders. When the piece is run, the lighting designer needs to be looking beyond individual cue states and paying attention to the developing visual dramaturgy of the production.

dramaturge can be key here in allowing the developing performance to drive the response of the lighting design rather than trapping the performance in a fixed view of what the lighting will do. Perhaps some evocation of mood the team planned to do with lighting is now being done powerfully by the performers — the lighting designer may need to back off here to avoid overpowering the performance. Conversely perhaps a sense of place and time the director hoped would be conveyed by the script is not coming over, and the lighting designer needs to work with the director to establish location or time of day.

Whatever the particulars of the production, there is usually little to be gained from fixing the lighting on the set dressing in a state where the principal performer remains unlit. The priorities of the production may change from day to day or even from hour to hour. Working to those changing priorities is something that requires artistic sensitivity, technical understanding and excellent people skills — and is a normal day's work for a professional lighting designer.

Lighting notes

Depending on how many runs are available to watch and take notes, the lighting designer may wish to concentrate on different things for each run. Perhaps the finished states at one run and the transitions at another, or the stage near the principal performers first and the rest of the look later. This approach acknowledges that there are limits to how much can be achieved, both in taking notes and in doing the fixes with the programmer, show-caller and crew afterwards. Each production is likely to be different. An experienced lighting designer will have a good grasp of what has to be fixed before the next run, and what can wait.

Often there are details of the design which need the performance to develop in the space before they can be fully addressed. The lighting designer's role as visual

Taking notes

To take efficient notes, the lighting designer will have to do several apparently incompatible things at once: closely observe the stage, legibly record the note and the cue number or the state the note applies to.[1] On larger shows, this is where an assistant can be invaluable. If the lighting designer's eyes are on the stage, the assistant can be writing down the notes and discovering the cue numbers, either from a monitor linked to the console or by asking the operator over the head-sets. When no assistant is available the lighting designer has to work out other ways to take good notes. The strategy adopted will depend to some extent on how many notes the lighting designer thinks might be taken in that particular run. If the piece is still quite raw there may be little alternative to watching from the production desk,

---

[1]The need to write notes while still looking at the stage can be solved in a couple of ways. A lighting designer who can touch type can continue to observe the stage while typing their notes into a lap-top. More traditionally, with a little practice many people can write legible notes on a notepad without looking at it. This method means notes can be taken even while sitting amongst the audience.

close to console monitors and a work-light to illuminate a notepad or computer key-board. As the piece becomes closer to the lighting designer's vision of a finished work, fewer notes will be needed and they can more easily move away from the production desk. Many become quite good at writing in a notepad without looking at it; use large letters and stick to one or two notes per page on a reporter's style notepad, with plenty of abbreviations and this can be effective. Using a voice recorder can work well too. The lighting designer can speak the note quietly into the machine, and the background noise from the stage recorded at the same time will help to locate the comment in the piece. Using a wireless earpiece linked to the show-callers talkback channel can keep the lighting designer aware of the current cue number (and of whether the mistakes in the lighting are down to them or to operator error, e.g. the wrong button being pressed at the wrong time).

Voice recordings of notes or written notes, taken at the production desk or elsewhere in the auditorium, can be a great way of gathering the information required to refine a lighting design — to ensure the focus is always in the right place, that there are no unwanted distractions and that the states and transitions support the production. Notes may include changes in level of individual channels or groups, changes in moving light position, beam or colour, and changes in timing — both in the recorded cue times and in the placement of cue points. They might also include notes for discussion with other departments; can a fly cue run slightly slower to aid the drama of a reveal, or a scene be played in a slightly different place to avoid casting a distracting shadow? In some productions notes of this second kind will be welcomed as a useful contribution to making the show better for everyone, whilst in others they will be seen as interfering by the lighting designer in matters that don't concern them. Once again they will need to be

using people skills to decide the best way of working in each different production.

Once the notes have been taken, they need to be acted upon — states re-recorded, times altered, focus positions up-dated, cue positions changed, whole cues cut or new cues added. During this process, the lighting designer must keep their paperwork up-to-date (another job for the assistant on those occasions when the lighting designer is lucky enough to have one). For example, to work on the focus of individual lanterns or groups requires a full knowledge of the use made of those lanterns through the whole piece — there is nothing to be gained from re-positioning a lantern to work in a scene in act two if by doing so it no longer works in act one. Likewise with cue states and timings, if a new cue is to be added, the lighting designer must know where in the sequence of existing states it is needed so that it gets the right number. If a cue time is to be successfully extended there may be other consequences that need to be taken into consideration — is there still enough time for the moving lights that go out in that cue to move while dark to their required positions for the following cue?

Without up-to-date paperwork — which will include focus plots, track sheets,[2] cue synopsis with timings, script or score with cue positions marked in — the task of refining the lighting will be almost impossible. If all these things are in place, the lighting designer can use dedicated work sessions or stolen time to develop, refine or even completely change the lighting for small or large sections of the piece. In theatre, dedicated time slots for the lighting designer are usually called Lx notes sessions. There will be an expectation that general working light will not be used during an Lx notes sessions, though other work may be happening in the space at the same time and may need localised illumination arranged by the lighting department. The lighting designer will need to let

---

[2] These days the track sheet is a screen or printed document produced by the lighting desk showing the level (and other things) of a particular channel in every cue in the show. A lighting designer can use it to see if a particular lantern already has a significant role in lighting states, or if it is free to be used for some new purpose.

others know if they intend to use the session to do work with lantern focus or with cue states since different personnel will be required for each type of work. Refocusing will probably need the whole lighting team (but perhaps not the programmer) while working on states and timings will need the programmer, hopefully the show caller, and perhaps the director and other designers.

It is usually possible to get an Lx notes session into even the busiest production day but often it will take some organisation by the lighting designer and the production electrician. Perhaps the notes session can happen while the stage crew are at lunch, provided they leave the stage set up in a useful way and the lighting department has sufficient staff to provide a programmer over lunch time.[3] Perhaps it can happen at the end of a call for the performers (who are often given time to get out of costume and make-up before the end of a work session) again provided others co-operate to allow this to happen. The canny lighting designer will be able to give notes even in the small breaks that happen during a rehearsal session — as long as in doing this the lighting department does not hold up the process of re-starting the rehearsal. The lighting designer needs to record that a note has been acted upon, otherwise time will be wasted looking at cue states that have already been fixed.

The lighting designer needs to be clear about what can be achieved with what can be made available. For example, in a piece with several sets, is it better to have a specific one, or to work on a bare stage? Often this will depend on what is being fixed. If it is about the lighting down stage centre in several scenes or the look of the cyc, perhaps working on an open stage is alright, but if it is about the balance between background and foreground or fixing a focus that currently flares on a set, the full setting may need to be on stage.

Very often the lighting designer works around other activity. The schedule for a day mid way through a week of production rehearsals in a theatre might look like this:

8:00	Call for house crew to open the building, turn on systems. Stage department re-set the stage for the morning's work.
8:15	Stage crew begin repairs or modifications on stage under general working light.
9:00	Lighting department begin rig check.
9:30	Stage department break for breakfast, working light can be turned off while lighting department do ½ hour of timing notes or focus adjustments (since the stage is not set with any particular setting, it is unlikely to be possible to do detailed notes just yet).
10:00	Stage department return to work on stage under working light. The lighting designer and the lighting department break for breakfast, followed by preparations for the rest of the day, which might include up-dating paperwork. The lighting team has an opportunity to correct any faults in the lighting system, make any required changes, and replace burnt out colour.
12:30	Stage department, having finished repairs and modifications and put the act one set on stage ready for the afternoon rehearsals, break for lunch. Lighting do notes on act one with reduced crew — probably just the lighting designer, the programmer and one other. The show running crew will be at lunch, returning for the half hour call.

---

[3]Generally once production rehearsals begin, lighting designers don't get as many breaks as their crew — taking every opportunity to work on the states and transitions. This does not mean the lighting designer should neglect their own physical needs such as food, drink and sleep. A tired and hungry lighting designer is unlikely to do their best work, and very likely to become grumpy and short tempered with poor people skills!

| 13:00 | The stage management team arrive on stage to set up for afternoon rehearsals at 14:00. DSM/show caller joins the lighting designer at the production desk to update cue positions and timings in the book. |

| 13:25 | Half hour call[4] for the afternoon rehearsal — show crew prepare for rehearsal. Perhaps the lighting designer takes the opportunity to chat to the director over coffee, or to show the director states on stage that have been worked on in the preceding session. |

| 14:00 | Run of act one on stage, lighting designer takes more notes. |

| 15:10 | Run of act one ends, director working with cast on stage, lighting designer working with show caller and lighting programmer to refine states, cue positions and timings. Some sections may be run again, to check changes in blocking, lighting states or cue timing or for other reasons. At some point there will be a break for the performers. There will be crew breaks to fit in too. The lighting designer will often want to keep working through breaks. To do this, however, they will have had to make suitable arrangements with the head of the lighting department. The lighting designer does as much work as is possible/practicable, remembering to stay in touch with both the director and the head of the lighting department/production electrician. |

| 17:00 | End of rehearsal session: stage department re-set the stage for evening rehearsal, performers and stage management (and some of the lighting department) break for evening meal — another chance for the lighting designer to catch up with the director and other members of the production team, and to eat, while the stage is unavailable for lighting. |

| 18:25 | Half hour call for the evening rehearsal, another chance for the lighting designer to do some notes or catch up with the director/head of the lighting department. |

| 19:00 | Run of act two on stage, lighting designer takes more notes. The pattern will be much the same as the afternoon rehearsals, with work on cue states continuing over the rehearsal and during breaks on stage. |

| 21:30 | Performers leave the stage to get out of costume and perhaps receive their notes from the director. Stage management may be available to work with lighting to facilitate a short notes session for the lighting designer before … |

| 22:00 | End of the formal working day (for most departments). It is likely that formal and informal meetings will continue with the production team and others, reflecting on the day's work and planning sessions for the coming days. Engineers, scenic artists, or others may take over the stage to do their work overnight. There may be an element of this that involves the lighting department, in which case a night crew will need to be briefed. |

By making the necessary arrangements the lighting designer has secured some dedicated lighting time; the late morning session with the set on stage, away from the pressure of rehearsals with the performers. This

[4]In the British tradition, all calls to prepare for the show are timed to five minutes before scheduled start time. In this system, zero is the beginners call.

session happens after the lighting team has had an opportunity to fix or adjust elements of the lighting system and get it working well, and some of the session can happen with the show caller, making sure times and positions of cues are correctly recorded in the book. An hour is not a lot of time, especially with a complex show, so the lighting designer will have to work with the head of the lighting department to ensure the lighting team is focused and ready to work quickly when required.

The lighting designer is also able to make use of short periods of unscheduled time too. During the day, time can been found to do more fixes or adjustments to the focus or colour of individual units (perhaps during the performer's breaks), to talk with the show caller and adjust cue placement and timing, to work with the programmer and adjust recorded states and times, and to talk with the director and other members of the creative team, to make sure everyone's goals for the piece are still coherent. And time for a little food and drink, too.

Notes from the director, set designer and others

As we have said many times, making performance is about collaboration, and that involves taking on board the opinions of others in our work. The director will hopefully express opinions about the lighting, and not all of them will be complimentary all the time. It is quite likely that the designers will also give notes on the lighting design. If there is good communication between the lighting designer and the rest of the creative team, these notes and comments will be part of the dialogue that informs the development of the piece — the evolution of the visual dramaturgy along side other dramaturgies. However, when communication has broken down the lighting designer may find themselves blamed for anything from the inaudibility of some performers to the dull colours of the costumes. Lighting has

even been blamed for a whole piece not working. (If only the acknowledgement that sometimes a piece only works because of the lighting was more common.) A lighting designer needs to listen to the comments and complaints of their collaborators, and then decide what to do with the information these notes contain.

The trouble is that much of the language used by an experienced lighting designer to describe their work is quite technical and precise — non-specialists often use much less clear language when they talk about light in performance. When a creative team has worked together on several productions they will have developed an understanding of what each member of the team means by what they say. But even between members of experienced production teams there will be plenty of scope for mis-communication. We have already mentioned the potential for misunderstanding inherent in the use of the terms warm and cool, and between silhouette and shadow. It does not stop there. Often the best way for the lighting designer to approach these situations is to show collaborators the light on stage. In meetings away from the stage, however, this is not possible, and even with the stage in front of the team, there are times when it seems director and lighting designer are talking in different languages.

The people skills of the lighting designer may be tested to the limit. What does the director mean by saying something like 'Is the sky too blue in act one?' This note could be about the colour in the cyc floods lighting the sky, but it could just as easily actually be about the intensity of the cyc, or the balance between the cyc and the rest of the stage, or it could be a reaction to the 'warm' look on stage in front of the cyc at that moment.[5] The note could also be a way of saying, 'Didn't we talk about having clouds in act one? Where have the clouds gone?' The note could be something the director is really concerned about, or something said more or less in passing, because the director was trying

[5] Remember the subjectivity of our response to colour — our perception of the colour of a particular element depends on other colours in the whole visual field.

not to think about the leading man forgetting his lines again.

It is not always a good idea to respond instantly to every note with a change in the lighting. Some notes need interpretation and some need further discussion. Notes that impact on the lighting designer's key ideas may need to be challenged in a way that is appropriate to the particulars of the production situation, and the relationship between lighting designer and director. The lighting designer may find themselves needing the support of all that dramaturgical research into text and context that first informed the design, and the support of other members of the creative team too — and may still not win every time.

Placeholder cues

Sometimes the lighting designer will be caught without a clue as to how to proceed; unsure of what the director means, except that they are not happy with what they presently see. The idea of a placeholder cue can be useful here — something that lights up the stage but which we know is not what we will finish up with. The production team agrees that they will need to come back to look at this part of the piece again. This often happens near the beginning of lit rehearsals, before the visual language of the piece has developed. With luck, as things proceed a good solution to replace the placeholder cue will become clear.

In theatre, generally speaking the director is boss — what they say goes. As a member of the creative team behind a production, the lighting designer may sometimes need to close their eyes during a particular scene because the director insisted on their own aesthetic over that of the lighting designer. Hopefully this will be a very rare occasion, for the proficient lighting designer is just as good at persuading others of their vision as they are at creating it on stage. In lighting design, as in the rest of life however, one needs to choose the battles one fights with grim determination and those one withdraws from gracefully.

The last days before opening night

Many theatre productions have a run of several preview performances before the official opening. The piece is played in front of a paying audience, but is acknowledged to be still developing, and the ticket price is slightly lower as a result. The lighting designer is expected to watch these preview performances, taking notes, and working with the rest of the creative team to refine the production. In the world of live music touring, the same thing happens, the lighting designer watches the first shows before leaving the lighting director to run the rest of the tour, but the ticket price is rarely reduced.

Generally speaking there is little major that can be done with the design at this point, and the lighting designer needs to spend time polishing what is there, not dreaming of what they would like to be there. We may not be able to move the entire front of house lighting rig to compensate for the fact that every key scene now takes place on a platform mid-stage as opposed to in the many places on stage where they were originally set. Nor may we be able to replace all the profile moving lights with CMY wash lights which seem far more appropriate now that every planned gobo look in the piece has been cut. This can be hard to come to terms with, but at this stage in the production, life for the lighting designer becomes about achievable goals. However, there is no reason not to push for as much as can be achieved. A few well chosen FoH lanterns moved and their levels carefully replotted in the appropriate cues; some underused moving profiles removed and a couple of CMY wash-lights introduced to provide a kick to key scenes; both may be possible with enough negotiation and planning.

There will be a lot that can be done with through balancing intensity and colour, and tweaking timing, but sometimes these small adjustments will have unexpected results. Performers and/or crew may be taking lighting cues as their personal cue: 'When the moving light goes red I prepare to enter — and tonight it didn't go red!' Another example might be the need to introduce back stage working light[6] as a result of reducing the intensity of some scenes or reducing the area of stage that is lit; both of which would result in less spill light in the wings, which might in turn make preparing for a scene change more difficult or a compromise a quick costume change. In a way, that is why these shows are previews. Once a show is up and more or less running, it can become a complex interlinked machine, where even small adjustments to one element can have knock-on effects on other seemingly unconnected elements. The lighting designer needs to make sure that there is time to try out changes (especially if they involve moving lights) and make sure they don't have unexpected consequences further down the line.

Opening night and after

There comes a point in most productions where the lighting designer needs to be able to say their work is complete. The lighting design may not be what was originally conceived, it may not be something the lighting designer is completely happy with, but time has run out. The show opens and hopefully everyone is still talking to each other, and the next night it is someone else's responsibility to maintain the lighting design and make sure the lighting works as best it can to support the performance.

For long-running shows, the head of the lighting department will usually take day-to-day responsibility for maintaining the equipment in a proper state to keep the show looking as it should. This person may take some responsibility for making small changes to the cue states or timings to accommodate changes in the performance. Hopefully these changes will be sympathetic to the original lighting design. This is more likely to be the case if the lighting designer has been able to share their vision with the team looking after the show. On a long-running show, the lighting designer will usually be paid a royalty. This ongoing commitment will usually include an agreement to come and watch the show from time to time and then work with the resident team to do Lx notes.

For shows in repertory, that is when several shows play on the same stage in rotation, the lighting rig will have to be re-focused to each show as it comes back onto stage. In these situations it is normal to have a designated member of the lighting team take responsibility for ensuring the show looks as good as first night every time it is played. The same thing frequently happens when shows tour from one venue to the next. A designated member of the lighting team takes responsibility for ensuring the quality of the lighting design is maintained. This requires a good level of paperwork to support the lighting design, including accurate lighting plots, focus plots, stage management cue lists and console cue sheets, and the lighting console memories and other data, stored and backed up securely.

Sometimes shows have another life. If a production is particularly successful, it may be reproduced in another city or country. It is usual for the lighting designer to oversee the lighting of the new production, though they may send a trusted associate in some circumstances. Whoever goes, a reproduction is something that will test the accuracy and completeness of the lighting paperwork. Is the focus of every element of the rig fully documented so that it can be reproduced in the new city? Has what the unit does been recorded so that if the throw is different, suitable adjustments can be made? Are all the cues correctly copied to the hard-drive of the new lighting desk, and all the cue positions correctly recorded in the new book? On top of this

---

[6]It would not usually be the direct responsibility of the lighting designer to ensure the show running lights — usually low level blue light in the wings and immediate back stage area — are fit for purpose. This is most often the responsibility of the stage management team who run these areas. Members of the lighting team will work with stage management to get the right units in the right places. However, it is a good idea to keep an eye on what is planned, since light escaping from the wings and other back stage areas can have a detrimental effect on the lighting design.

there is all the supporting production lighting paper-work, equipment specifications, patch, colour and gobo calls, power and dimmer requirements, and much more. Keeping track of all this information is where dedicated lighting design support software comes into its own.

Then there is the matter of changes to the production, both technical and artistic. Equipment design may have moved on or the equipment used on the original show may have proved to be unreliable on a long run. Artistically the director and/or writers may have developed ideas, written a new ending or just cut a few verses from a song. All these factors will need to inform the modified lighting design.

Even if the show has no afterlife, for all kinds of reasons the lighting designer may wish to keep records of it: production photographs and favourable reviews for a portfolio, a scrap book, or a promotional web site; notes of particularly successful (or even unsuccessful) colour combinations for future use (or to avoid); rigging positions and other specifications of a space that they might work in again, and any of a number or other reasons. There is also the personal stuff from any production — new friends made, new restaurants discovered, and perhaps some reflection on how well the whole thing went, and what has been learned.

The post mortem

How does a lighting designer think about how to get a better result next time? The rest of this chapter is about just that. The things mentioned here though are not meant to be exhaustive, and not everything mentioned will apply to every production. This is a starting point only.

We will start by considering three interlinked areas of practice we have talked about before in relation to the job of performance lighting designer. We talked about the art stuff, the tech stuff, and especially in the last chapter, the people stuff. We can also split the production process into the time before we get into the space and the time in the space. (For shows that tour or have another kind of afterlife there will be further phases, but let's stick with two here.) We can try to map various

FIGURE 1. ONE OF A NUMBER OF MOONLIGHT SCENES FROM *BULLIE'S HOUSE* (DIRECTED BY MICHAEL WALLING, SET DESIGN BY JAMIE VARTAN, 2004).
HOW WELL DID WHAT I CONTRIBUTED HELP TO ACHIEVE THE INTENTION OF THE PLAYWRIGHT, THE DIRECTOR, THE PERFORMERS?
HOW WELL DID I ACHIEVE WHAT I WANTED? WHAT I HAD PROMOSED? WHAT DID I LEARN FROM THAT SHOW? WHAT WOULD I DO DIFFERENTLY NEXT TIME?
EVERYTHING FROM CHOICE OF COLOUR AND INSTRUMENT TO THE WAY I COMMUNICATE WITH THE ACTORS AND THE STAGE MANAGER. HOW CAN I GO ABOUT BUILDING ON WHAT WAS ACHIEVED HERE OR REPAIRING ANY DAMAGE?

parts of the job of producing a lighting design against each of the three areas of skill.

Let's look at some of these areas of the job in detail, from the point of view of a lighting designer who has just opened a show. Remember that what we are trying to get out of this post mortem is a way to do better next time. This might be to produce better lighting, but it also might be to have more fun doing that, to use time better, or to build better relationships with the people we work with and to build a long term career. The post mortem is

TABLE 1. SOME OF THE ACTIVITIES OF A LIGHTING DESIGNER IN THE PRE-PRODUCTION PHASE

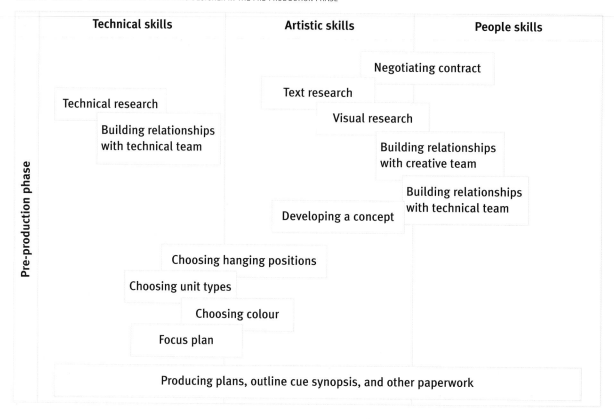

not there just to congratulate the lighting designer on a job well done, to vent spleen at poor treatment by management, or make excuses for why we did not do the good job we wanted to do.

The job starts with the first enquiry, perhaps the lighting designer approaches the producer, or more likely the lighting designer is approached by the set designer, director or producer. The concept is discussed, dates and availability are checked, fees may be mentioned. This is the beginning of negotiating a contract. The contract may be a completely formal document setting out in detail everything about the lighting designer's role on the production. Much more likely it is an outline agreement, setting out dates, e.g. for submission of plans and equipment list by the lighting designer, when they are expected to be on site or in rehearsal; and terms of payment, e.g. one third of the fee on signing the contract, one third on submission of a lighting plan, and one third on opening night.

Equally important for the lighting designer is the informal side of the contract; what resources are available, it terms of time, money and staff, who are the key personnel in the lighting team — chief, production electrician, programmer — and how long they will be around.

This is only scratching the surface of the negotiations undertaken when a lighting designer takes on a major show and in these cases much of detail will be negotiated by an agent. For most lighting designers, however, these negotiations over the non-contract terms and conditions must be handled personally, with the producer or production manager, probably in an on-going way.[7]

[7]The Association of Lighting Designers currently provides advice on contract terms and suggests a rider for contracts for lighting designers. More information at www.ald.org.uk

On the morning after the first night, looking back on these discussions, a lighting designer might ask:

- How good was I at asking for resources? Were there things I should have asked for that I forgot about or did not know about?

- How good was I at getting the resources? Did I ask the right people at the right time? Did I accept 'no' too easily or did I make a fuss over things that I didn't really need — with what implications?

- Did I accept contract terms I could not really live with such as an early date for submitting a plan, or an unrealistic budget restriction?

- How happy am I that the fee paid reflects the work done?

- Were there any disputes resulting from different interpretations of terms in the contract?

- How well did the management stick to their agreements, and how well was I able to stick to mine?

- What will I ask for next time that I did not have this time? What will I reject next time?

- What is worth fighting to be put in writing, and what can be left as a verbal agreement?

Many of these questions, and especially the last two points, have been major topics of discussion between all kinds of professionals working in live performance. One way of generally improving the working conditions of lighting designers and others is to share information about these things and others. In the UK the Association of Lighting Designers (ALD) provides a forum for this kind of sharing, with the object of raising the profile and status of the performance lighting designer.

After the agreement to work on a project has been made comes research; into the text and/or the music, into the people we are going to work with, into the technology we may be using, and into visual images that might feed the design concept. Here are some more questions that might be useful:

- To begin, how good was my analysis of the text/music? Did I read the text/listen to the music early enough? Did I really know the stories, the themes, the sub-plots and the details? Did I ever find myself caught out in discussions?

- How about the context of the original work? If the piece is not original, did I research the original? If I did, was that useful and if I did not, should I have?

- How good was my visual research and how am I measuring that? Was I able to bring appropriate visual references to discussions and use them to inform my design? Through research, am I expanding my own stock of visual reference or continually falling back on what I already know?

- What tools am I using for visual research? Am I making the best use of these? Could I use different ones? Are there galleries or collections I found useful/useless? Why? Was I able to make use of my own drawing or photography? Or my own visual experience?

- Am I expanding my technical knowledge? Did I try out anything new? Did it work? If it didn't, should I have known/could I have tried it out somewhere else first?

- Am I relying on others to inform me? (Could be waiting for the director or set and costume designer to give me keys to the text, or my chief to tell me about how I can use some unfamiliar unit type.) Is that OK (this time)?

This last question may be uncomfortable to ask. However, in part it acknowledges that as a single human being with only 24 hours available to you each day, you can't do everything. There will be times when it is entirely appropriate to take the research of the director and set designer as the basis for a lighting design, just as there will be times when it is appropriate to trust the production lighting chief to specify equipment that they know will work for you. All I would say to aspiring lighting designers is don't let this become the only way you work.

We have said a lot about building relationships, developing the concept, and making choices earlier in the book. The post mortem offers an opportunity for the lighting designer to examine how effective their current strategy in each of these areas is, and what (if anything) they need to improve on. Rather than a set of specific questions in these areas, think about using one of the following tools.

The first is the SWOT analysis. In our context try taking a particular element of your practice — say equipment choice — and analyse what are your strengths and weaknesses in this area, and what are the opportunities and threats presented. So for example:

SWOT analysis – choosing equipment

STRENGTHS	OPPORTUNITIES
Good knowledge of beam angles of a range of lanterns commonly available in the UK Fair knowledge of a limited range of moving lights	Can use present knowledge base (and contacts) to offer myself as assistant to an established LD Can build on existing knowledge working as assistant to established lighting designer in the coming months
WEAKNESSES	THREATS
Not comfortable assessing when and how to use zoom fixtures Limited feel for how much useable light comes out of different types of lantern	Likely to make mistakes in equipment selection leading to time lost changing units, consequent loss of respect and poor results. Do this too often and will lose opportunity to work with establishes LD!

We can see from this simple case how difficult it is to treat any specific task in isolation, especially when it comes to the consequent opportunities and threats. Here, for example, a lack of knowledge in one area — the relative useable intensity of different types of lantern — raises a threat to progression in the chosen career! This type of analysis is able to highlight threats, but will only be useful if the result is acted upon. In this case, it might be a good idea to gain a better feeling for the amount of useable light produced by the lanterns in common use quickly — perhaps by doing some work focusing from behind these lanterns — before the next design job leads to more mistakes.

Another approach available to any practitioner wanting to reflect on their practice is stop/start/continue. Here is an example:

Stop/start/continue — building professional relationships

STOP	START	CONTINUE
Relying on calling everyone 'darling' because I don't know their name	Taking better notes of everybody's names. Finding ways of remembering names.	Making time to say 'Hello! How are you?' to creative team members and crew
Being so keen to defer to the opinions of others, even when I have done research to support a contrary opinion	Respecting my own opinion when I have done the work to back it Keeping better records of e-mail and phone numbers	Researching into the work my collaborators have done – formally and informally to establish common reference points and potential social connections
Taking everything said in the pub at face value	Building social relationships as well as professional ones	Thinking about what the way I dress says about me, and what I want to say by the way I dress

Again this is a simple but potentially effective analytical tool.

The last tool we will look at is a variation on stop/start/continue. Ask 'What am I doing now that works?' and 'What am I doing now that doesn't work?' and finally 'What is missing?' This does not have the potential to build new practice that the previous two tools have, but it can be useful when we look at specific areas of a job such as calling the focus in the next phase of the production process or the production of paperwork in this one.

'What works?' analysis — the lighting plan

What works?	What doesn't work?	What is missing?
Using a computer package to generate plots and a linked database of other important information. Changes to the plot reflected in the data file and vice-versa Can print out new plot on standard A4 colour printer and stick sheets together when necessary	Channel numbers too small — can't read them under dim work light. <u>Find out how to do this</u> Default equipment schedule — <u>need to find a better format</u> that presents all the useful information in a clear way, both on paper and on computer screen Final plot is not really user friendly either — <u>find someone who does better plots and find out how they work</u>	Being able to take the patch file from the drawing package and use it in the lighting desk — <u>find out how to do this</u> Linking the dmx 512 output of the console to the display of my laptop — <u>again find out how to do this and cost</u> Can't produce drawings in a format suitable for printing at our local graphics shop — <u>how can I save drawings as PDFs on my laptop?</u>

Of course, none of these tools will be of much use if they are only used to look backwards. The reflective practitioner needs to use their reflection to inform future practice, to build on strengths and to fill gaps in knowledge and skills. Here we have introduced action points underlined in the table beside some of the negative comments. These can be copied into a 'to do' list for personal and professional development, alongside the 'find a way of helping me to remember people's names' and 'make approaches to assist an established LD', both taken from the previous tables.

Any of these methods could be used more or less interchangeably to look at my performance in any of the areas outlined in table 1, though some activities will suit one kind of analysis better than another. Stop/start/continue for research might be just as effective at highlighting what worked best for me as the list of questions, and SWOT could be a very useful way of looking at my performance building professional relationships.

Let's look at activities in the performance space.

If we imagine that the three areas of skill we have talked about — the technical, the artistic and the people skills — occupy different areas of the brain, we can see from table 2 that the lighting designer's brain is going to be very busy once the show gets into the performance space. Let's have a look at some of the areas in detail, starting with the focus:

■ How well prepared were you for doing the focus? Notes in order, torch, pens and pencils and bottled water available, names of crew learnt and a clear idea in your head about what each lantern would do, for example.

■ How well did you manage the focus? Did it all get done? In the allotted time? Without any cursing or cross words? Were you able to be flexible when required; to work around problems such as faulty equipment, continuing to focus other lanterns while one was being fixed, or swapping the function of two units because they happen to work better that way?

TABLE 2. SOME OF THE ACTIVITIES OF A LIGHTING DESIGNER IN THE PRODUCTION PHASE

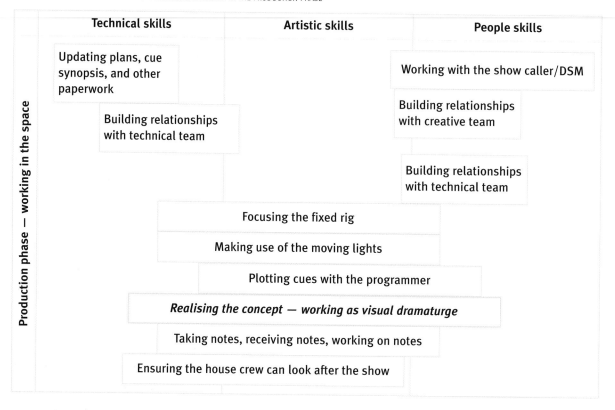

- How much of it worked? Beams fitting together as planned, covering what was planned, doing what was planned?

- How well covered were you for the bits that you thought might not work? Did they work or not? Should you have tried them out anyway or in retrospect should you have known they could not work? Or should you have had more confidence in your idea and not wasted time rigging and focusing a backup that you didn't need?

- Did you have to go back to any lanterns to re-focus them? How many? Because you got it wrong first time or because things changed? How did you cope with asking the crew to go back to units they had already focused?

- How good was your focus crew? Any whose name and phone number you've got for the next time you need someone good? If you might come back to this venue, it is a good idea to note who does what best on the crew — do you know?

- How well did you brief your focus crew or did you finish up working slowly for the first hour while they learnt your way of working?

- Did you focus the rig in the right order? If not, why not and what would be the right order?

- Did you have to compromise the focus of any part of the rig? Why? (For example, your miscalculation, faulty equipment, or crew could not get what you wanted?)

- What was the impact of the compromise? How did you cope? Did it turn out to be more or less serious than you first thought?

Some of these questions may seem harsh — they are. Most performance lighting designers are freelance workers. They do not have the benefits of a friendly boss coaching and supporting them through difficult time, and helping to identify strengths and areas that need to be worked on. They have to do it for themselves. If you are lucky you may develop an ongoing professional relationship with someone you do a lot of work with, maybe a director, a set designer, or a production manager, and this person may be able to help you identify the things you are good at and the stuff you need to work on. However, when it comes to the application of specialist knowledge it is unlikely that anyone other than another lighting practitioner will be able to help, and even then, this person will probably not know all the ins and outs of the particular job. Only you do, so you have to be able to ask yourself hard questions and to answer them honestly: Was the reason that a particular wash didn't work because 'someone' decided to dead the bar at a different height, or because you misread the section or didn't do the beam angle calculations and just guessed (wrong)?

Let's have a look at another box, notes. Starting with your own notes:

- Do you manage to take as many notes as you would like?

- Have you found your perfect way to take notes? If not, what might help you? How can you access that help? (How much will it cost?)

- Do you manage to prioritise well, taking and fixing the right things first?

- How well were you able to stay on top of which cue number the show was in during runs? While you were at the production desk? Away from the production desk?

- How easy do you find it to interpret your notes when you get time to fix them?

- How well did you plan and use the time given to you to do fixes based on notes?

- Were the show caller and console programmer both clear about what you were asking of them all the time? If there was confusion, where did it come from?

- How long on average do you take to fix notes concerning removing rogue channels from a cue state? (How long does it take you to locate a channel that is messing up a state?)

- How quickly were you able to fix a state that needs intensities to be balanced?

- What about cue timing and cue placement?

- How well did you handle notes from the director and others? Were there notes you found it difficult to act on? Were there things that were asked for you successfully argued against?

- Did you misinterpret notes from anyone else? Why? And what impact did that have on the show, on your relationship with the note giver?

- Is each cue in the show being called correctly? If not, why not? Is the show suffering? Is there anything you can still do about that?

Clearly there are elements of practice touched on here which could be put in other boxes than the — working with the programmer/operator and with the show caller/DSM for example, and relationships with other members of the creative team. The point is that many areas of the practice of lighting design depend on each other, affect each other and overlap with each other. Different individuals in different productions will want to ask different questions. By looking at the detail here we hope to find a way of asking the big questions, and answering them: how well did I light the show?

- Does my lighting design support the piece as best it can, given the constraints of time, money and people available to the lighting department and to the production?

And there is a supplementary to this one:

- What would I have done with more money and/or time and/or more or different people?

How is my career developing?

- What did I do well on this show? What did I learn? What will I do better next time?

- Do I want to work with any of these people again? What opportunities already present themselves to do that? How can I make the most of those? What opportunities might present themselves in the future? How do I stay in touch and in the frame for those future opportunities?

- How can I make the most of this work? Have I got good photographs of my lighting? (Do I have the right to use those images?) Can I put them on my web site? On another useful web site? Is the lighting mentioned in any reviews? (Is there anyone I can get to review the lighting for a specialist publication or web site?) Is there anyone I want to send reviews or images to? Or bring to see the show? (A potential agent, designer or director perhaps.)

This last point brings us to the final box in table 2: can the house crew look after the show? While others may take some part in ensuring this, ultimately it is the lighting designer's responsibility to provide the means for this to happen. Of course it is in their best interest to make sure their work looks good for the whole run of the production as well. Providing a complete, user-friendly show bible of important paperwork is only part of the job. How well will the chosen equipment continue to do its job? How easy is it to fix if and when it does fail? Is the cost of keeping the show looking good within the budget of the production? For example, if the deep blue in the cyc floods needs to be replaced every second show, is there someone with time to do that and is there money to buy the colour media. If a unit is suspended high above the set, can it be accessed for cleaning/re-lamping/re-focusing if necessary, or will it remain hanging but unused should the lamp blow? What impact will this have on the show? Some people argue that such matters should not concern the lighting designer, and perhaps they are right — in an ideal world. For most of us, however, taking some account of how the design will be maintained does inform our practice.

No sooner has one show opened than the next is on the drawing board — or at least that is what we hope for — building on the success of yesterday to inform the practice of tomorrow. But an artist should not try to develop in isolation. I would strongly advise going to see the work of other designers, and not just those working with light or in performance. This not only allows a wide range of influences to inform your design practice, but it will give you a growing set of reference points for discussions with the director and other designers of the next project.

FIGURE 2. A VISUALISATION AND THE END RESULT. EVEN THOUGH THE VISUALISATION IS RELATIVELY CRUDE, IT WAS ENOUGH TO PERSUADE THE CLIENT TO INVEST IN FIVE 10M HIGH SCREENS FOR THE SHOW, ALONG WITH A NUMBER OF MOVING LIGHTS.

11

looking ahead

An alternative title for this chapter could be Provocations. It is not in the nature of any practice associated with live performance to stay the same over time, and lighting design is no exception. In this final chapter I would like to provoke a discussion about where the practice of lighting design for live performance might be heading. What follows is meant as an introduction to some of the practices and arguments that will probably be part of the future world of lighting designers, and not a full description of that world. What we are talking about here is speculation on the future and what I want to do is to ask you some questions.

What is the carbon footprint of your show?

Richard Cadena, the excellent American writer on lighting technology, has recently calculated that it takes about one medium-sized bucket of coal to generate enough electricity to run a PAR-can for a show. The average unit count in the West End, on Broadway, and elsewhere has been steadily rising, probably ever since electricity was first introduced into the theatres at the end of the 19th century! It is not uncommon for the build period of a large commercial musical to begin with the installation of a new and increased electricity supply.[1] Concert lighting, too, has substantially increased its demand for power in recent years. It is now not uncommon for a show touring arenas to need over 500 kiloWatts of power (800 amps per phase in the UK and Europe) where as only 15 years ago 200 kilowatts was the norm. As well as the increased demand for power for the lighting, the heat generated by these lighting rigs has to be dealt with by the building, be it theatre or concert hall. Air conditioning and ventilation for the auditorium (and back stage areas) also consumes greenhouse gas emitting power.

Measures to combat global warming would seem to indicate that this practice will not be allowed to continue unchecked. The inefficient incandescent lamps that have been at the core of most performance lighting designs for over 100 years may soon be consigned to the history books. We are all almost certainly going to be under increasing pressure to make better use of the power available to us in the coming years and to use substantially less of it as time goes on.

How long before an additional constraint on the lighting designer is a consideration of the carbon footprint of their work?

LEDs, fluorescent lamps, and . . .

Incandescent lamps are not a very efficient way of producing light from electricity. Most domestic incandes-

[1] In part this is due to the power demanded by the extensive automation of the scenery as much as it is the demands of lighting.

cent light bulbs are woefully inefficient, converting around 5% of the electricity they consume into light, and 'wasting' the rest as heat. Some countries have already legislated to effectively ban their use in the very near future. How will the performance lighting industry react? It is all very well being told we have to use fewer units but to have no incandescent fixtures — surely this is a disaster? Before we all panic it is best to have a few facts. The metric used to compare light bulbs usually lumens per watt. Here are a few comparison figures from General Electric:

Lamp type	LPW	Notes
Incandescent	7 to 25	The lower the wattage the lower the efficiency, so while domestic lamps are around 7 to 10 LPW most theatre lamps are over 20 LPW (the halogen gas used to fill high wattage lamps helps too).
Compact fluorescent	30 to 63	It is often stated that compact fluorescent lamps (CFLs) are at least four times more efficient than domestic incandescent light bulbs. Generally there is a trade off between efficiency and colour rendition index (CRI). Lamps that emit a 'nice' light sit at about 40 LPW.
Standard fluorescent	30 to 100	These are the long tube lamps seen in any commercial and industrial applications. Again, the highest efficiency lamps emit a 'cold and unfriendly' light. There are difficulties inherent in the way fluorescent lamps work that make them unusable in a focusable lantern. They are difficult, but not imposable to dim, and are used successfully for cyc lighting and soft-light.
Metal halide discharge (e.g. CSI, HMI, etc)	75 to 125	These are the lamps used most often in moving lights, projectors, and industrial fixtures. They come in all kinds of different shapes and sizes. CRI can be made close to perfect without too much loss of efficiency.
High CRI white LEDs	15 to 19	This may come as a shock since LEDs are often put forward as super efficient — and many are — but not yet the white ones.[2] There are problems getting rid of waste heat in any LED fixture since the devices themselves don't work well when they get hot, and this limits the power of any individual fixture.

On the horizon are higher efficiency incandescent lamps (spring 2007: General Electric announced a new technology for incandescent lamps that doubles their efficiency at domestic wattage, and the potential for these new technology lamps to be least as efficient as compact fluorescents.) These new technology lamps could be just what many performance lighting designers are hoping for — a way of keeping the dimmable incandescent source on stage.

The real threat to this, however, comes from the compact source metal halide lamps that already exist. Just to give you a small taste of the energy savings possible with these lamps, a 150W metal halide lamp in an ETC Source 4 profile produces as much light as a 750W conventional lamp — and lasts a lot longer. GE are marketing a PAR 64 metal halide lamp as a direct replacement for their 1000W incandescent PAR 64. The marketing talks about better colour rendition with the

---

[2]This is statement is true as I write now in 2007. Since some of the largest labs in the world are researching into making the efficient high power white LED by the time you read this, things may well have changed. In all probability there will still be problems producing a compact enough light source with a high enough output to be useful in say a theatre profile lantern.

new lamp and it uses only 150 watts instead of 1000! This increase in light per watt, or rather decrease in watts per unit of light on stage, is a pressure it will be hard to resist. New performance spaces are still being built with dimmer racks — the assumption is that we will carry on the way we have for a while yet, however with Australia and California[3] both joining the list of territories banning the use of incandescent lamps in the foreseeable future, how much longer will we be able to argue that we are a special case?

Energy efficient moving lights — part of the solution?

The moving light manufacturers realised early that discharge sources produce more light per watt than incandescent lamps, even though they still produce a lot of heat. The lamp of a moving light generally stays lit (and therefore continues to draw power) for the whole show where as a conventional lantern only 'burns coal' when it is shining light on the stage (or anywhere else for that matter). We can reasonably assume that since the moving light is replacing several conventional lanterns, at least one of which would be on most of the time, the total power consumed would stay more or less the same whether the rig was mostly conventional incandescent lanterns or discharge lamped moving lights[4].

For several reasons, power companies prefer consumers to use a more or less constant amount of electricity rather than using it in big surges and this favours moving light rigs over incandescent rigs. It is possible that a producer could negotiate a lower price for power to a moving light rig, even if the moving light rig actually used more power overall. Of course, there are other cost advantages to be negotiated by the canny producer or general manager. If the moving lights replace enough conventional units (each of which previously needed a dimmer) there may be a cost saving in the hire or purchase of equipment, and possibly in the number of personnel needed to run and maintain the lighting system.[5] Let's look at how this move towards extensive moving light rigs has affected lighting designers working on some of the most prestigious stages.

Pros and cons of large-scale moving light rigs

Many of the largest repertory stages in the UK, Europe and North America have introduced extensive moving light rigs. In the UK this includes all three stages at the National Theatre and the main stage at the Royal Opera House. Before the introduction of moving lights these institutions were often forced to keep the majority of their lanterns in fixed focus positions, providing a general area cover for the whole stage area. The visiting lighting designers had to use these lanterns as the basis for every lighting design, adding a strictly limited number of specials specific to the shape, colour and atmospheric requirements of their show. This was because the institutions could not dedicate the time or man-power to refocus large numbers of lanterns every time the show on stage changed — perhaps as often as every day in a large opera house. Exceptions were made for prestigious shows, for example the management might agree to allow an extensive rig for just one of the shows in the repertory to be mounted along side the fixed focus rig. (Of course this assumes that there

---

[3]At the time of writing, the Australian government is proposing a three year transfer period, ending in 2010, after which 'the energy efficiency required by law will make it impossible to use incandescent lamps'; no mention of 'except in theatres and concert halls' there either. Californian state government is currently considering a similar proposals (spring 2007).

[4]However, since the lamp in the moving lights will be more efficient than the conventional lamps in the units it replaces. In practice most moving light rigs use less power per show than an equivalent conventional rig.

[5]As lighting systems become more technologically advanced, they require different skills from the people who look after them. In some markets at present there is a mismatch between what some producers and general managers see as the required skill level for lighting crew (and therefore what they are prepared to pay staff) and what lighting designers actually need to facilitate and maintain their designs. To some extent it is up to lighting designers to educate producers and others in these matters if they want things to improve.

---

is room to do this, and sometimes there was not.) With the extensive moving light rigs now available to lighting designers on these stages, lighting can be made much more specific to the production — to the shape of the setting, to the colours and atmospheres appropriate to the piece. On the whole this has benefited lighting designers by allowing them to extend their creativity outside the constraints of the fixed rig.

However, there are some potential drawbacks to working with a rig dominated with intelligent fixtures. At present, the first of these is the noise generated by fans used in cooling most of the moving lights presently in use, and by motors, gear boxes and other moving parts. This problem is being solved by manufactures who are beginning to produce units without fans, capable of very quiet movement. Next is to do with the very discharge source that helps to make these units more efficient: some lighting designers feel it is not as 'friendly' to their art as the incandescent source of conventional theatre fixtures. As already discussed, it is a different colour temperature and lower colour rendition index — discharge light does not look as 'nice' on skin and some other materials as incandescent light — and it does not dim in the same way that incandescent light dims. These issues too are being looked at by manufacturers: new lamps are being designed with a more complete spectrum — better CRI — and the new designs for dimmer shutters are resolving many of the concerns of both lighting designers and technicians.

Another problem, however, is somewhat harder to solve. When the director knows there are many moving lights around the stage, their temptation can be to begin to direct the lighting in just the same way as (some) directors direct the performers, effectively removing the lighting designer from much of the creative process and turning them into a facilitator of the director's vision rather than a collaborator. The lighting designer can find themselves in the same position the chief electrician had some generations ago.

Often, because (almost) everything is possible with a moving light rig, states are created in isolation, with no overall dramaturgical through line — no sense of overall design. Whilst this is not a problem faced by many of us (since there are still relatively few productions with both an extensive moving rig and the time for a director to direct lighting as well as everything else) it has led to some compromised designs appearing on our most prestigious stages, which does little to promote to a wider public the potential power of light in performance.

Another down side of working with moving light rigs is the supremely disappointing way in which they just don't quite do what we want them to do, in all sorts of ways. Everything from colour rendition to beam edge quality and light distribution across the beam have been criticised in pub arguments and in professional journals. Is this just the unfamiliarity of experienced practitioners working with new tools? Perhaps, but let's take colour as an example: if you compare the range of colour available from even the best moving light with a swatch book from just one filter manufacturer, the chances are that the swatch book wins in providing more choices that are more useable in more situations. Even if it does not, there are other manufacturer's colours available to use in a conventional lantern while with the moving light, what you have available is what is in the unit and nothing else.[6] Despite the many control channels taken up by today's moving heads, there is still a feeling that there is not enough subtle adjustment available to the designer — the moving light too often presents us with a 'take it or leave it' beam.

By making our lighting systems more able to do more things more quickly than ever before, are we as lighting designers losing control of our lighting? In the move to more efficient lighting systems, are we in danger of losing the ability to be subtle with light on stage?

---

[6]This is in part why ETC's Revolution™ has a scroller instead of dichroic colour filters. There was a time when it was common to see filters fixed to the front of moving lights. This clearly limits what else you can do with them, and although I have advocated the practice in the past, there has to be a better way.

Digital lighting or visual media on stage

What is usually meant by digital lighting is using a video projector on stage and visual media is the term used to describe the images the projector is projecting. Neither digital lighting nor visual media are entirely satisfactory terms; we are still searching for appropriate words. Strictly speaking everything we see on stage could be termed visual media and there is nothing necessarily digital about using a projector as a light source on stage. What we are talking about here is also called projection and video but both of these words imply something more limited. Usually what we mean involves the use of a projector or a video monitor or some other kind of display device such as an LED array. It also involves some kind of content which might be documentary footage, abstract imagery, or the output of a live camera or many other things. On the big budget stage we have the huge screens behind pop performers including Kylie and Robbie Williams, the CGI[7] scenery of shows such as Andrew Lloyd Webber's *Woman in White*, and the re-rendered film footage of *Sinatra*. But visual media in live performance is not restricted to big budget shows. Although the largest, clearest, brightest projectors are still very expensive, smaller venues can make good use of something costing less than £1000. When it comes to creating content too, entry level video editing, image creation and image manipulation packages are now all available to the domestic computer user at not much more than pocket money prices. One thing that is still potentially expensive at any scale is the time and expertise of the few very talented people who understand both the content creation and the image production side of things.

I am not very interested in CGI scenery. To me it is a 21st century version of the painted cloth world that Appia and Craig rebelled against at the beginning of the 20th century. It is asking the three dimensional performer to inhabit an essentially two dimensional world and perform in front of a cinema screen. If a particular audience needs the hyper-reality of CGI let them go to the cinema, where it's presence does not compromise the ways in which the performers can be lit. (Think how hard it is to light an actor standing in front of a projection screen — putting enough light on them to ensure the audience can't see the projected image on their face while at the same time not washing out the image of the scenery on the screen.) However, other ways of using what we shall for now call visual media, do interest me.

Screens, whether for video or film, have become a common-place for most audiences world wide. On stage we can use them very easily to show documentary footage that gives a context to or passes comment on the live action. We can use a screen as a window into other worlds, as a comforting reminder of the domestic or as an alienating device. The use and manipulation of images from a live camera on a screen can give the audience additional perspectives on the performers and the performance — a kind of live Cubism on stage — or it can give a performer an opportunity to play to (or with) a disembodied version of another actor or even him or herself.

Escaping the tyranny of the projection screen

A problem with video images on stage is often the very commonplaceness of the screen — as soon as an audience sees a white or pale coloured surface, roughly rectangular in shape, there is an expectation that it will soon be filled with images. For the most part, a screen remains a screen for all the time it is on stage, even if at times it has no images on it, and this can be problematic, at least for me as an audience member. The continuing presence of a screen is further enhanced by the not quite black light that most video projectors emit, even when the image is black. This picks out the clearly defined rectangular shape we know as a screen even if the projected image has been cropped to some other shape. This 'ghost screen' remains present in

---

[7]CGI stands for computer generated imagery as used in countless contemporary action and adventure films, and also on some live stages.

227

black outs and has a tendency to draw attention to itself. The audience is reminded of the presence of a screen and the projector and this may not be what we want.

One description of digital lighting involves using the projected image as a light source to illuminate something other than a dedicated screen — perhaps turning a tablecloth or a bed-sheet into a temporary and impromptu screen, or perhaps using the light from a projector to light a performer — the potentially moving coloured gobo in a shaped beam. Suddenly there are all kinds of new levels of meaning possible, as well as an almost infinite variation in colour and beam texture. Place a projector in a moving yoke, with pan, tilt, a dimmer shutter, and a zoom lens and beam shaping, and perhaps we have the next generation of moving light. At present, there are limits to this, and they go beyond cost. Affordable light-weight projectors are mass produced items made with other uses in mind. At present the light from the otherwise most suitable projectors is not particularly optimised for lighting most skin tones — there does not appear to be much red in it. More difficult to solve perhaps are ways of organising and delivering content to the projector. Media server systems can provide several different outputs to several moving projectors, but the number of different outputs remains low at present. The time it can take to prepare images and program systems can be immense.

We will discuss the thorny issue of content later, but assume for the moment we have some; and now we can choose where it is displayed. If we avoid formal screens, what alternatives are there? Théâtre de Complicité recently used a back wall made of strips of thick industrial plastic of the kind that covers the doorway into a warehouse or cold store. This was treated to make it opaque and it formed a projection surface that performers could walk through.[8] Robert LaPage has used a curved surface that allows him to appear to spray the image onto the screen, and to move around inside a projected room. Lower tech solutions have included stretching white lycra material between bodies or posts, and slowly revealing the presence of a projected image in a space by filling it with bodies, or by pegging out washing on a line, or by controlled use of smoke. It is important to have a dramaturgical reason for anything that appears on the performance stage, and the projected image is no different. At the same time there is room for playfulness in making performance, and the unexpected appearance of a projected image can be part of that spirit too.

Can we ever have too much choice?

One of the differences between working with a fixed rig and a rig of moving lights is not so much the increased number of choices available, but the fact that so many choices can be delayed until the technical rehearsal, or even later. With a fixed rig, the focus, colour, beam shape and edge of each unit is set at the focus. To change any one of them during rehearsal requires us to stop rehearsals and get someone up to the lantern to make the change. This encourages thoroughness in preparation — make sure you get it right in the focus or everything else will suffer. With moving lights, it is relatively easy to change a colour, a focus position, a gobo or a shutter cut, from the console, during a rehearsal; so we do. Introducing the possibility of using any of the millions of video colours and shapes and any static or moving image you can get the rights for, presents us with whole new worlds of choice. Making choices takes time, and with this number of possibilities to chose from even getting started can be intimidating — deciding when you are finished can be just as hard. I think the possibilities inherent in digital lighting are very exciting, but there are potential pitfalls if the lighting designer abandons a rigorous approach to preparation. Consider the following example.

---

[8]Complicite works with some very expensive projectors that do very good black, i.e. almost no light at all when the image is black to give away the screen.

On an open stage we have a scene set in a cathedral. The production team decide that it would like to set the time and place by using an image of sunlight through a high window somewhere on stage. With conventional lanterns, we might choose to use a glass gobo of a stained glass window in a good quality profile from an appropriate angle. The gobo would take some time to research, a high quality image would need to be found and the gobo produced. This might take several days or even weeks and once the gobo is made it cannot easily be changed. Once the lantern is focused the position of the image on the stage is set — it cannot be changed without somebody climbing up to it and refocusing it which would take time and stop the rehearsal. The likelihood is that sufficient care would be taken to get this focus right first time. The lighting designer, set designer and director are likely to have collectively thought through the implications of using a particular place on stage. In the tech, the director is most likely to work with this agreed position of the image on stage rather than stop the rehearsal to ask for it to be changed.

If the gobo is in a moving light, we still have to research the image and select one to be made up into a gobo — if we are lucky there may be an opportunity to use up two gobo slots in our moving light and have a choice of gobo. Once we get to the cathedral scene in the tech, the position of the image on stage can be decided. If we are not quite happy with the position at the next rehearsal, at the twist of a controller on the lighting console, the image can be moved across stage to a new position. It can probably be made bigger or smaller too. The lighting designer and director both know this, and so in all likelihood have only talked in vague terms about a final position — well, they didn't need to think too hard about it because they can always change it in the space.

If the image is produced by a video projector, we can have the designer's entire collection of cathedral windows from medieval to modern, stored as static images or even as movie files on the hard disk. We can re-size them, re-colour them, pre-distort and colour balance them, edit two or more together, all in the space. And this is on top of our ability to move the image to a new place on stage and zoom it larger or smaller. But have we got time to do any of this? Are we more or less likely to make better work with all this choice we can make in the space than we made when we were forced to think hard in advance about what and where the image should be?

Whose job is content creation and preparation?

In any performance that has a plan to use visual media this question needs to be answered clearly, as early in the production process as possible. It may be that the project starts with some specific media ideas in mind, or that the need for media emerges from the devising process or something in-between. Whatever the situation, somebody will need to either make or find material and prepare it in a way that is suitable for use on stage. These two jobs involve a mix of skills, very often including those of film maker, computer programmer, editor, art director, video engineer and performance operator. Is it any wonder there are not many of these people about? It is a specialist role and needs to be valued as such. Because the material delivered on stage is a kind of light, even when there is no projector involved, it has often fallen to the lighting designer or at least the lighting department, to make it all happen. No lighting designer should take on this role lightly, but neither is it wise for the lighting designer to be too distant from the process. If the images are going to relate to the rest of what is on stage, then there will clearly have to be a good deal of collaboration and cooperation between whoever is responsible for the images and the lighting designer.

Several different models have emerged and these have worked more or less well in different situations. In the world of large budgets — the concert tour or the large scale theatre show — a specific department has usually emerged, staffed by people with skills in video engineering and projection, screen technology (for large format LED screens), digital video editing and computer networks, and headed by a media designer or video director. The team might also include camera operators if there are images from live camera to be integrated into the content, and a lighting console programmer if that is the chosen route for controlling playback in performance. Where the set designer has taken a major role in creating content, the structure or the department will reflect this. The video department becomes responsible for appropriately reformatting the images provided by the set designer and their associates, and for getting them onto the stage. The set designer (or scenographer) supervises the creation of the images, or perhaps creates them themself, and oversees the technical production of those images on the stage.

On the smaller scale, roles are less likely to be so clearly defined. The technical problems are likely to be of a more manageable scale, so that the lighting department is more likely to be involved in solving them.[9] The issue of who will produce the content and who will be responsible for getting it onto the stage still needs to be resolved. If the displayed images need to be shot on camera, the lighting designer will often be involved in making sure the look is right for the piece. There may not be budget for a professional lighting camera operator so the lighting designer may be asked to step in — don't assume this is easy stuff. Do some homework: think about how big the final image will need to be on stage, do the images need to be created in 'hi-def' (at extra cost), buy a decent light meter and make sure you have time to make a few mistakes along the way.

The lighting designer will usually want some say in what is projected or displayed where and when. The brightness and colour of the images will need to be considered both for how light from the image might impact on the lighting state and for how the lighting state might wash out the image. (This is in addition to the need to have some relationship between the displayed image and the way the lighting reveals the stage image.) Before you offer your services as video content director, remember the problem of too much choice. If the lighting system is relatively simple and the number of cues is small perhaps you may have

time to do both — if you are really on top of the video system and can make changes quickly. Otherwise it might be best to delegate this function to another member of the team.

It may be more appropriate to give the set designer responsibility for the images. Apart from other considerations, the work load of the set designer gets lighter at the same point that of the lighting designer gets heaviest — around the tech. Few set designers are presently skilled in the techniques of digital image manipulation, but there is an argument that if they want to use this stuff in their designs then — at a certain scale — it is useful to know how to use it.

Many of those currently practising in these emerging arts began as lighting designers and that is for a reason. As we have said before, visual media on stage is basically coloured light. If this area of lighting interests you, here is a non exhaustive list of skills that might be useful.

- Camera operation, framing and lighting for camera.
- Image researching and rights clearance.
- Photoshop and other image manipulation techniques.
- Video editing — both on line and off line.
- Video cable standards and interconnectivity of systems.
- Projector specification, set-up, and basic maintenance.
- Video monitor set-up and basic maintenance.
- Digital image storage and retrieval systems.
- Computer networks and backup systems.
- Video server systems, and other ways of controlling and playing back video images.

And all this on top of dramaturgical skills and aesthetic appreciation — enjoy!

....

[9]However, in some theatres for historic reasons it will be the sound department that looks after projectors and other video equipment.

....

Another kind of digital lighting

The concert and entertainment TV worlds offer another model, and another practice that could be called digital lighting. The lighting designer employs multiple surfaces, often blocks of LEDs rather than projection surfaces, as part of the lighting design. These multiple LEDs are not controlled as individual channels from a lighting desk, but as pixels, each mapped to a virtual screen position, and fed with video data from a media server. The LED blocks can be stacked to form a large single screen, and the video information fed to them creates an image on that screen — it can be any kind of video image, moving or static. The resolution will depend on the LED devices — generally it will be fairly low since these fixtures have a spacing between pixels (called the pitch) that is considerably larger than even the biggest dedicated display screen. However, if seen from far enough away, a reasonable version of the original image can be seen.

Things get much more interesting when the LED blocks are arranged in other ways than just as a continuous screen — perhaps as a much larger screen with holes in, or wrapped round the performance area almost at random. The programmer can still assign each unit to a particular area of the virtual screen, and the colour and intensity of the light from each cell in the block will be controlled by the colour and intensity of the pixel that the cell is mapped to. The blocks can be arranged as an animated background, or as units providing light on stage, or as both. The content displayed on this fractured screen can be abstract patterns or moving video footage, including live camera. These fixtures and the media servers that provide the content to them have been designed to be integrated into high specification lighting systems, so naturally the first people to use them have been lighting designers (and lighting directors on TV). The systems as they exist at present are more suitable for the brash and colourful world of live music and light entertainment television than the theatre stage, but in the last year or two we have seen controllable RGB[10] LEDs in soft goods such as drapes and nets. We can expand the ideas used on concert stages with hard blocks of LED fixtures into these soft arrays, perhaps draped over irregularly-shaped objects, perhaps tracked on and off stage on standard theatre curtain tracking systems, perhaps at times bunched up and at other times spread out. These LED arrays can more easily disappear than the hard blocks, but can potentially display the same low resolution graphics — and perhaps in time higher resolution images as well.

When this happens it is unlikely that the lighting designer will remain sole arbiter of content as they are so often at present. There are also limits to the level of sophistication possible with a lighting console controlling such a system. New ways of working will undoubtedly emerge as new ways to use this technology on stage become clear, and another kind of digital lighting practice begins to be defined.

The possibilities of precision

How much more can the cinematographer do with light than the theatre lighting designer — and usually with far fewer units? Of course, with camera we have a single point of view at a fixed distance, and in live performance most often we do not have that. But there is another factor — in film, the performers stand where they are told to, move only when they are told to and look only where they are told to. If they don't, and because of that the take does not work, then they do it all again. This is a possibility that is not generally available on the live stage. But imagine how you might light a performer who moved to the same precise spot every night? Generally dancers do, and perhaps this is one reason why some of the most ambitious lighting on many stages is for dance. Some practitioners have taken this idea even further. Robert Wilson has recently used tiny beams to pick out

---

[10]RGB stands for red, green, blue, the three colours used to make TV pictures. Each cell of an LED device that can be driven successfully as a pixel needs all three colours to be present discretely.

---

just the hand of a performer. Over 40 years ago Samuel Beckett wrote *Not I*, a play that demands the only light on stage picks out just the mouth of a performer. The realisation that precision has potential is not new, but now we can do things Beckett only dreamed of.

Imagine how you might light a performer whose precise position you could track, and your lights could respond to each move? Several systems based on radio location have been developed, none quite as good as the very best human follow-spot operator. The lanterns used to follow the performer in these tracking systems, however, can be anywhere in the rig, which presents some advantages, and there can be multiple units tracking multiple targets — a big advantage if you have a show in the round, for example.

Imagine a system where you could project, say, a single word onto the hand of a performer, and have that word stay on their hand wherever they moved it, as long as it faced the projector. This kind of trick can be accomplished using infra-red camera images to control the output of a projector.

Imagine writing lighting cues designed to happen on precise beats of a complex piece of music, not in a regular fashion, but exactly the same every night. No operator could learn the music so well without a good deal of time and training, but if the music is prerecorded or running to a click track we can make it happen. The recording needs to have some kind of time-code embedded in it. This can then be read by the lighting console. Each cue state is stamped with a specific time from the time code, and each time the music is played — the cues happen as programmed.

The thing about knowing you have a high level of precision available is that you can be much bolder. As a lighting designer, if you know precisely where the performer will be at the moment of the cue, you can light them with a tight special rather than a broader wash. If you know the direction they will be facing and the tilt of their head, you can place one or two fixtures to do the perfect job, rather than have to add in several more in case they are not doing it that way tonight. If you have a tracking system you can trust, you can follow four performers as they run around stage, knowing each will always be lit without the need to spoil your lighting

state with a slab of general cover. And if you want to do something for each tympani beat in the finale of the *Carmina Burana* it can be a bold statement because you know it will be right on the beat every night. It is not always what you want to do — it is not always what the performance calls for — but when want to be bold you often need precision.

Interactivity — giving the performer (or the audience) control of the lighting

I have an experiment I would like to run one day at a large outdoor event such as a fireworks pageant. I would usually light the general setting and the surrounding trees and structures to provide a frame for the event but not provide any front light. Instead I would give a proportion of the audience powerful rechargeable torches, with instructions to shine them at whatever attracted their attention on stage at any time. The front light for the performance would be controlled by the audience, who would see what they chose to see not what we chose to show them — true interactivity.

Lighting operator as performer

In the tradition of the called show, the lighting operator hits a GO button as instructed by the show caller. The object is to make sure the lighting is the same every night, and although a good operator can have a small impact at the margins, the scope for being an interactive part of the show is limited. In the concert lighting world, however, the lighting operator is often able to respond in the moment to what is happening on stage; to push a build a little faster, hold a fade a few moments longer, add an extra flourish or most directly, help to stimulate audience response with some extra sweeps and flashes. The lighting operator for a live concert can add something to a performance, and conversely can also take something away from it, too — lighting operation as performance. This is true for follow spot operators as well. Really tight operation can lift the whole performance, both for the watching audience and for the leading performers, just as slack operation can take something away from the performance.

For a while technology seemed to inhibit the ability of the operator to respond in the moment. The concert lighting designer would stick to running the conventionals on their fader desk, while the operator ran the movers by pressing buttons to playback pre-program sequences. Better moving light consoles and more imaginative programming techniques have enabled the moving light operator to re-enter the role of performer — and I can tell you it is quite a buzz to get a whole show completely right in the middle of a large and enthusiastic crowd.

But what about the lighting operator as part performer on the dramatic stage? Away from the commercial imperative of the called show, traditions in Eastern Europe evolved which were much more sympathetic to this notion. The lighting men (and mostly they were men) watched the rehearsals and were part of the evolution of the piece over months. Eventually when the piece arrived on stage, they knew it as well as the cast and responded to it with light in much the same way — no fixed cues, no show caller, no single lighting designer. Well, that's not going to work for us is it — we will all be out of a job, and in any case, who is going to pay for the lighting crew to sit in on months of rehearsal? Is there another way?

If the lighting systems were less complex, if the consoles were more interactive, if the theatre operators were more interested in taking on this role — that's a lot of ifs. Would it make for better performance? Better lighting? Almost inevitably some of the time the result would be worse — all performers have off nights and so would the lighting operator. But sometimes it might be better: if the leading lady changes the tempo of her exit and the light changes its tempo to match or if the leading man delivers a soliloquy from the wrong side of stage but the lighting seamlessly illuminates his new position rather than is original one. The tradition of called shows enables complex performances to happen

in a repeatable way, minimising the risk of physical harm for performers moving between heavy trucks and under hanging scenery but it also restricts the ability of the lighting operator to respond in the moment to the performance and this is sometimes not necessary.

Should lighting designers leave space for the operator in their designs from time to time — the operator as performer?

Towards more art in lighting for live performance

This discussion began by talking about how much coal (or gas or oil) we burn to make our shows. While some repertory stages have introduced moving lights as part of a programme to save money on running costs, this has rarely been the main motivating factor and cutting down on power consumption and the amount of waste heat has probably hardly ever been a consideration. But while car and truck makers are being pressured to reduce the impact of their products on the environment and air travel is becoming as socially unacceptable as smoking in some quarters, how long can we carry on without considering how much CO_2 goes into the atmosphere every time we push up a fader? Should we begin to reject the idea of lighting the stage with lots of lanterns for environmental reasons as well as for aesthetic reasons? In the medium term we have almost certainly already lost the battle to retain large numbers of inefficient incandescent lanterns on dimmers. Even if GE's new technology provides a temporary stay of execution, we will probably have to get used to lanterns that don't change colour as they get dimmer — and who knows we might even learn to like that. Multi-fixture cover systems for lighting the stage grew up around the demands of Broadway and the West End spectaculars, where the lighting designer often had to deal with many different sets, locations times etc. Jewel lighting[11] developed as a

---

[11]Jewel lighting is essentially a development of the area cover approach. The rig is arranged to enable the lighting designer to light from multiple angles into each area, with a choice of colour and lots of intensity. The object is to be able to make the dramatic focus of the stage picture sparkle like a jewel in its setting. At its best it is an effective and flexible approach to lighting proscenium theatre. It is, however, an approach that uses a lot of lanterns and a lot of electrical power!

---

way of coping with these demands. The practice spread to drama lighting where it is probably not appropriate, and even into studio spaces where scaled down versions of jewel lighting are not only inappropriate, they don't work.

In the past the practice has been to fill the stage with light from many lanterns combined to make a wash, and then use relative intensity to guide the audience gaze (amongst other things). How often do we still need to work this way? The design aesthetic on many stages is moving away from cluttered spaces and back towards a more open stage. Do we need a multi-fixture wash for this kind of space? Would it be better to do the washes with fewer large units and use moving lights as specials to guide audience gaze?

The more complex the lighting system the longer it takes to get it in the air and focused, and usually the longer it takes to make the cues. Then there is the thing about too much choice, and finally the potential inflexibility of a complex system — designing out the operator.

If the lighting designer were able to fully participate in the devising of the piece, to offer lighting solutions to the director and others at a point where these interventions could enhance the production without overloading the lighting system. If there were enough time given to lighting the piece in the space so that each lighting state could find its solution in the right light from the right direction, in just the right colour and at just the right intensity … would we be making progress?

If we are going to be useful collaborators with our directors, rather than technical facilitators, we need to be steeped in the dramaturgy of the pieces we light. In the words of Dutch lighting designer Henk van der Geest,

'Understanding the piece makes you ready to make decisions later — when you don't have time to talk'.

If we have to cut down on power, on numbers of units, on incandescent lamps, let's make what we have left work hard for the productions. Let's have the right kit in the right places, because we have the same vision of the piece as the director and other designers. Let's be properly prepared to make the scenes we have agreed on (and have a little something ready if one or two of them don't work). Let's make light work to tell stories, add psychological nuances and paint the pictures on stage. No more turning up to the focus wondering what play we are doing today; no more putting a lantern on every available hanging position 'just in case'.

Let's make creating performance lighting more like making art.

Appendix

Performance semiotics

Semiotics is the study of signs, and can be a very useful tool to analyse how the communication between performer and audience works. We can look at the communication between artist(s) and audience(s) as a language or set of languages of signs. Humans communicate through signs, and it seems we have a natural disposition to attempt to make sense of them. The shapes on this page represent words which you can read individually, and which form parts of a larger communication of ideas. We are so used to using the language of words to communicate that we often forget that there is no natural meaning to the signs they represent. The letters F, I, R and E in the English language together stand for the sound you make if you read aloud the word *fire,* and in turn that sound is a sign for something burning, or a signal of command to discharge weapons. There is no natural link between F, I, R and E used together and what it stands for in the English language — to understand the word, *that is to read the sign in the way it is intended to be read*, you need some knowledge of the language. Semiotics treats all communication, not just words, as a set of signs. For communication to happen successfully, the signs must mean at least approximately the same to the sender as they do to the receiver.

Some terms

As we have said, a sign is anything that stands for something else in a communication process. Ferdinand Saussure, an influential figure in the study of languages, called the mental concept the sign stands for its *signified* and the sign itself the *signifier*, whilst the actual thing itself is the *object*. In the play *Cyrano de Bergerac* the moon is mentioned several times in the text. Consider a production of this play featuring the projected image of the moon in a night scene. The *signifier* is the pattern of light and shade that makes up the image of the moon. The *signified* is the idea of moon in the mind of each audience member, and the *object* is the actual moon, revolving round the earth and not actually visible to anyone in the theatre. The influential American writer C.S. Peirce, sometimes called the father of modern semiotics, divides signs into three classes:

Iconic signs look like the thing they stand for. An example is the clouds on a TV or newsprint weather map. They are not graphical representations of real clouds, but they look enough like real clouds for us to understand their meaning in that context. In our production of *Cyrano*, the image of the moon looks enough like the real thing for the audience to know what it is meant to represent — it is not important for the communication process for it to be the real moon.

Indexical Signs point to or otherwise imply the existence of the thing they signify (*The Signifier*). An example is a knock at the door, which is an indexical sign that there is someone on the other side. Another example is the smoke from a chimney, which is an indexical sign of the fire below. Again in our *Cyrano*, for with some knowledge of theatre lighting techniques, the image of the moon 'points to' the fixture that is projecting it.

Symbolic signs are signs with no direct link to there signified objects. They can only be read with some more specific cultural knowledge. Many religious images are loaded with this kind of symbolic meaning. The Crucifix in a Catholic church may be only a representation of a man upon an ancient instrument of torture for some, but for Catholics it has a much richer signification. Symbols carry cultural meanings far beyond their representational meaning. To get this full meaning, the readers need some cultural knowledge. In our *Cyrano*, the projected image of the moon stands for the real moon, but also symbolises the idealised unrequited love of the soldier poet of the title — but only to those familiar with that cultural use of the idea of the moon in this way. (In *Cyrano*, the point is made several times in the text, which makes the sign easier for the audience to read.)

So then, for Saussure a sign is made up of the physically present signifier, and the associated concept, the signified. For Peirce and his followers the sign may be an icon, an index, or a symbol for the object it represents — and the object can be a concrete thing, such as the moon, or a concept, such as idealised un-requited love.[1]

It is important to realise that the signified and the signifier cannot exist independently of each other. For anyone who can read English, F I R E (and the sound that goes with speaking the word) *and* our concepts associated with the word exist together. For speakers and writers of other languages the equivalent speech-sounds and the written symbols that represent them, will be different (and it can be argued that the signified will be different for them too, but that is a much more complex argument than there is space for here). It can be argued that only for someone with no language can the concept exist without the word — and for them there is no sign — only the object itself. (This too is a contested point but again this book is not the place to debate it.) To make the units of any language they must be harnessed to concepts, whether we are referring to a written and spoken language such as English, or a language of lighting signs associated with a particular production.

Some performance traditions have evolved a complex language of signs used in very formal dance to tell stories. One example of this is the Balinese dance tradition observed by the French theatrical Antonin Artaud.[2] He wrote about his interpretation of the many hundreds of gestures used by Balinese dancers per-forming traditional story dances, based on the effect they had on him as audience member. Just like a spoken language, many of the gestures used by the Balinese dancers were essentially arbitrary. The dancers undergo extended training to make the precise body shapes and moves for each sign unit. The traditional audience needs to observe closely each gesture, which they have also spent a long time learning to interpret. Many of the meanings Artaud attributed to particular gestures are not even close to the intended meaning of the dancers, which tells us something about the difficulty of attributing meaning to performance signs from a standpoint outside the culture within which the performance was made.

Saussure argued that the essentially arbitrary nature of the link between words and the things they stand for gives verbal and written language its complexity, richness and depth of potential meaning. Conversely, this must mean that there will be limits to the range and complexity of meaning available to the (usually) less arbitrary languages of signification used in (for example) scenography. In any case, we have to acknowledge that signs only fully work within a community with a common understanding of those signs. The English language only reveals its full meaning to competent users of it, just as the intricate gestures of Balinese dance only reveal their intended meaning to audience members who understand the signified concept associated with each signifying gesture.

In performance, there are often many 'languages of signs' to be read by the audience. These may include the language of words, gestural languages, including forms of dance, languages of meaning encoded in costume and setting, and of course the signs created by light, all of which we would normally aim to be part of a coherent set of languages communicating the story and ideas, feelings, emotions, etc, to the audience. In most

---

[1] This is not the only way semiotics defines the sign. A much fuller definition of semiotic analysis is available in Daniel Chandler's *Semiotics the Basics*. The French writer and academic Patrice Pavis has written extensively on the semiotics of performance and many of his essays are available in translation.

[2] For Artaud in English, see *Collected Works* in several volumes translated by Victor Corti and published in 1974 by Calder & Boyer (London).

---

models of performers in place, can become a useful story-board. In some circumstances, for example when specialist small scale lighting equipment is not available, a single photograph of each configuration of the set, printed out on suitable paper, can be used as the basis of sketches to show positions of performers and lighting effect.

Towards a cue synopsis

Using the lighting score or something like it, and/or a story-board, the lighting designer can record ideas and requirements for each lighting scene. As they work through the whole piece, recurring themes will often emerge and a rhythm too, that hopefully the lighting can work with. For example:

■ In multi-location drama, the rhythm of interior and exterior scenes is rarely accidental; from reading or listening to the piece and in discussion with the director and other members of the creative team, underlying themes may be played here. On a relatively open set, there are usually many possibilities for light (and sound) to work with these themes.

■ Looking at how the tempo varies through a piece may inspire an idea that can link dramatic tempo to intensity or colour choice at each moment.

■ A particular feeling or emotional state may build over a scene, an act or the whole piece. It may be appropriate to vary a particular lighting angle or colour in response to this.

Sometimes one or more key images will begin to crystallise in the mind of the lighting designer — perhaps a dramatic sunset building through the final act or an architectural curtain of light sculpting the space of performance for a particular purpose. Practical considerations, such as light for entrances or faces also emerge, perhaps as secondary to the main image, but hopefully as an integral part of it.

Light and signs

If we take the semiotic approach to performance outlined in the appendix, we can think in terms of the signs and signifiers available that will help communication with the audience. Hopefully a close reading of the text and discussions with the rest of the creative team will have revealed a range of things which will need to be signified at different moments. The creative team (hopefully lead by a rigorous and informed lighting designer) need to agree the signifying roles of lighting in each moment and through the piece. These may include:

■ Different locations — in the multi-location drama, is there a particular colour or quality or physical arrangement of light that might signify each different location?

■ Different times — when there is a need to signify different times of day, could long shadows from low angled light signify dawn or dusk, would a colour change work?

■ Particular events such as a storm or a fire which may be happening on stage or somewhere off stage.

■ Emotional or psychological states — can a particular colour, quality or angle of light be used as a signifier? Blue light for 'the blues' and pink for a love song, or perhaps predominantly steep angles in psychologically tense moments, or 'broken beams' causing performers to move in and out of light as they cross the stage, could this be a signifier of loss.

■ Different levels of reality such as dream-states and natural states — could a distinctive colour pallet for each help with the signification here?

There will also be things which need to be signified through the whole piece, not least the genre of the performance. This might come down to comedy = bright or musical theatre = colourful. There may also be signs that need to build in significance through the piece (growing foreboding, increasing despair).

Natural signs — the signs of nature

How might the performance lighting signify events in nature? Flashes of 'lightning' for a storm, a flickering red or amber glow for a fire. Soft-focused gobos for light through trees, a crisp projection of a photographically accurate moon. At many points in discussions of this type, the lighting designer will need to decide if they wish to imitate the light of nature, and if so, how closely. To achieve 'natural' light on stage the lighting designer will need to have made a close study of light in nature, perhaps using an extensive collection of photographs as a reminder, but essentially relying on their own observation of light in nature. For some productions, however, it might make more sense to adopt a more or less stylised approach, often following a lead set by the design of the set or perhaps the language of the text or the style of the direction and performance. Whether the design choice is an attempt at reproducing the light of nature or something else, a consistent approach will usually help the audience decode the signs offered while working against other systems of signification on stage will only confuse the reading.

Framing and focus

Performance lighting will usually define which parts of the stage are seen and which hidden. What will be the signification generated by these choices? It will usually set both frame and focus of attention for the audience, both actions pregnant with the possibilities of signification since they are able in large part to establish the mode of audience reception. Take a production of *Hamlet* with a naturalistic set representing a castle and the famous 'To be, or not to be . . .' soliloquy. Consider the signification of each of these lighting set-ups:

1 Hamlet in the castle, lit for night time — no overt change in the lighting for the famous soliloquy.

2 Hamlet in his own 'lighting special' which appears for the speech. The castle still visible, but this time as background rather than the place where he stands.

3 At the beginning of the speech, Hamlet is suddenly in a follow spot on an otherwise dark stage.

The first example would normally be read as naturalism — Hamlet wandering the space where he lives, his contemplation part of the general world of the play. The audience is hearing the words because the character Hamlet is actually speaking them out loud in that world. The second choice is perhaps signifying that what we hear is going on in Hamlet's head rather than actually being spoken by the character; that we are seeing an inner dialogue that could not be heard by any other inhabitant of the performance world of Elsinore Castle.

The last example breaks the conventions used in most productions of Shakespeare in the UK by intro-

ducing an overt sign usually associated with other genre of performance — the follow spot. It could be so disruptive for a traditional audience that their attention is focused on the follow spot rather than the words and meaning of the text as delivered by the actor. If, however, the context enabled the audience to remain focused on the meaning of the text, this sign (the follow spot) could enhance audience understanding of the performance. For an audience more used to concerts than plays, the follow spot signifies a 'solo', a section that requires more attention, and this could work to enhance communication between stage and audience.

Live rock and pop music concerts are not often subject to this sort of analysis, but let's try. This time imagine a concert by a band with a charismatic lead singer who likes to get the audience up and on their feet at the beginning of the show. How can the lighting designer help? There are two issues, first signalling to the audience that they have permission to join in the performance and get on their feet to dance and sing. Second to enable the singer to see this activated audience — bearing in mind that he will usually have at least two bright follow spots in his face from the moment he walks out. In most medium-sized concert lighting rigs the lighting designer has at least two tools to play with, moving lights with beams that can be swung into the audience and 'audience blinders', usually several clusters of units able to throw bright white light into a large part of the auditorium. The audience blinders are usually there specifically to allow the artist to see the audience, to build up their energy by responding to that of the audience. But if these are used too early they will tend to reinforce the 'us/them' stage set-up by emphasising the division between 'stage' and 'not stage'. The audience will tend to remain passive observers back in their seats. The moving lights can be made to break down this division by sliding beams from stage to auditorium and back, by creating a look which unifies the singer with the (front rows) of the crowd. Whereas lighting the audience space as separate from the stage reinforces the difference between the two, creating a single space for the lead singer and the front section of the audience gives performance genre, these signs are intentionally set up by the performers and collaborators to help the audience understand the piece, be it an opera or a pop song.

Aberrant readings

Inevitably there are times when the makers of performance fail to get across to the audience their ideas. In semiotic terms, the reading of signs is not as the creators of the performance intended, and this disrupts the communication between performers and audience. Semiotics calls this kind of miss-communication an aberrant reading. Disruptive signs can be one-off accidents, such as be an exposed light that illuminates what should not be seen in a black out, an actor forgetting lines and coming out of character, or the sound of a police siren from outside the theatre at a moment of tension in a play. Disruptive signs can also result from a lack of good collaboration on the part of the production team; an actor standing in the dark to deliver an important speech, medieval costume worn with modern shoes, or any production element that is not properly integrated into the performance and grates with some audience members. Disruptive signs break the necessary suspension of disbelief required in many performance genre to create the performance world.[3]

A lack of attention to detail can distract the audience from the intended reading of the performance. In most live performance, the audience is bombarded with signs and information. We talk about the multi-channel nature of live performance. For a play this means that the audience not only *read* (in the sense of receive and interpret) words they hear from the actors, but every other part of their experience of that night out; from the posters, reviews and advertising that got them into the theatre in the first place, to every designed and undesigned element of the performance on stage, and everything about the performance space. Anything which can affect the audience experience of 'the show' should be considered as of some importance to the creators of live performance.

When a crown is more than a hat for a king

Let us look at another example of a sign in performance: an actor playing the part of Henry IV wears a crown as a sign to the audience that he is a king. The stage crown stands for a real crown, which we can assume would be too precious to be used on stage. The 'fake' prop crown signals kingship to an audience familiar with crowns on the heads of kings. There is an important distinction between the *standing in for* role of the crown, and the *signalling king-ness* of the crown. Using the definitions of C.S. Peirce, the stage crown is an *iconic sign* in that it looks similar to the real crown we assume it is *standing in for*. The king-making function of the crown is a symbolic sign, because there is no natural link between spiky ornamental headgear and kingship; to read the sign we need to have the cultural knowledge that men who wear crowns are kings. Now suppose that as part of a design the crown is made of rusty iron to signify the way in which this king came to power or his flawed nature. This would be another symbolic sign, and it would need the audience to share cultural assumptions with the design team about the relative worth and meaning of gold and iron, and the sign would need reenforcement from other signifiers in the production. It is important for us to acknowledge that the interpretation of these signs is not a *closed* given, but is *open* and will depend on many factors, including the preconceptions and cultural background of the audience and the way in which the signs are presented to the audience. The openness to interpretation is one of the things that can make live performance interesting and unique. The signs of performance can be read on many levels. In performance theory we say signs can contain multivalent meanings. However, the signs of performance may not always be interpreted as their creators would wish. For

---

[3]In contrast there are some styles of performance that use the disruptive effect of an un-unified production aesthetic to great effect, which goes to emphasise that there are really no absolute rules in performance.

---

example, some audience members may read into Henry's rusty crown that the budget for the show was too small to afford a 'proper' crown!

Signification and post-modern performance

Much avant-garde performance has abandoned the link between sign and signified, rejecting a responsibility for providing a fixed meaning for the work. Post-modern practitioners, influenced by Antonin Artaud, Jerzy Grotowski, Peter Brook and others, have abandoned the idea of intentional symbolic links as cultural arrogance on the part of the performance makers. Their work is presented to be read within the cultural context of its audience, not its makers, and so will have different meanings to different audiences. The theatre makers take no responsibility for deciding what that meaning should be, empowering the audience to make their own meaning from the piece. Whilst some critics rejoice in this practice, others, including the influential French writer Patrice Parvis, refer to it as the crisis of the post-modern and the avant-garde, and certainly some audiences seem unready to totally accept this additional responsibility.

There are significant challenges for the lighting practitioner working on post-modern performance, both in coming to terms with the theoretical approach, and in providing the visual excitement that is frequently key to the performance. In the work of Robert Wilson, the American performance maker most often cited in discussions of post-modern theatre of the late 20th century, the lighting practice is largely concerned with aiding the creation of beautiful tableau. As well as conceiving and directing his works, Wilson is also credited or co-credited with lighting, taking great care with each cue. Many other makers of post-modern performance make extensive use of beautiful lighting in their work.[4]

One word of caution when using any of the tools of performance analysis: each member of the audience brings their own unique set of experiences and knowledge into the performance space, informing their reading of the performance. Because of this each reading will be unique, and any generalised analysis will be that — a generalisation. At best, most of the audience will get most of the communication but that is part of what makes live performance exciting.

[4]Those of us from a scientific background can sometimes get carried away with the semiotics of performance, but to quote Patrice Parvis: 'To analyze the codes and signifying systems of a performance is not to rediscover what the author and director (sic) had previously established secretly once and for all. It is to organise the performance and the text into a possible circuit of meaning ... Theatrical Semiology is not trying to take the place of any existing theatre discipline. It does not claim to be a prophetic discovery or a religion for the use of the initiated ... research into signifying systems (may be) seen as a possible construction of meaning which occurs when an objective analysis of the performance data is joined to a more flexible attempt to take into account the audience's freedom of association and manoeuvre.' Patrice Pavis, *Languages of the Stage*, published by Johns Hopkins, New York 1982.

Index